THE SIXTH GUN

Book 4: A Town Called Penance

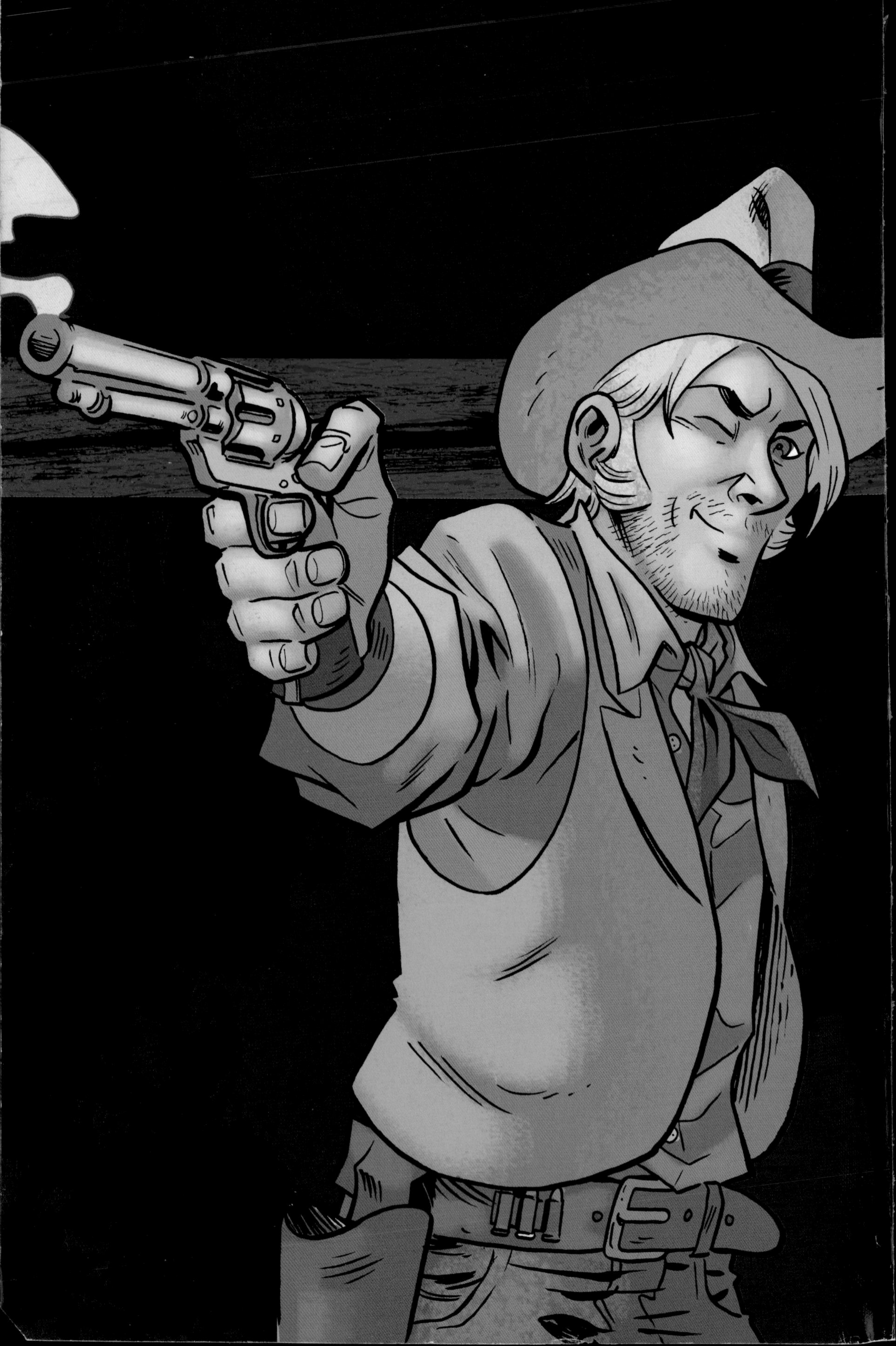

THE SIXTH GUN

BOOK 4: A TOWN CALLED PENANCE

WRITTEN BY
CULLEN BUNN

ILLUSTRATED BY
BRIAN HURTT

CHAPTER 6 ILLUSTRATED BY

TYLER CROOK

COLORED BY
BILL CRABTREE

LETTERED BY
DOUGLAS E. SHERWOOD

EDITED BY
CHARLIE CHU

DESIGNED BY
KEITH WOOD

THE SIXTH GUN™
BY CULLEN BUNN & BRIAN HURTT

PUBLISHED BY ONI PRESS, INC.
JOE NOZEMACK *publisher*
JAMES LUCAS JONES *editor in chief*
KEITH WOOD *art director*
GEORGE ROHAC *operations director*
JILL BEATON *editor*
CHARLIE CHU *editor*
TOM SHIMMIN *marketing coordinator*
AMBER LAPRAIM *marketing coordinator*
TROY LOOK *digital prepress lead*

THE SIXTH GUN: A TOWN CALLED PENANCE, NOVEMBER 2012. Published by Oni Press, Inc. 1305 SE Martin Luther King Jr. Blvd., Suite A, Portland, OR 97214.

This volume collects issues #18-23 of the Oni Press series *The Sixth Gun*.

ONI PRESS, INC.
1305 SE MARTIN LUTHER KING JR. BLVD.
SUITE A
PORTLAND, OR 97214
USA

onipress.com
Become our fan on Facebook: facebook.com/onipress
Follow us on Twitter: @onipress
onipress.tumblr.com

cullenbunn.com • @cullenbunn
theburttlocker.blogspot.com • @briburtt
mrcrook.com • @mrtylercrook
@crabtree_bill

First edition: November 2012
ISBN: 978-1-934964-95-8

Library of Congress Control Number: 2011933169

10 9 8 7 6 5 4 3 2 1

Printed in China

DRAKE SINCLAIR - A treasure hunter with a bleak past. He now holds four of the Six.

BECKY MONTCRIEF - A brave young woman who holds the Sixth Gun, a weapon that can divine the future.

BILLJOHN O'HENRY - Drake's friend. Killed at the battle of the Maw and raised as a golem-like creature by the power of the guns.

KIRBY HALE - A charming gunfighter and thief who betrayed Becky and tried to steal Drake's guns.

THE KNIGHTS OF SOLOMON - A secretive group dedicated to collecting ancient artifacts.

THE SWORD OF ABRAHAM - A religious order devoted to preventing Armageddon.

CHAPTER
ONE

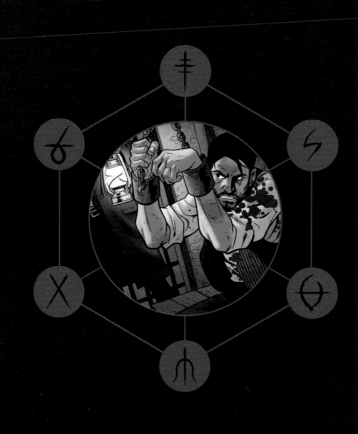

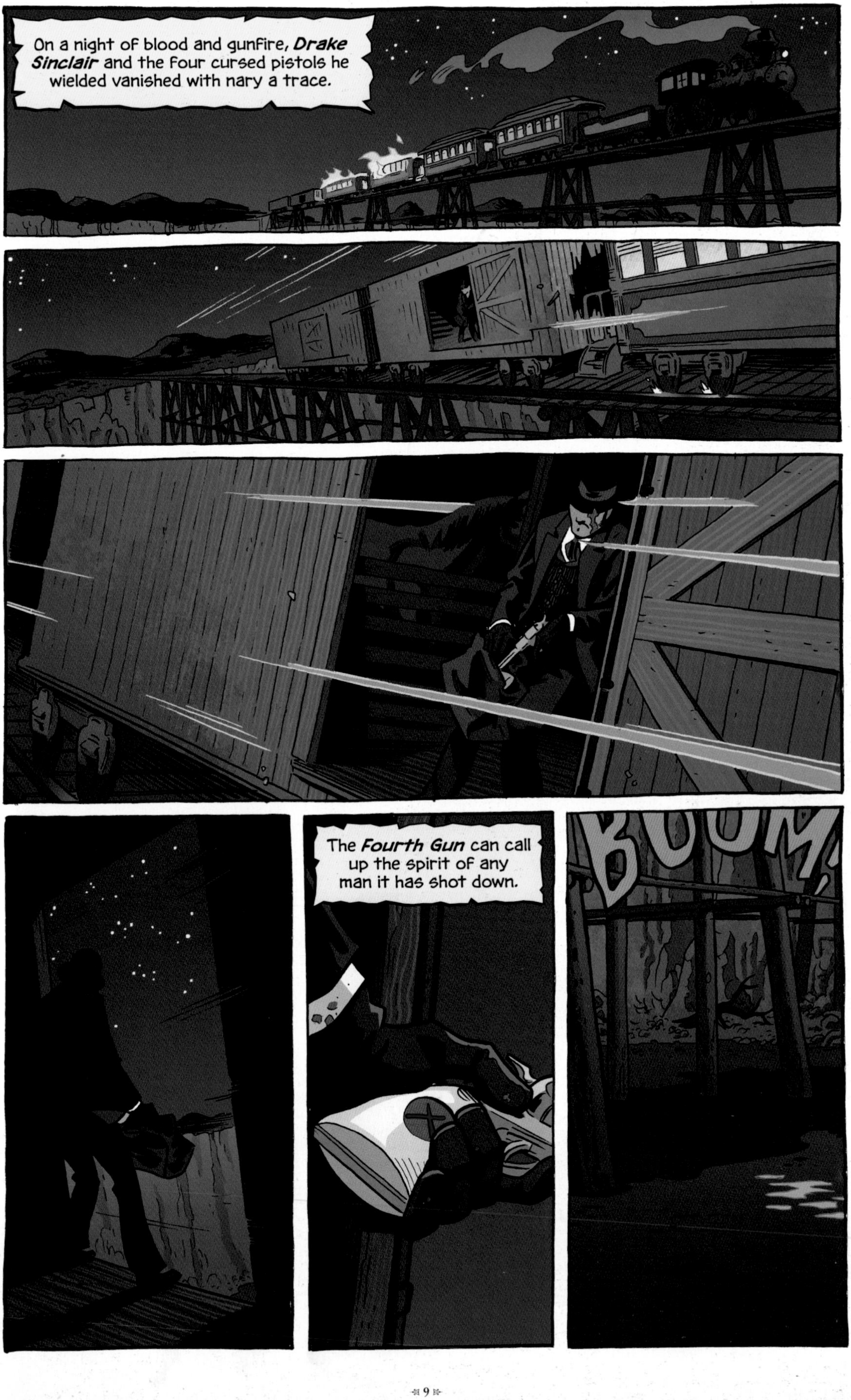
On a night of blood and gunfire, *Drake Sinclair* and the four cursed pistols he wielded vanished with nary a trace.
The *Fourth Gun* can call up the spirit of any man it has shot down.
BOOM!

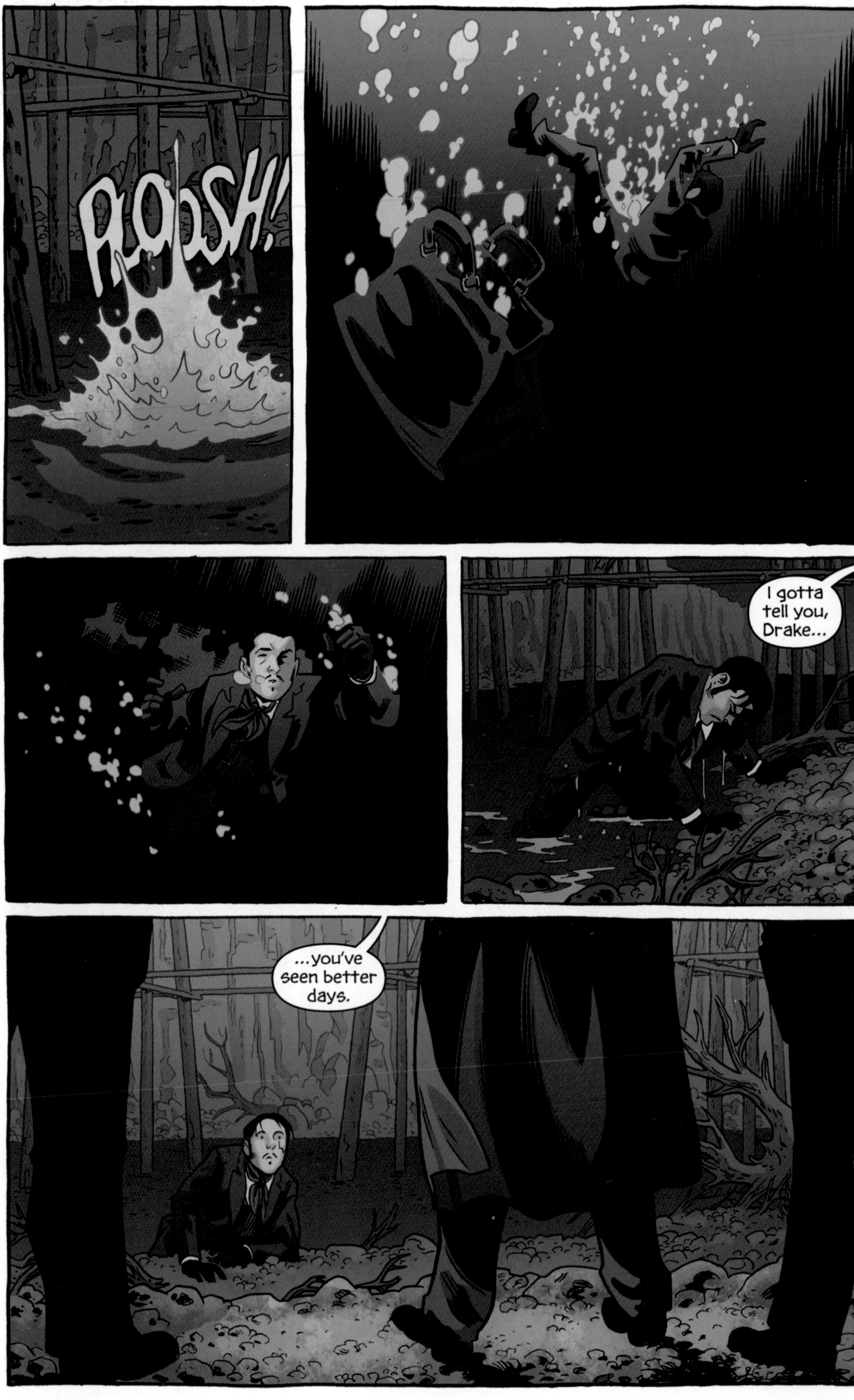
PLOOSH!
I gotta tell you, Drake...
...you've seen better days.

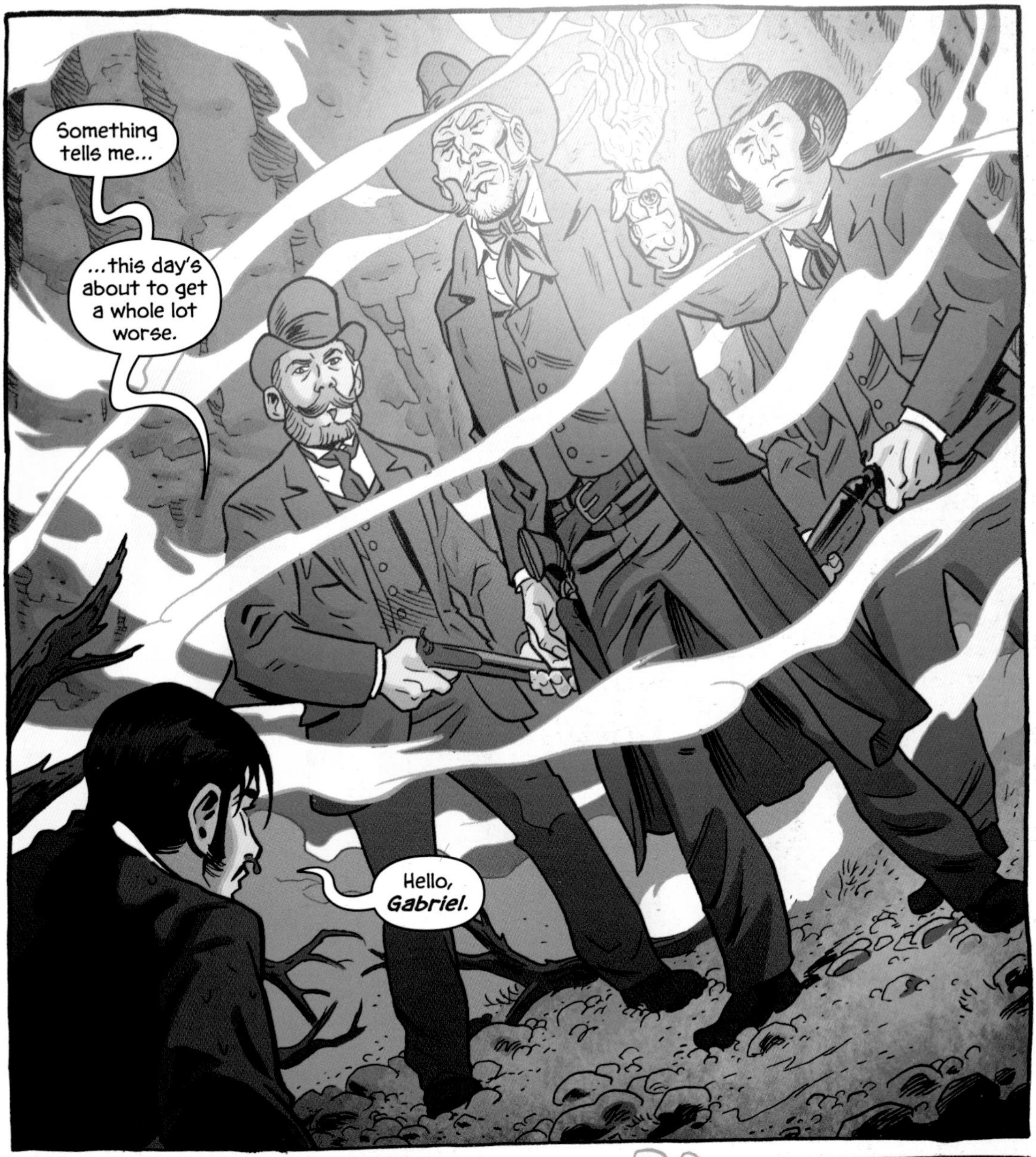
Something tells me...
...this day's about to get a whole lot worse.
Hello, Gabriel.

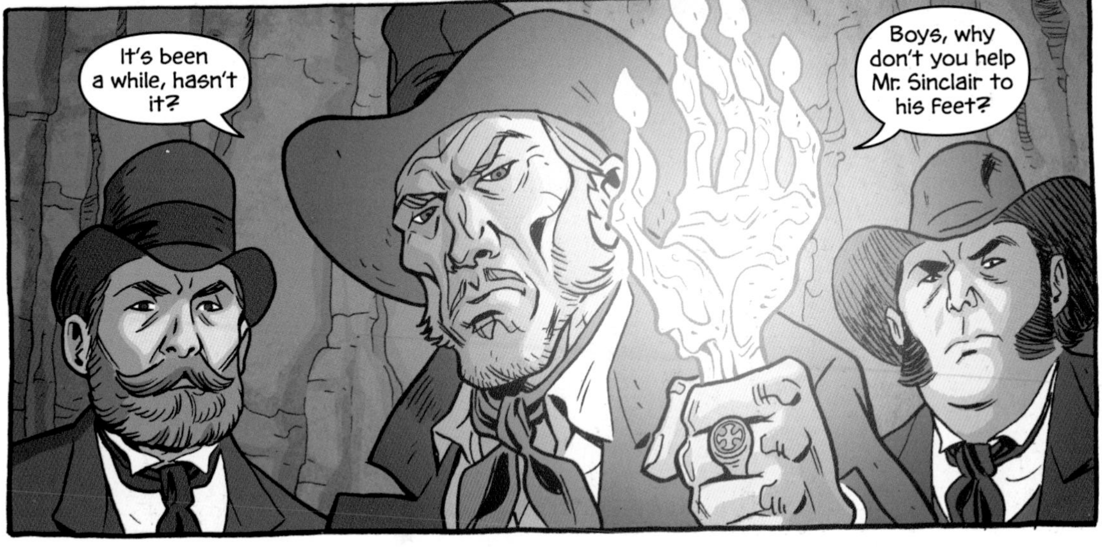
It's been a while, hasn't it?
Boys, why don't you help Mr. Sinclair to his feet?

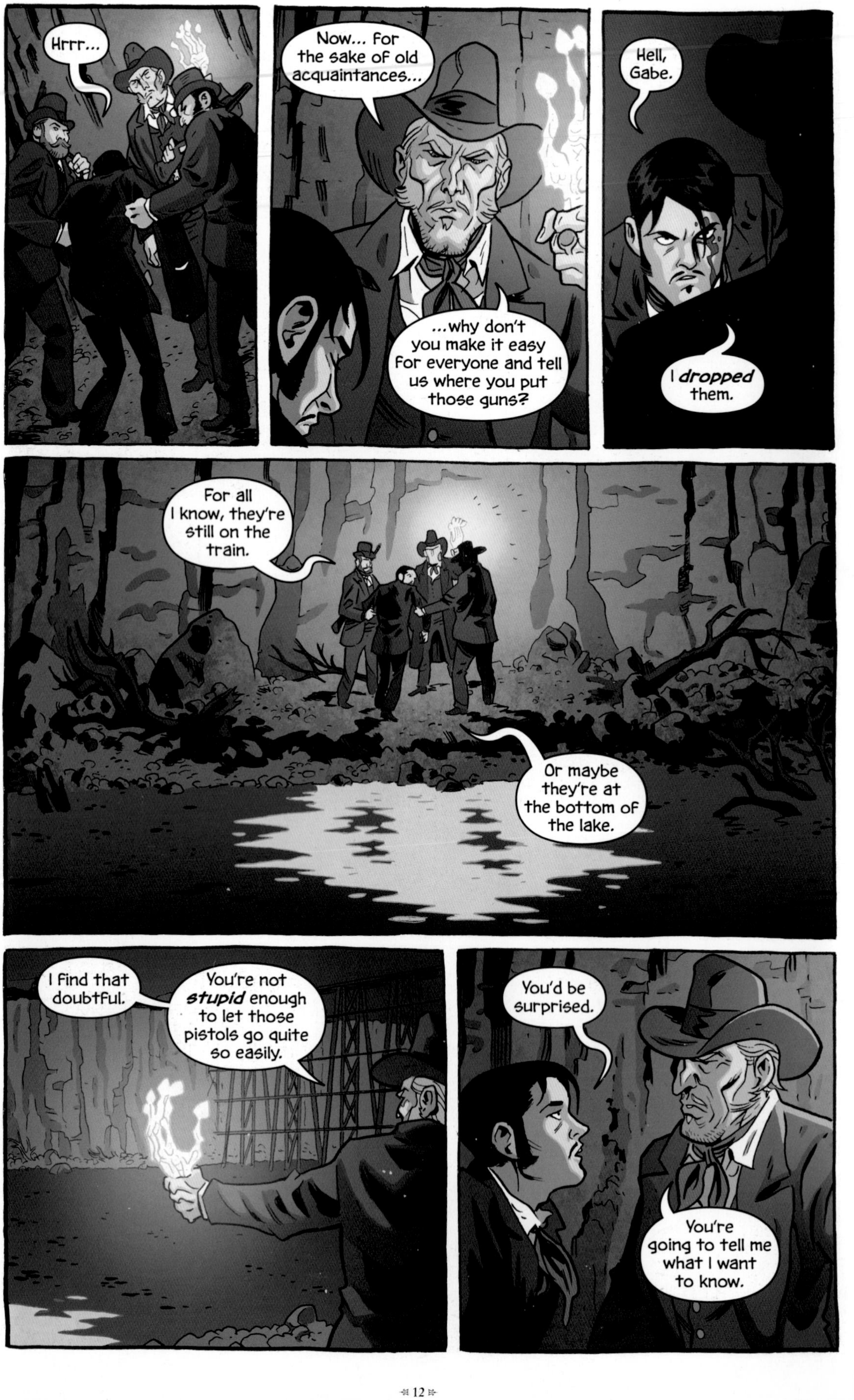

Hrrr...
Now... for the sake of old acquaintances...
...why don't you make it easy for everyone and tell us where you put those guns?
Hell, Gabe.
I *dropped* them.
For all I know, they're still on the train.
Or maybe they're at the bottom of the lake.
I find that doubtful.
You're not *stupid* enough to let those pistols go quite so easily.
You'd be surprised.
You're going to tell me what I want to know.

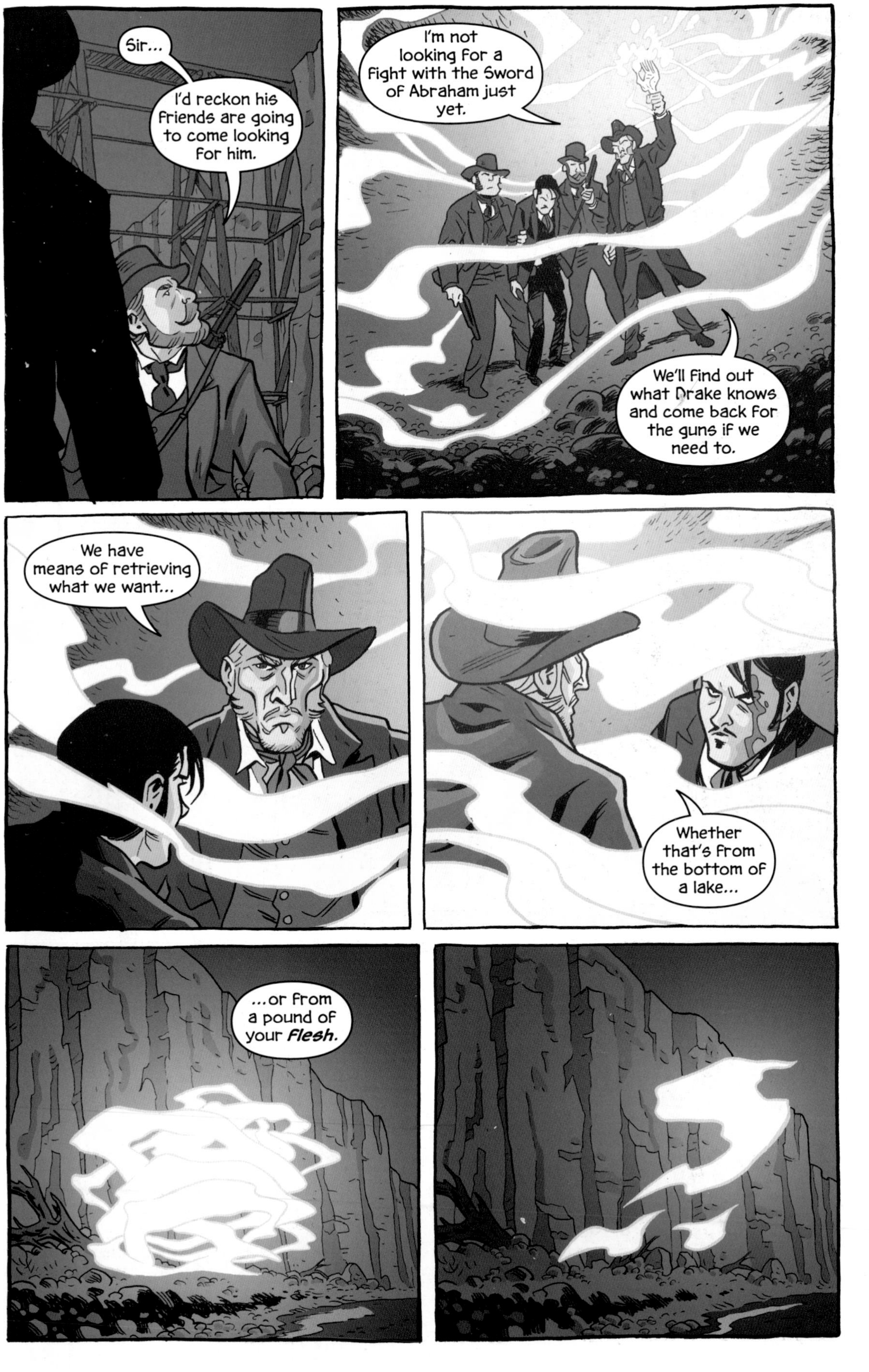
Sir...
I'd reckon his friends are going to come looking for him.
I'm not looking for a fight with the Sword of Abraham just yet.
We'll find out what Drake knows and come back for the guns if we need to.
We have means of retrieving what we want...
Whether that's from the bottom of a lake...
...or from a pound of your *flesh*.

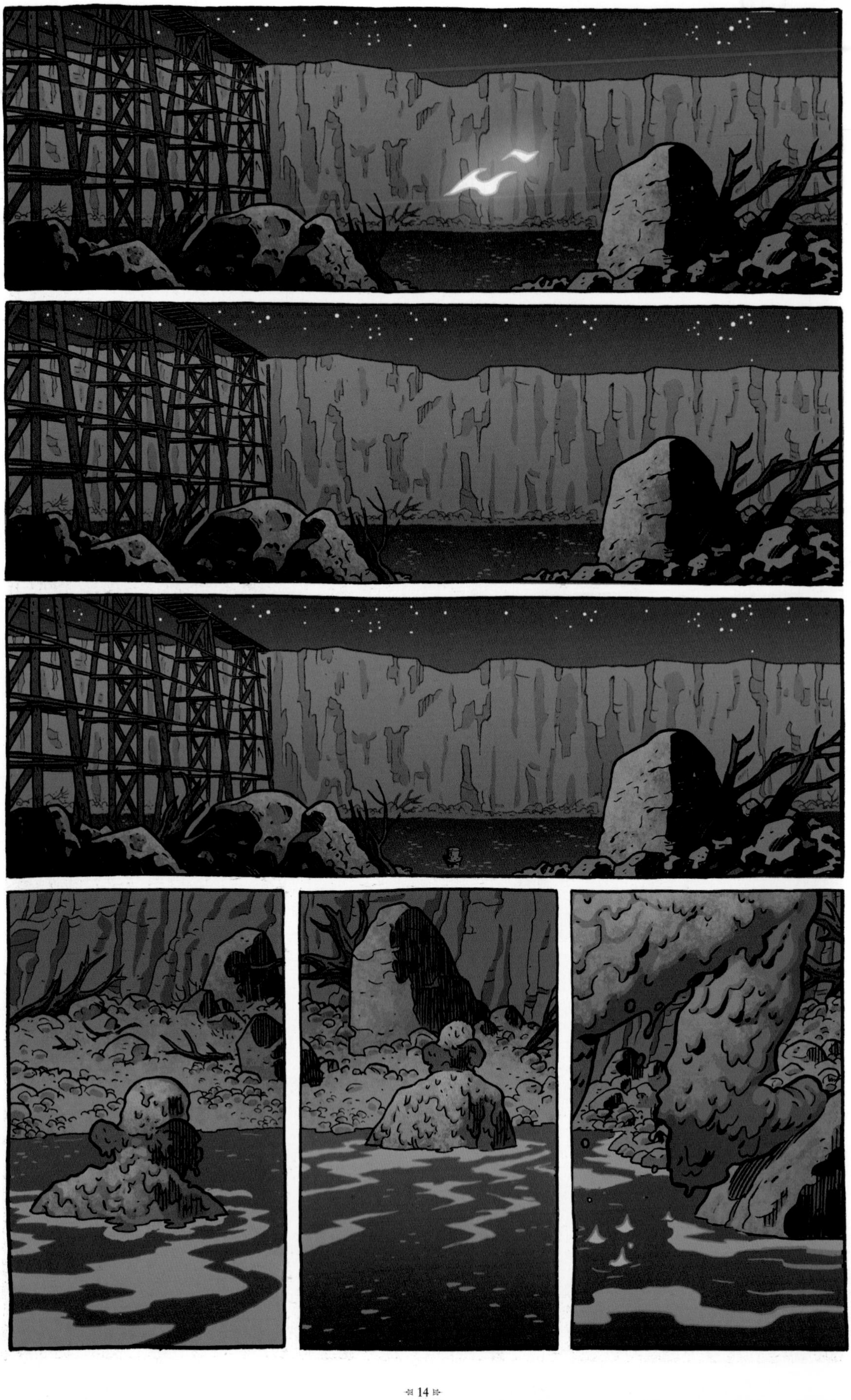

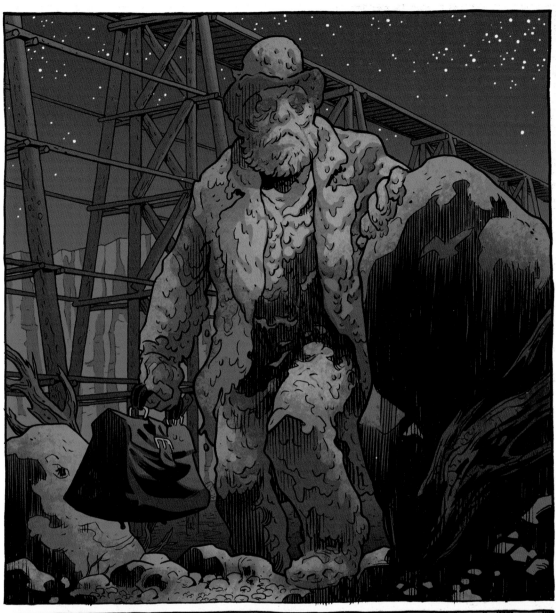

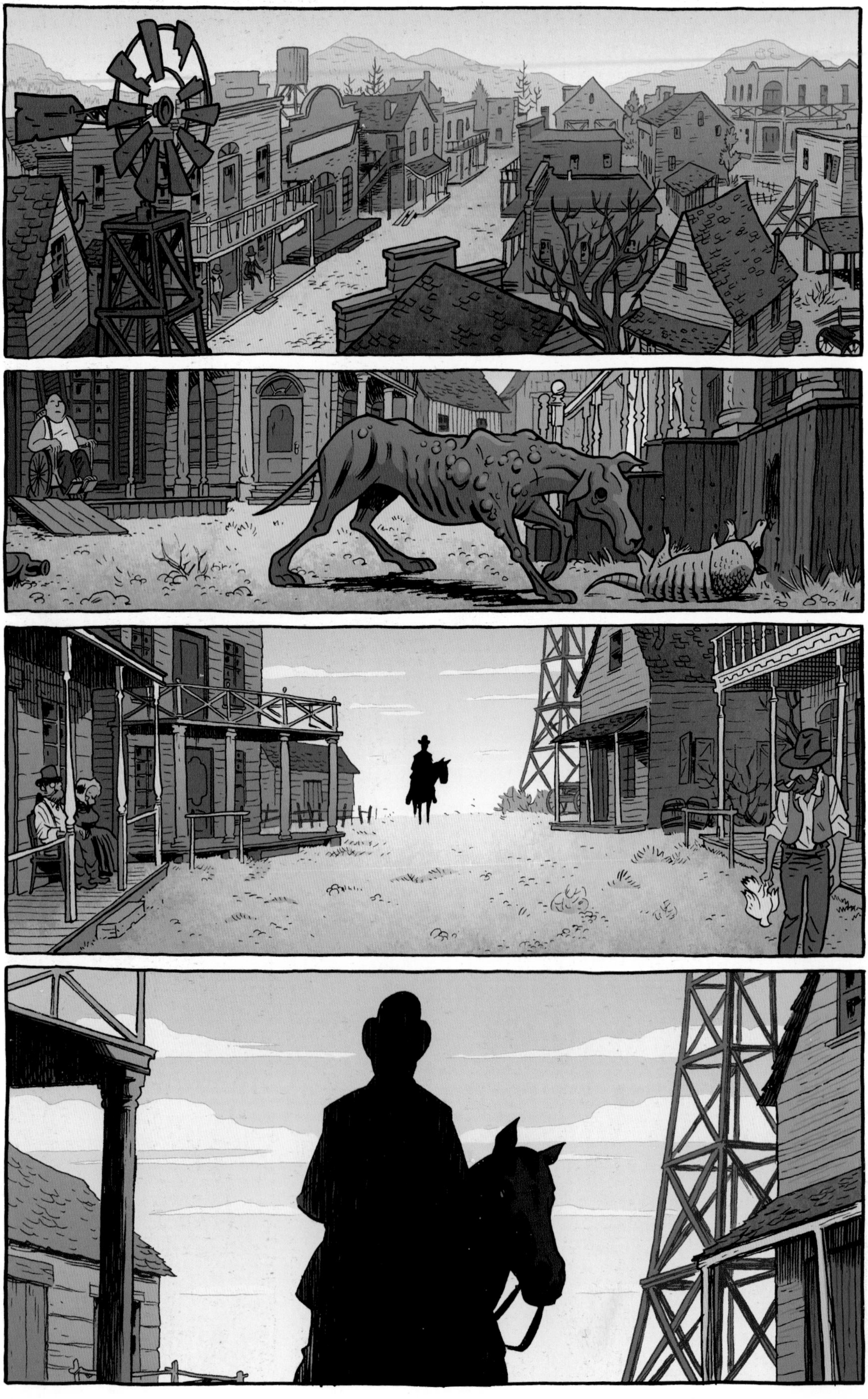

There's a rider coming, Maze!

Maze!

I hear ya.

Now keep yer voice down afore I feed ya to the worms just to shut ya up.

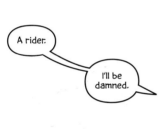

A rider.

I'll be damned.

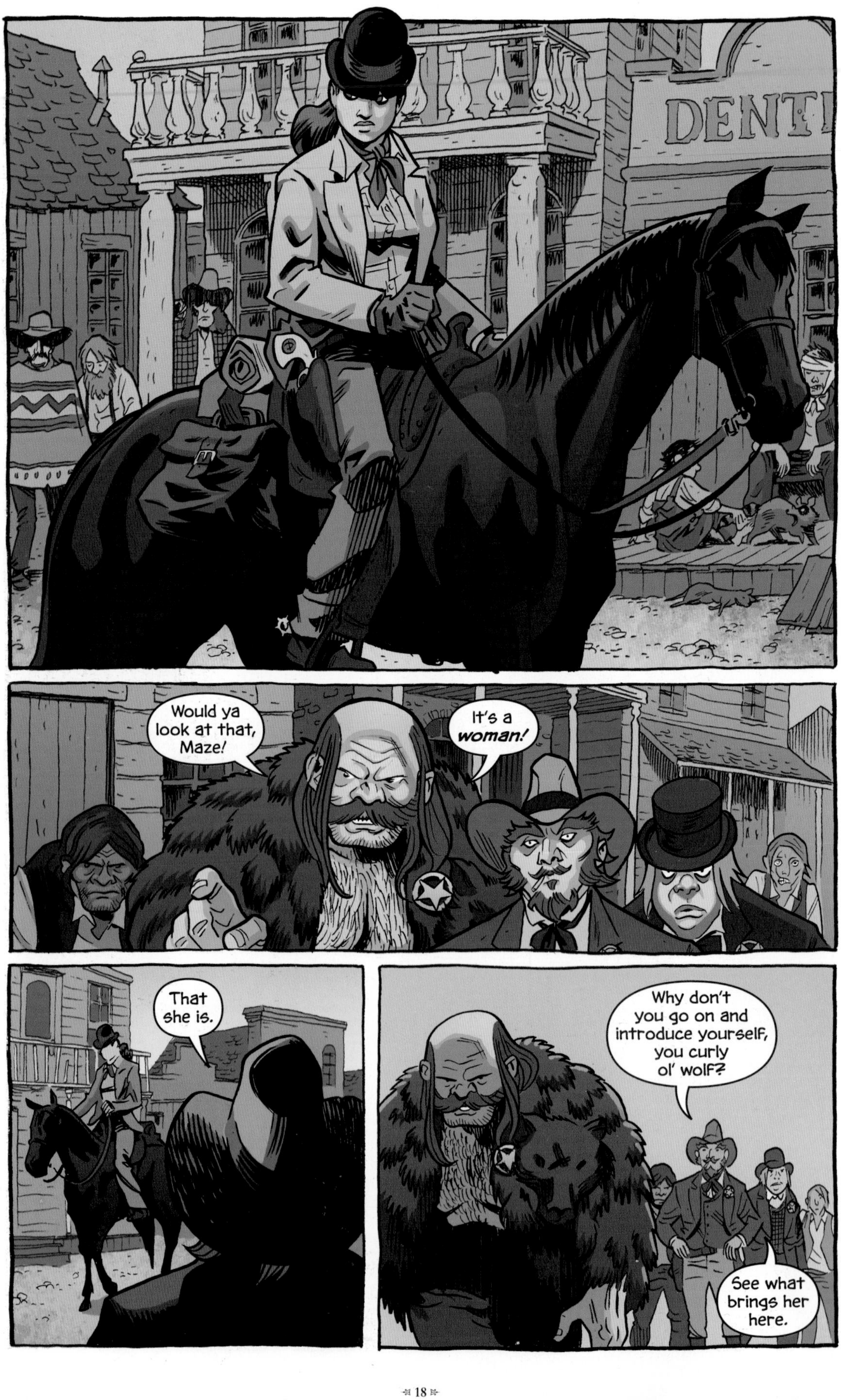
DENT
Would ya look at that, Maze!
It's a *woman!*
That she is.
Why don't you go on and introduce yourself, you curly ol' wolf?
See what brings her here.

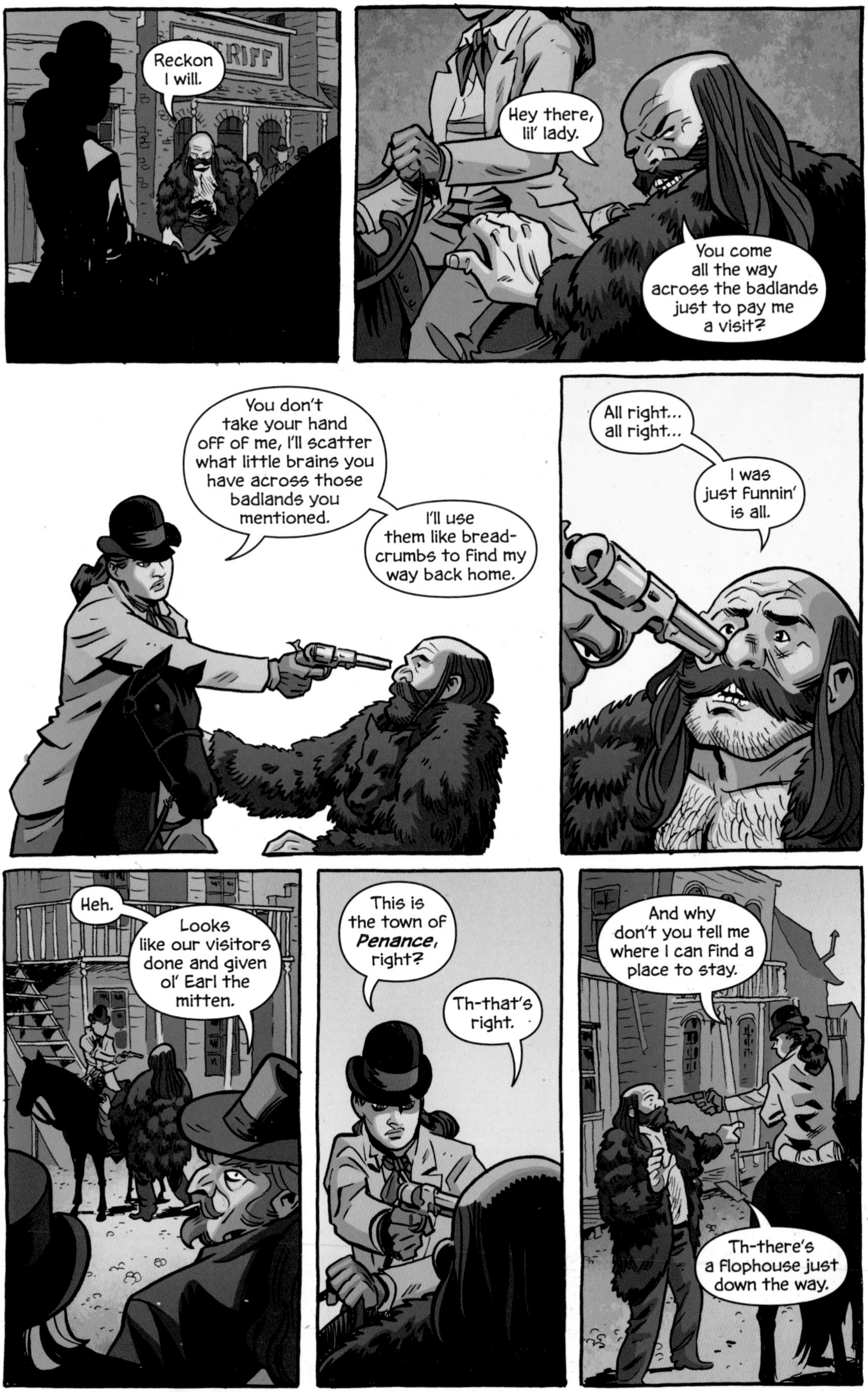
Reckon I will.
Hey there, lil' lady.
You come all the way across the badlands just to pay me a visit?
You don't take your hand off of me, I'll scatter what little brains you have across those badlands you mentioned.
I'll use them like bread-crumbs to find my way back home.
All right... all right...
I was just funnin' is all.
Heh.
Looks like our visitors done and given ol' Earl the mitten.
This is the town of *Penance*, right?
Th-that's right.
And why don't you tell me where I can find a place to stay.
Th-there's a flophouse just down the way.

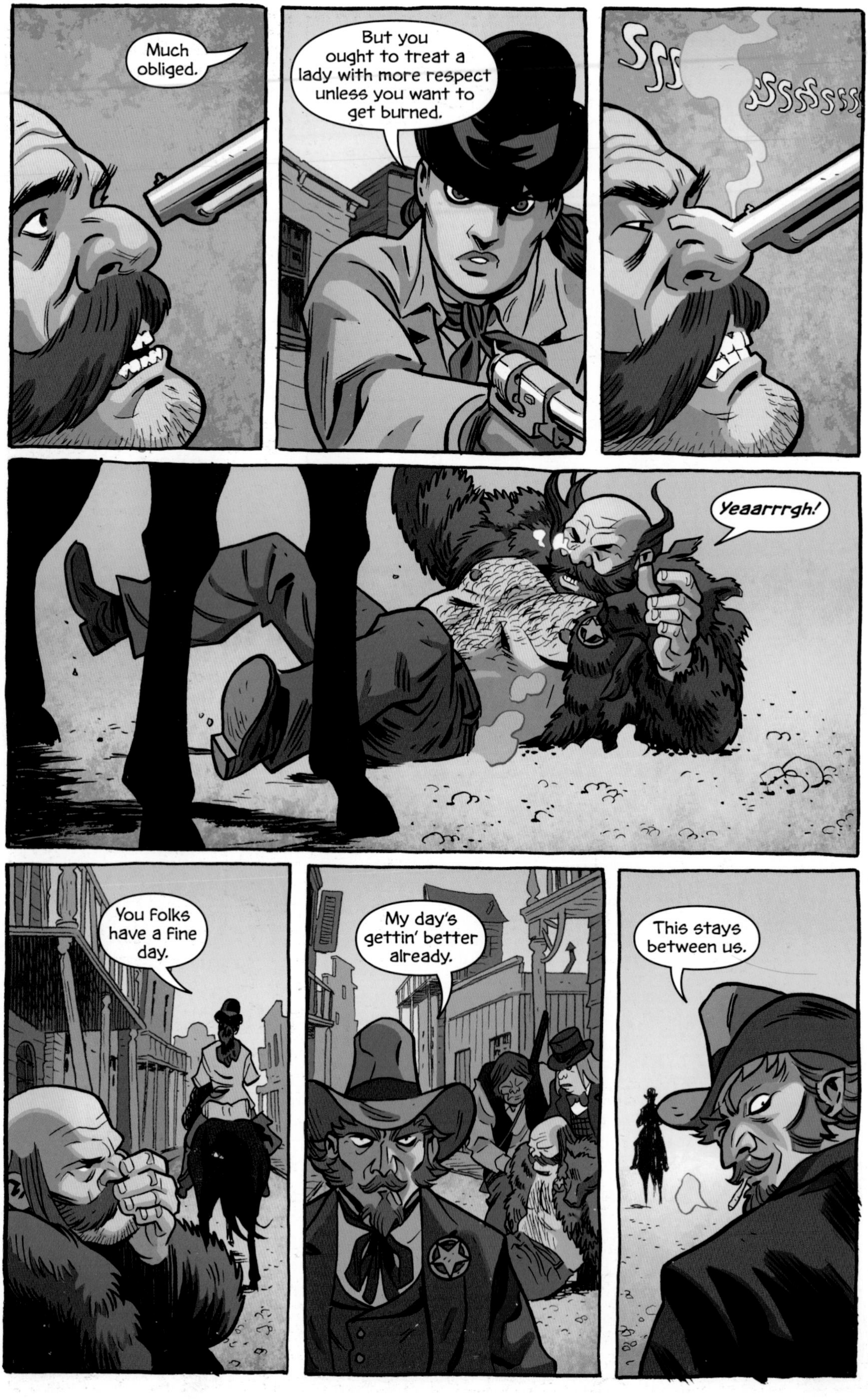
Much obliged.
But you ought to treat a lady with more respect unless you want to get burned.
Sss
Sssssss
Yeaarrrgh!
You folks have a fine day.
My day's gettin' better already.
This stays between us.

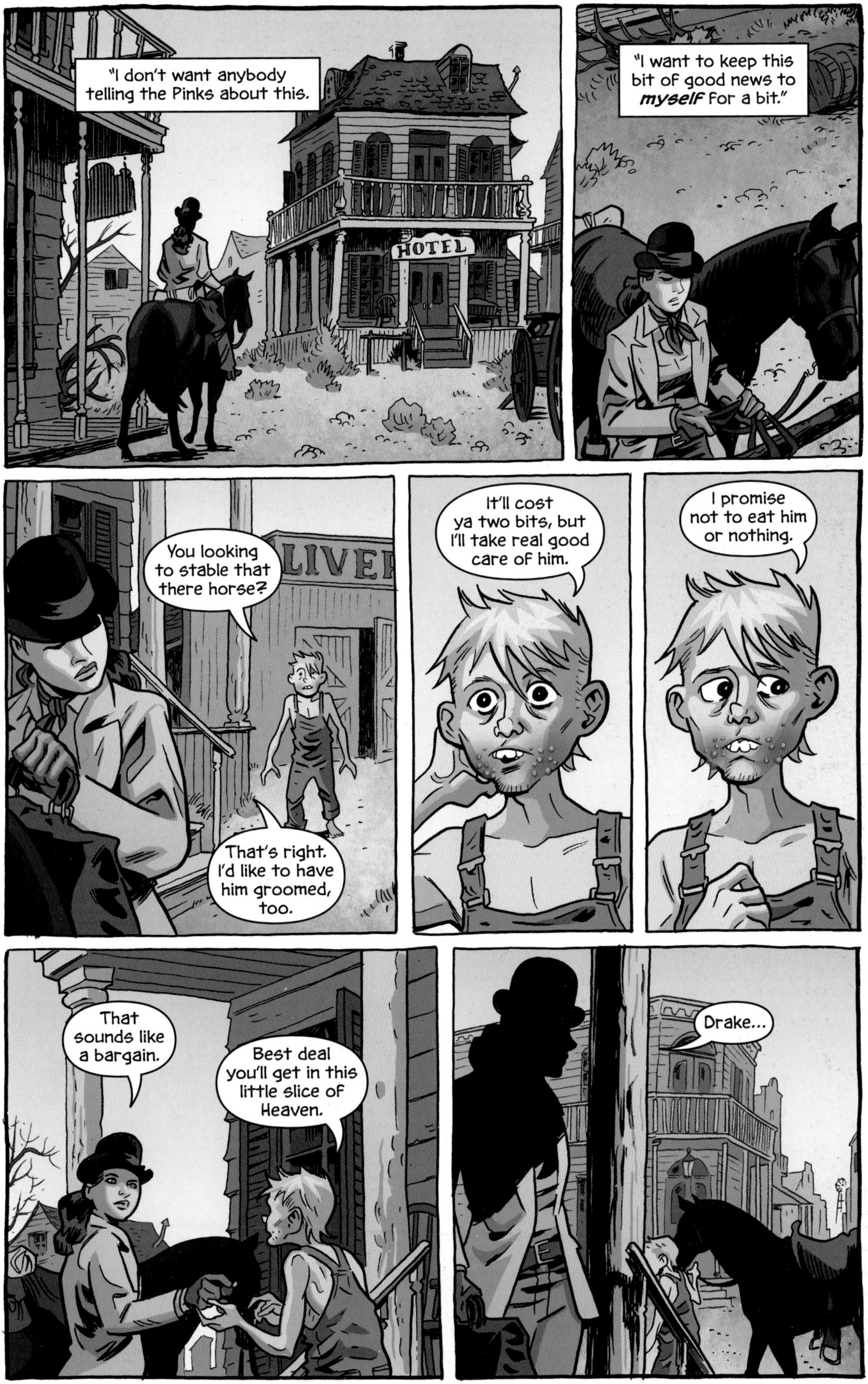
"I don't want anybody telling the Pinks about this.
HOTEL
"I want to keep this bit of good news to *myself* for a bit."
LIVER
You looking to stable that there horse?
That's right. I'd like to have him groomed, too.
It'll cost ya two bits, but I'll take real good care of him.
I promise not to eat him or nothing.
That sounds like a bargain.
Best deal you'll get in this little slice of Heaven.
Drake...

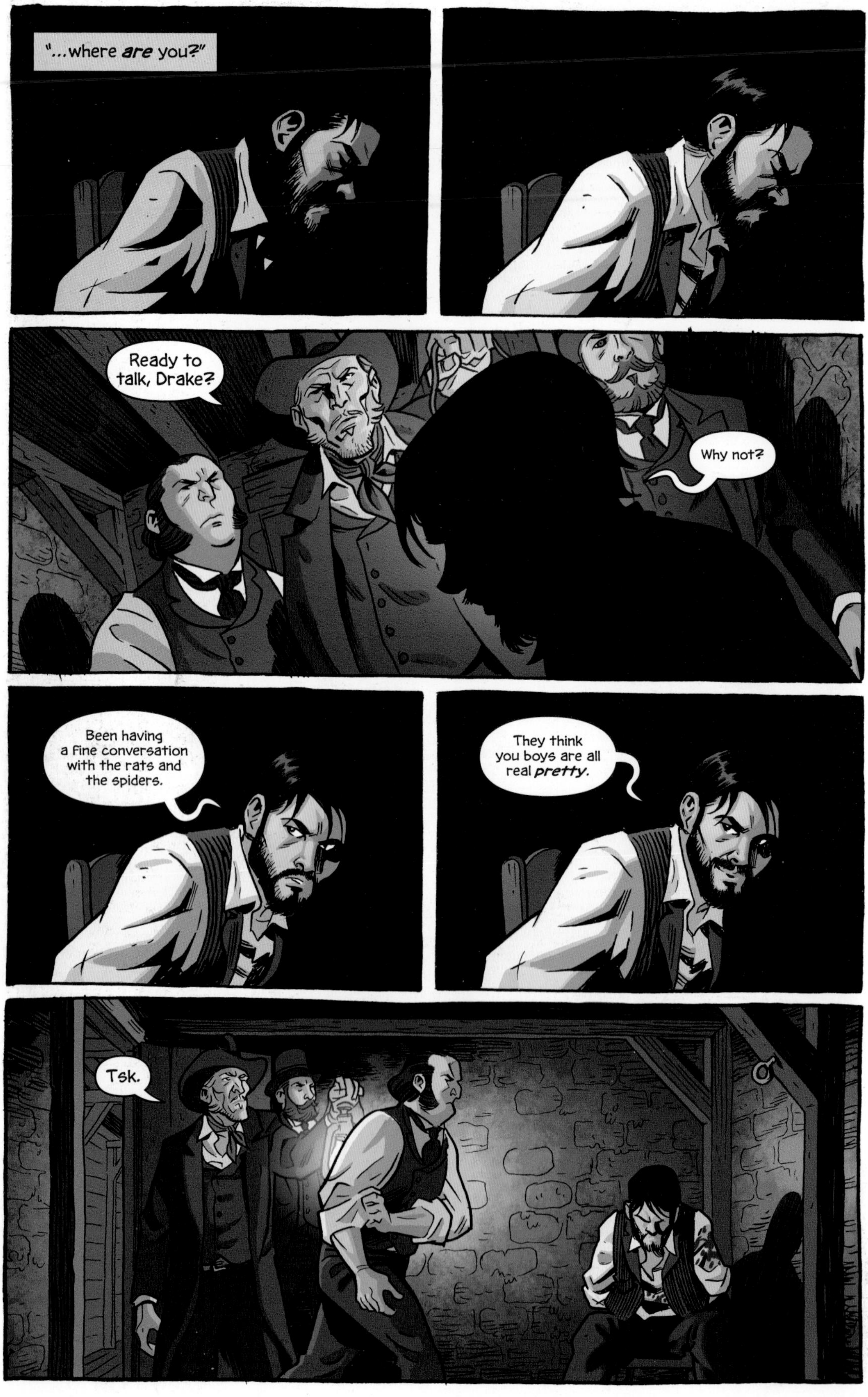
"...where *are* you?"
Ready to talk, Drake?
Why not?
Been having a fine conversation with the rats and the spiders.
They think you boys are all real *pretty*.
Tsk.

SMMCK!

Heh...

I... I already told you I don't know where those guns are.

If that's what you came to talk about, I ain't got much more to say...

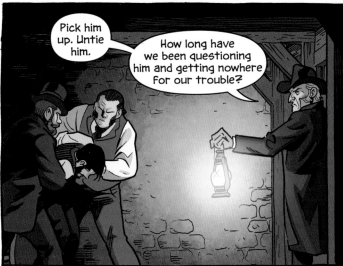

Pick him up. Untie him.

How long have we been questioning him and getting nowhere for our trouble?

It's time to try a *different* tact.

One that might better appeal to his *disposition.*

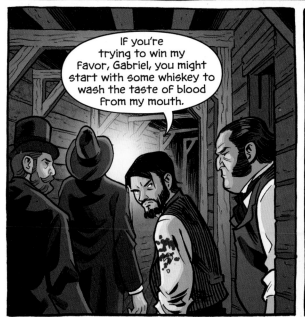

If you're trying to win my favor, Gabriel, you might start with some whiskey to wash the taste of blood from my mouth.

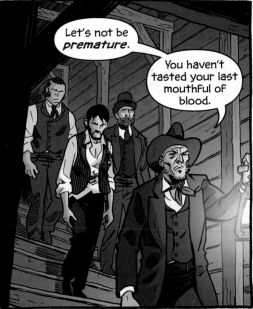

Let's not be *premature.*

You haven't tasted your last mouthful of blood.

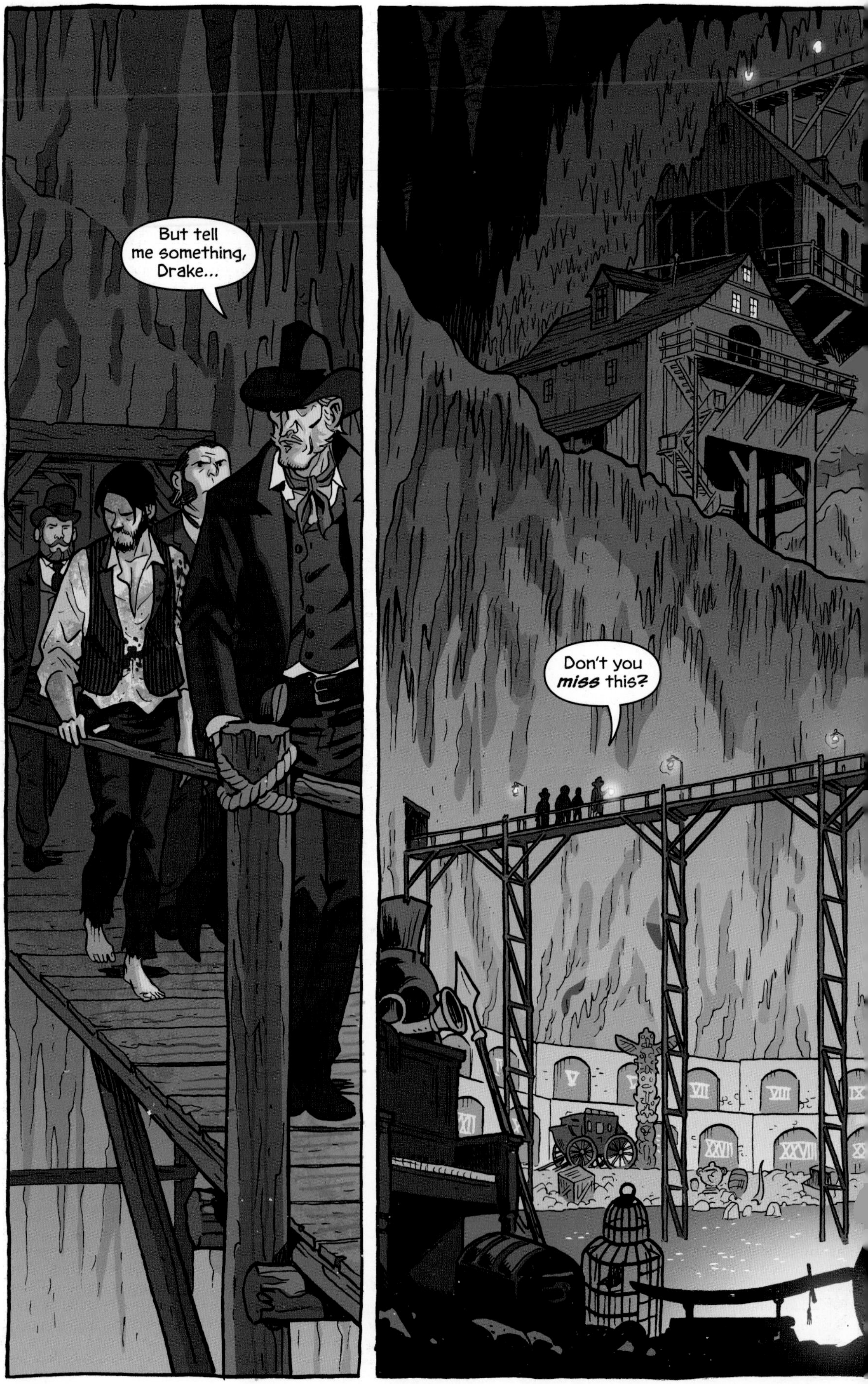
But tell me something, Drake...
Don't you *miss* this?

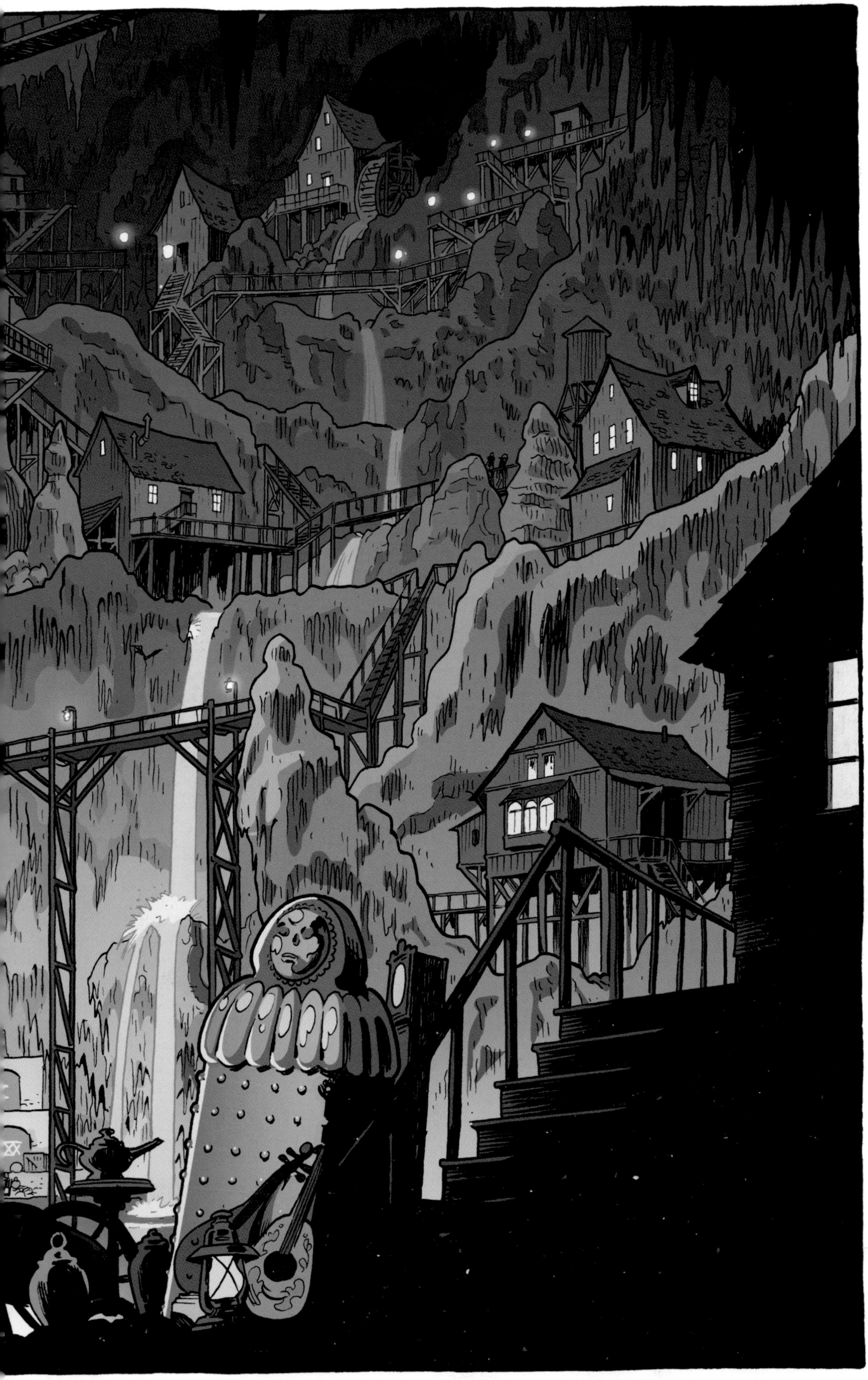

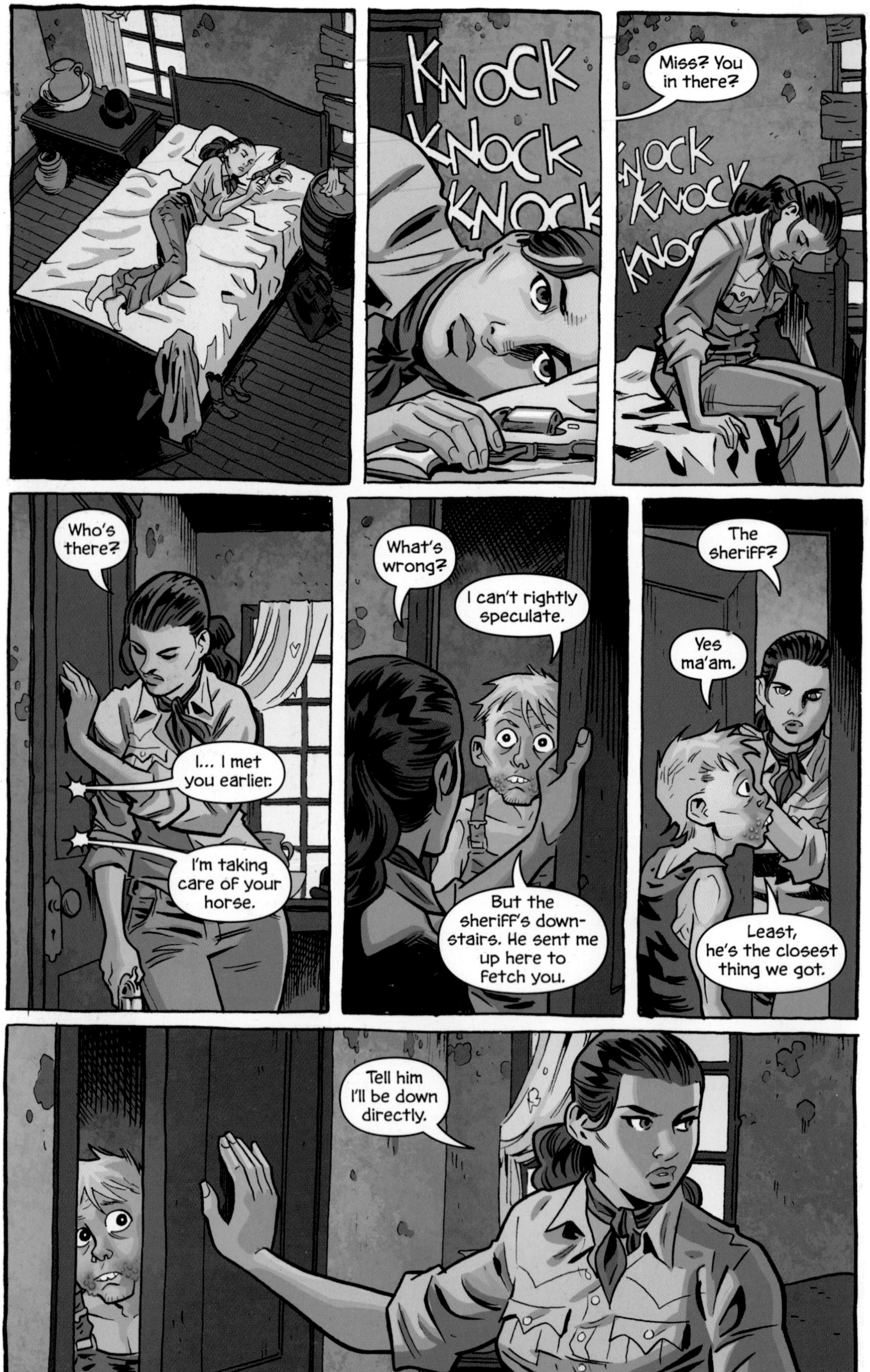
KNOCK
KNOCK
KNOCK
Miss? You in there?
KNOCK
KNOCK
KNOC
Who's there?
I... I met you earlier.
I'm taking care of your horse.
What's wrong?
I can't rightly speculate.
But the sheriff's down-stairs. He sent me up here to fetch you.
The sheriff?
Yes ma'am.
Least, he's the closest thing we got.
Tell him I'll be down directly.

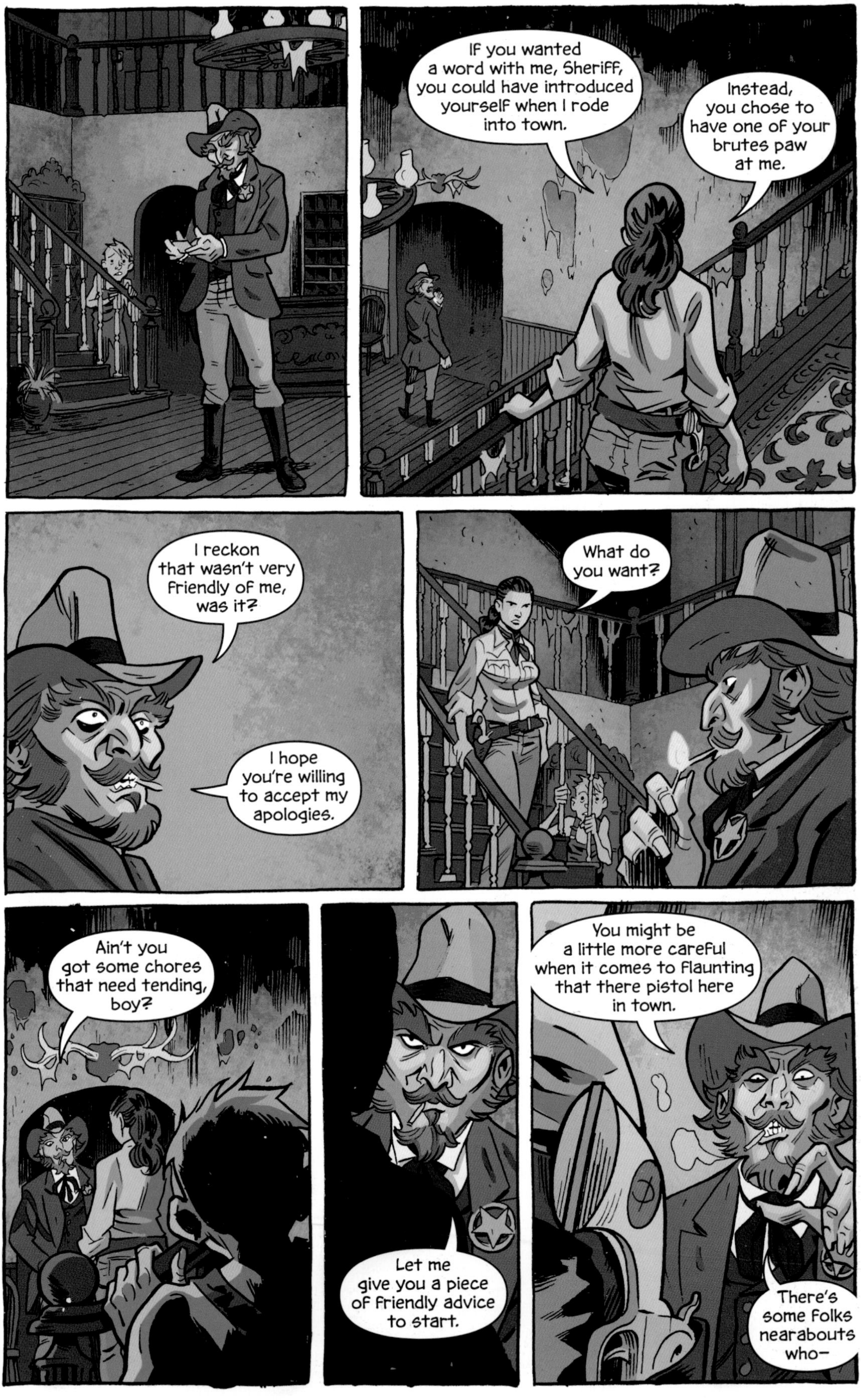
If you wanted a word with me, Sheriff, you could have introduced yourself when I rode into town.
Instead, you chose to have one of your brutes paw at me.
I reckon that wasn't very friendly of me, was it?
I hope you're willing to accept my apologies.
What do you want?
Ain't you got some chores that need tending, boy?
Let me give you a piece of friendly advice to start.
You might be a little more careful when it comes to flaunting that there pistol here in town.
There's some folks nearabouts who—

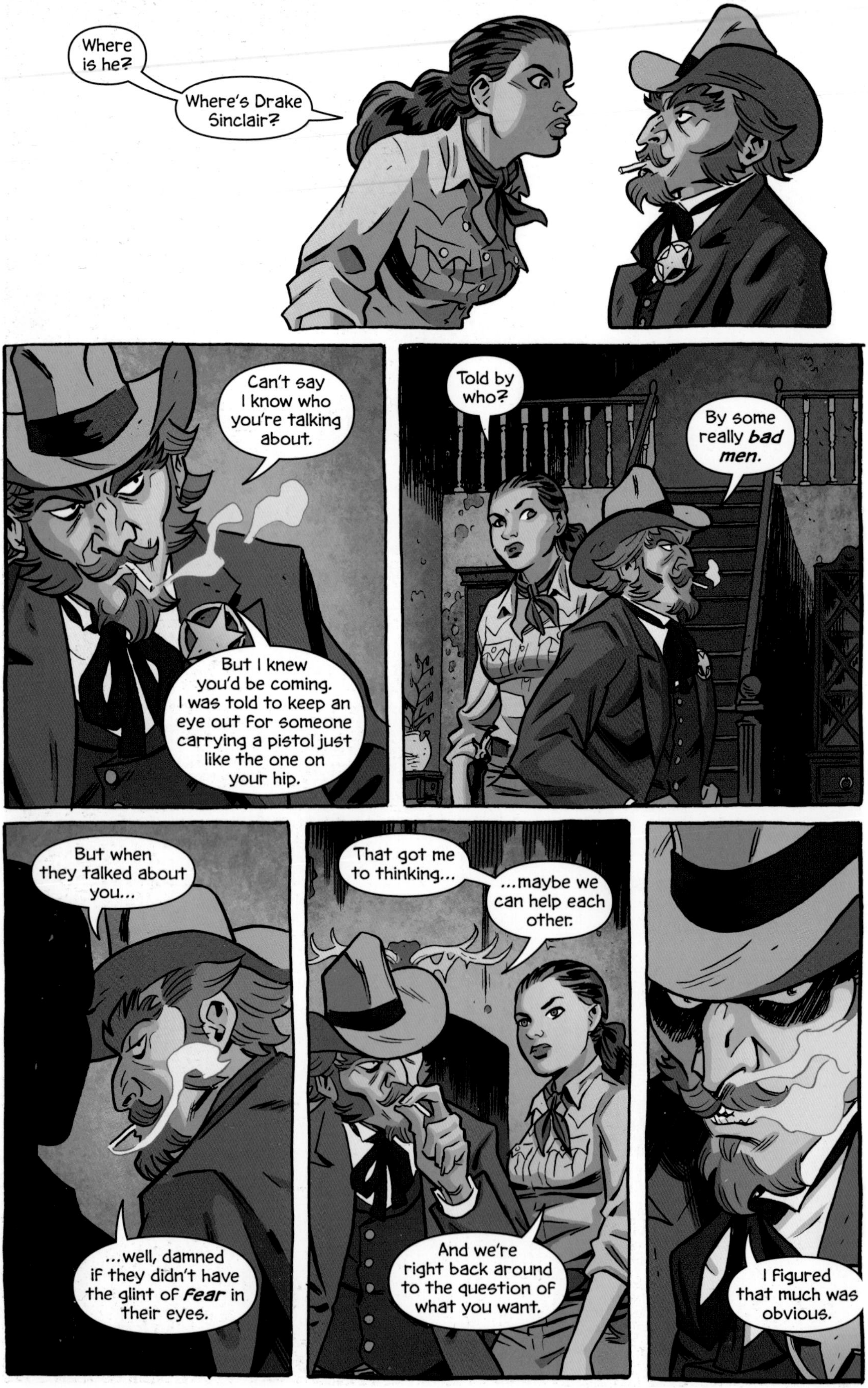
Where is he?
Where's Drake Sinclair?
Can't say I know who you're talking about.
But I knew you'd be coming. I was told to keep an eye out for someone carrying a pistol just like the one on your hip.
Told by who?
By some really *bad men*.
But when they talked about you...
...well, damned if they didn't have the glint of *fear* in their eyes.
That got me to thinking...
...maybe we can help each other.
And we're right back around to the question of what you want.
I figured that much was obvious.

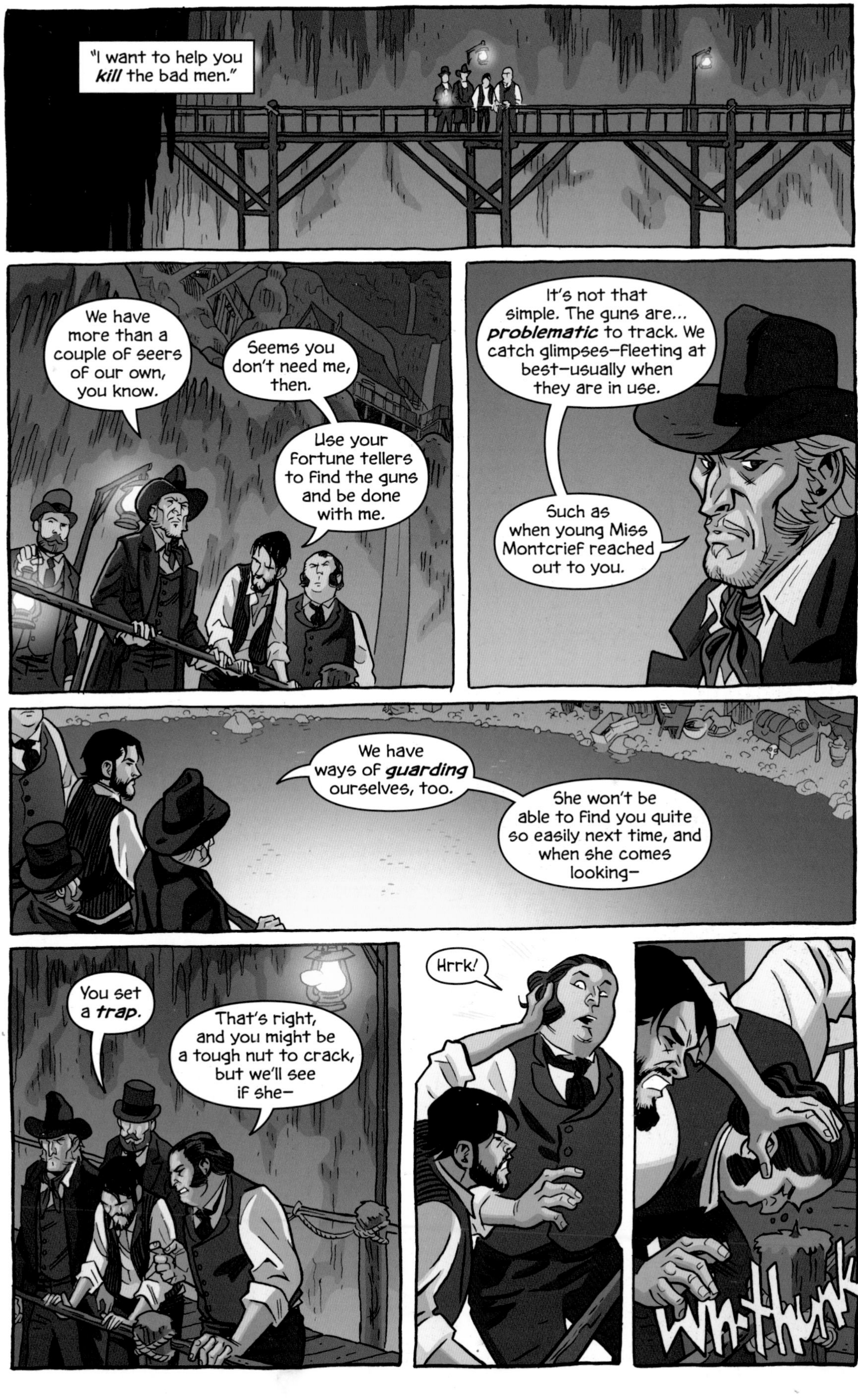
"I want to help you *kill* the bad men."
We have more than a couple of seers of our own, you know.
Seems you don't need me, then.
Use your fortune tellers to find the guns and be done with me.
It's not that simple. The guns are... *problematic* to track. We catch glimpses—fleeting at best—usually when they are in use.
Such as when young Miss Montcrief reached out to you.
We have ways of *guarding* ourselves, too.
She won't be able to find you quite so easily next time, and when she comes looking—
You set a *trap.*
That's right, and you might be a tough nut to crack, but we'll see if she—
Hrrk!
WN-THUNK!

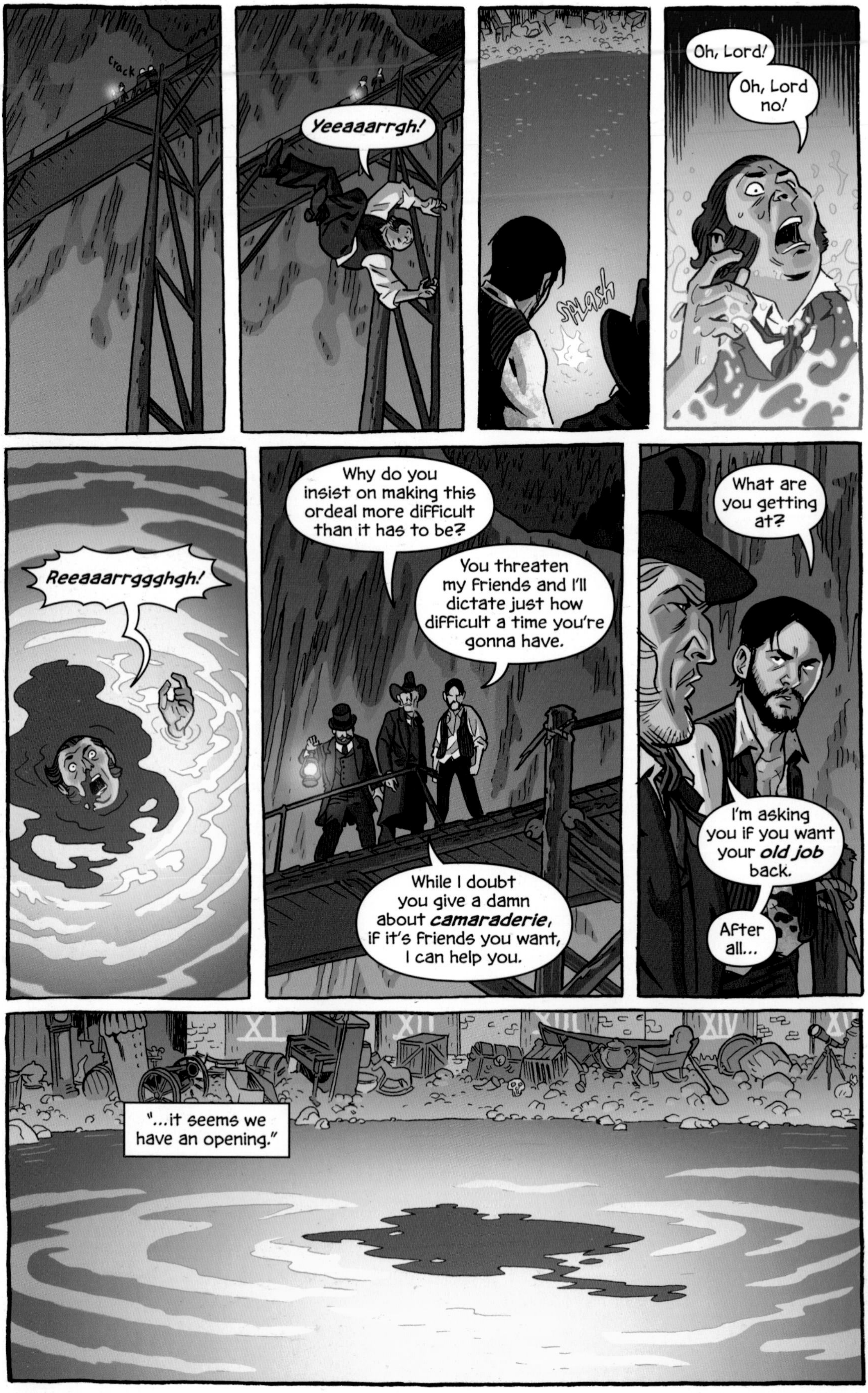
crack
Yeeaaarrgh!
SPLASH
Oh, Lord!
Oh, Lord no!
Reeaaarrggghgh!
Why do you insist on making this ordeal more difficult than it has to be?
You threaten my friends and I'll dictate just how difficult a time you're gonna have.
While I doubt you give a damn about *camaraderie*, if it's friends you want, I can help you.
What are you getting at?
I'm asking you if you want your *old job* back.
After all...
"...it seems we have an opening."

CHAPTER TWO

The *Sixth Gun* was a weapon forged by hatred and oiled in betrayal.

To carry the gun— even unwillingly— came with a price...

...a *penance* that likely could not be satisfied without loss of life and immortal soul.

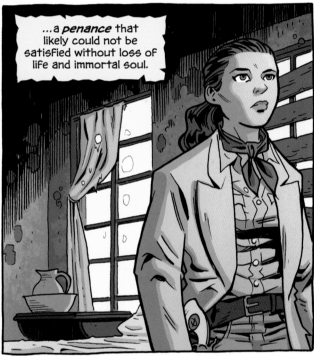

But the gun had a soul of its own... and a desire to play a part in its own fate.

The gun *schemed.*

A dream of trickery uncoiled blackly within the gunmetal like a serpent through the garden.

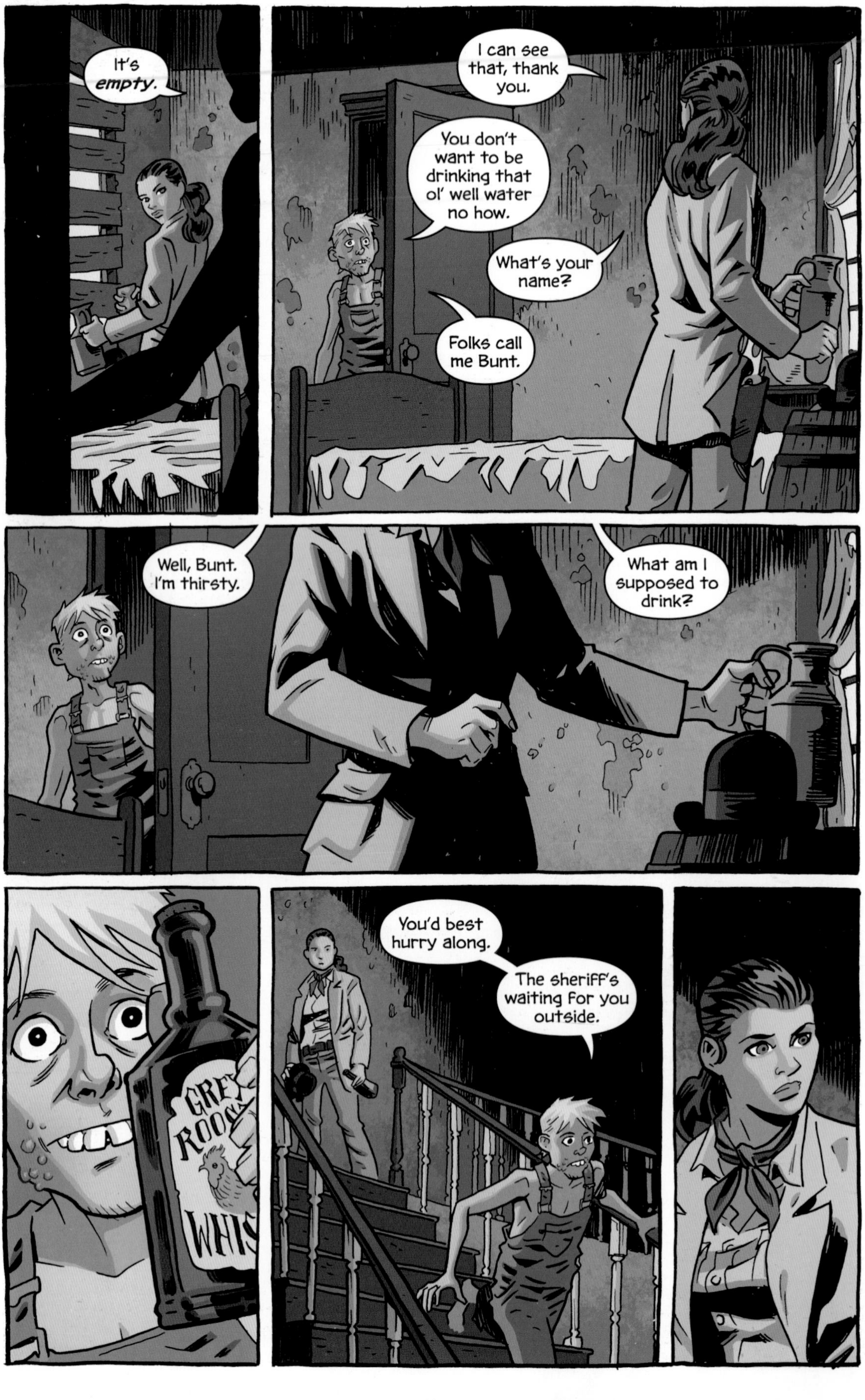
It's *empty*.
I can see that, thank you.
You don't want to be drinking that ol' well water no how.
What's your name?
Folks call me Bunt.
Well, Bunt. I'm thirsty.
What am I supposed to drink?
You'd best hurry along.
The sheriff's waiting for you outside.

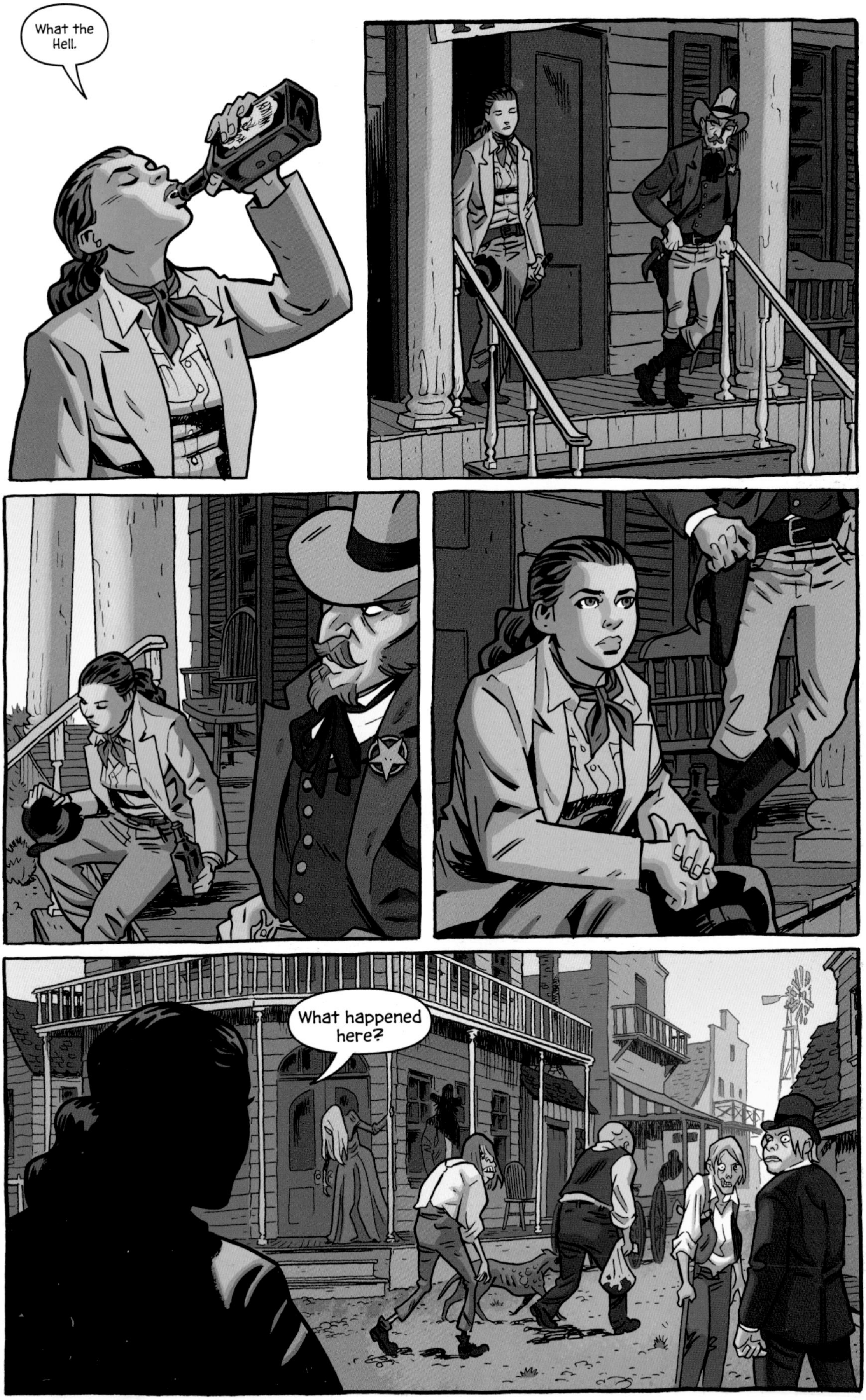
What the Hell.
What happened here?

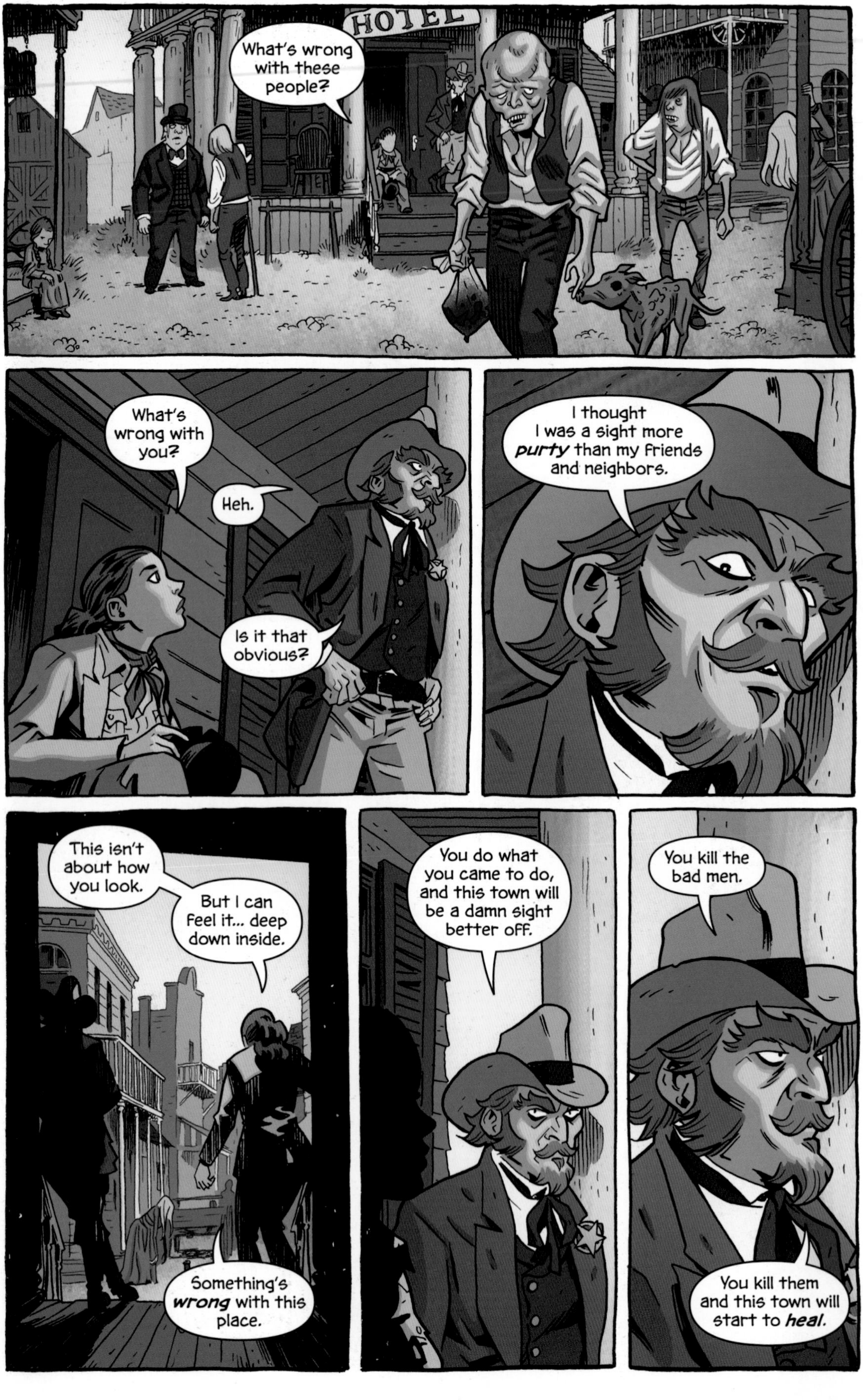
HOTEL
What's wrong with these people?
What's wrong with you?
Heh.
Is it that obvious?
I thought I was a sight more *purty* than my friends and neighbors.
This isn't about how you look.
But I can feel it... deep down inside.
Something's *wrong* with this place.
You do what you came to do, and this town will be a damn sight better off.
You kill the bad men.
You kill them and this town will start to *heal*.

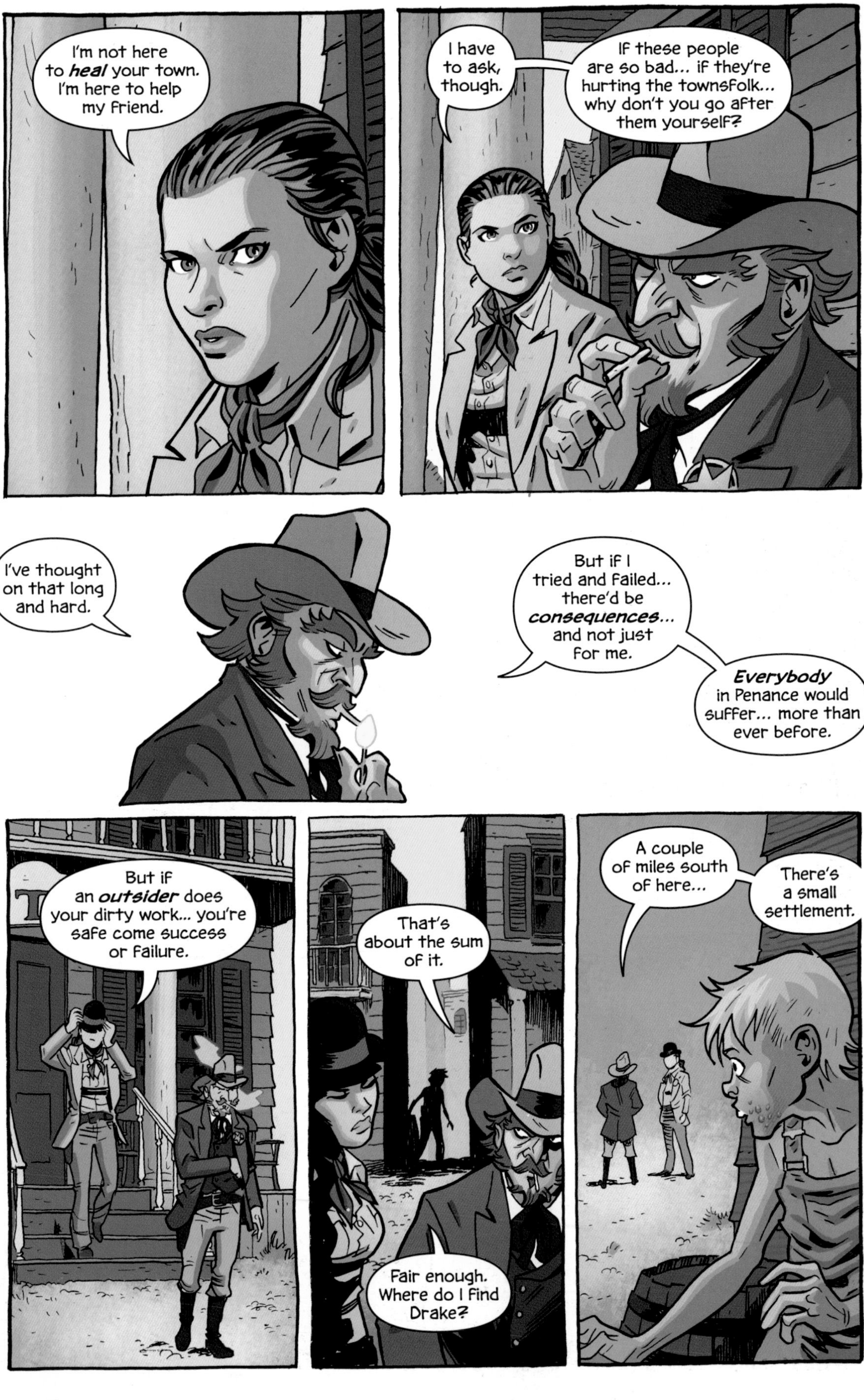

I'm not here to *heal* your town. I'm here to help my friend.
I have to ask, though.
If these people are so bad... if they're hurting the townsfolk... why don't you go after them yourself?
I've thought on that long and hard.
But if I tried and failed... there'd be *consequences*... and not just for me.
Everybody in Penance would suffer... more than ever before.
But if an *outsider* does your dirty work... you're safe come success or failure.
That's about the sum of it.
Fair enough. Where do I find Drake?
A couple of miles south of here...
There's a small settlement.

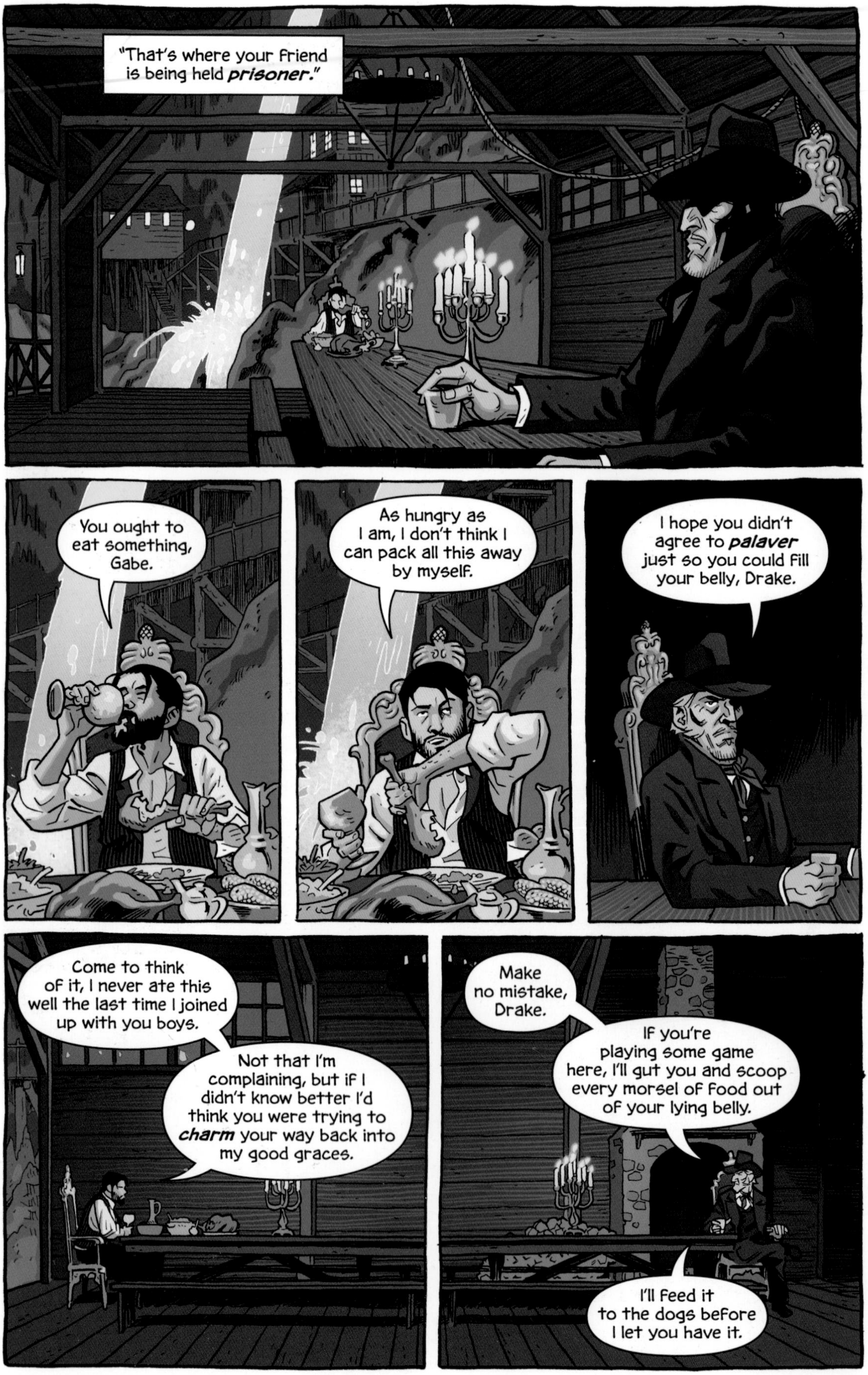
"That's where your friend is being held *prisoner.*"
You ought to eat something, Gabe.
As hungry as I am, I don't think I can pack all this away by myself.
I hope you didn't agree to *palaver* just so you could fill your belly, Drake.
Come to think of it, I never ate this well the last time I joined up with you boys.
Not that I'm complaining, but if I didn't know better I'd think you were trying to *charm* your way back into my good graces.
Make no mistake, Drake.
If you're playing some game here, I'll gut you and scoop every morsel of food out of your lying belly.
I'll feed it to the dogs before I let you have it.

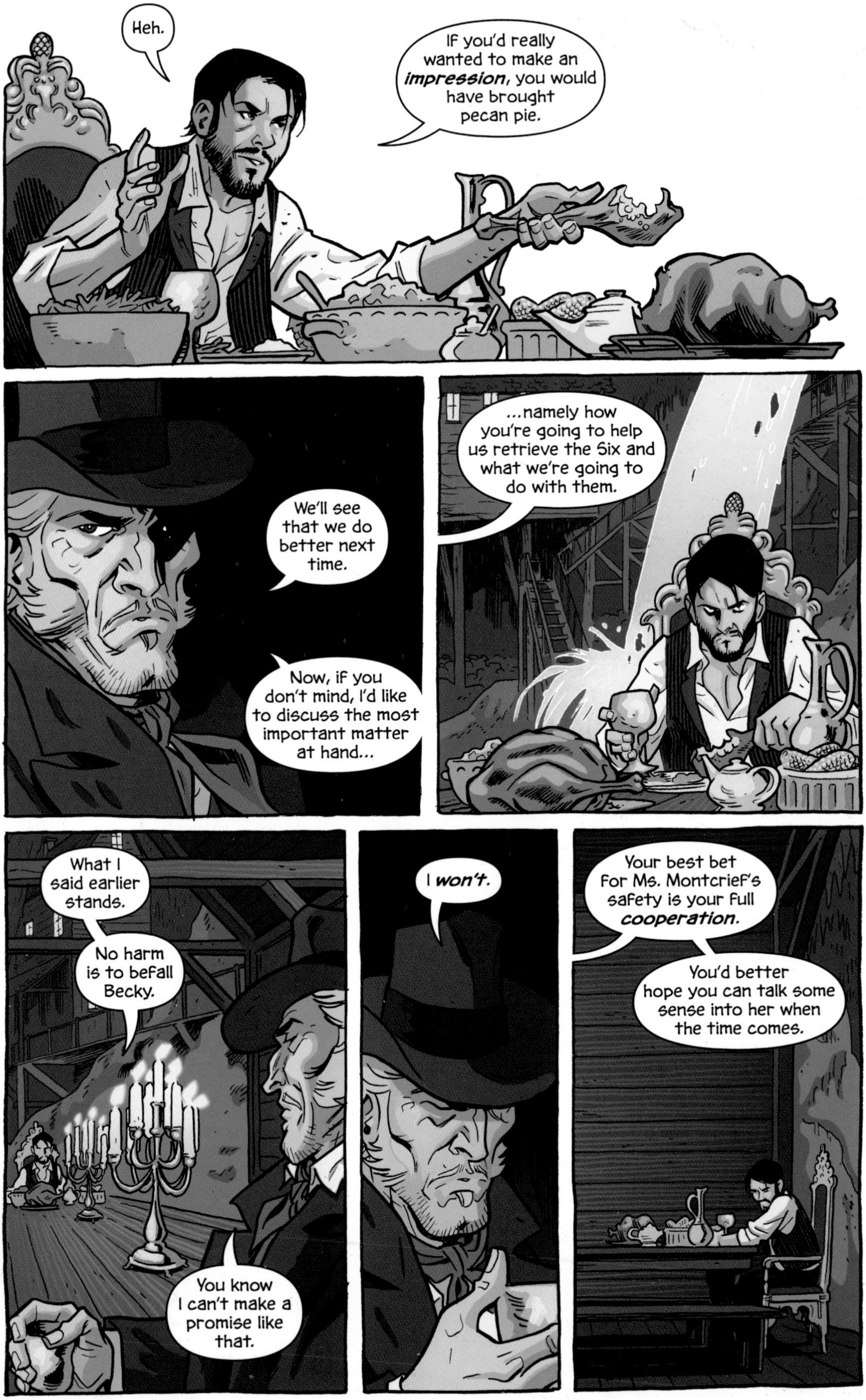
Heh.
If you'd really wanted to make an *impression*, you would have brought pecan pie.
We'll see that we do better next time.
Now, if you don't mind, I'd like to discuss the most important matter at hand...
...namely how you're going to help us retrieve the Six and what we're going to do with them.
What I said earlier stands.
No harm is to befall Becky.
You know I can't make a promise like that.
I *won't*.
Your best bet for Ms. Montcrief's safety is your full *cooperation*.
You'd better hope you can talk some sense into her when the time comes.

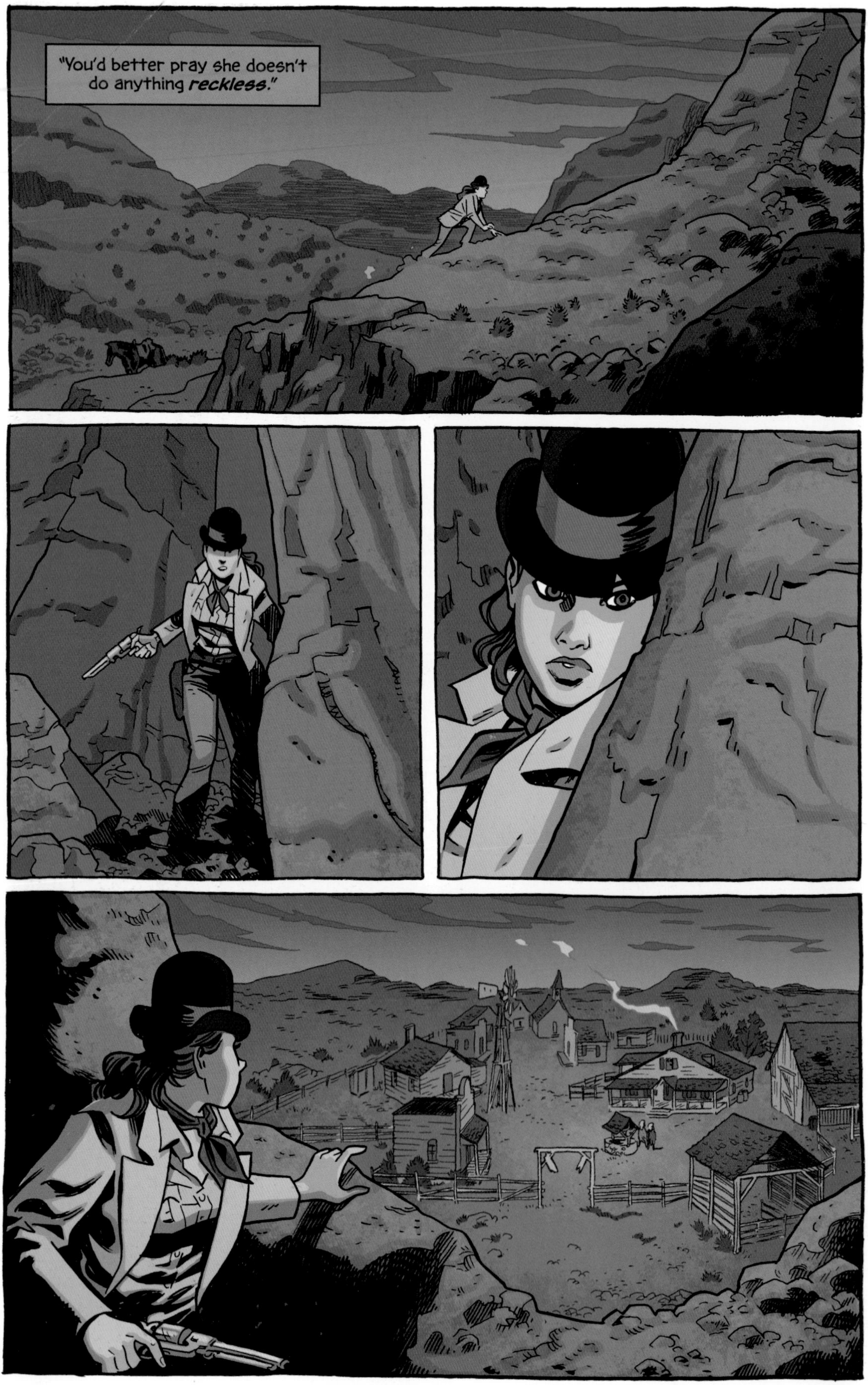
"You'd better pray she doesn't do anything *reckless*."

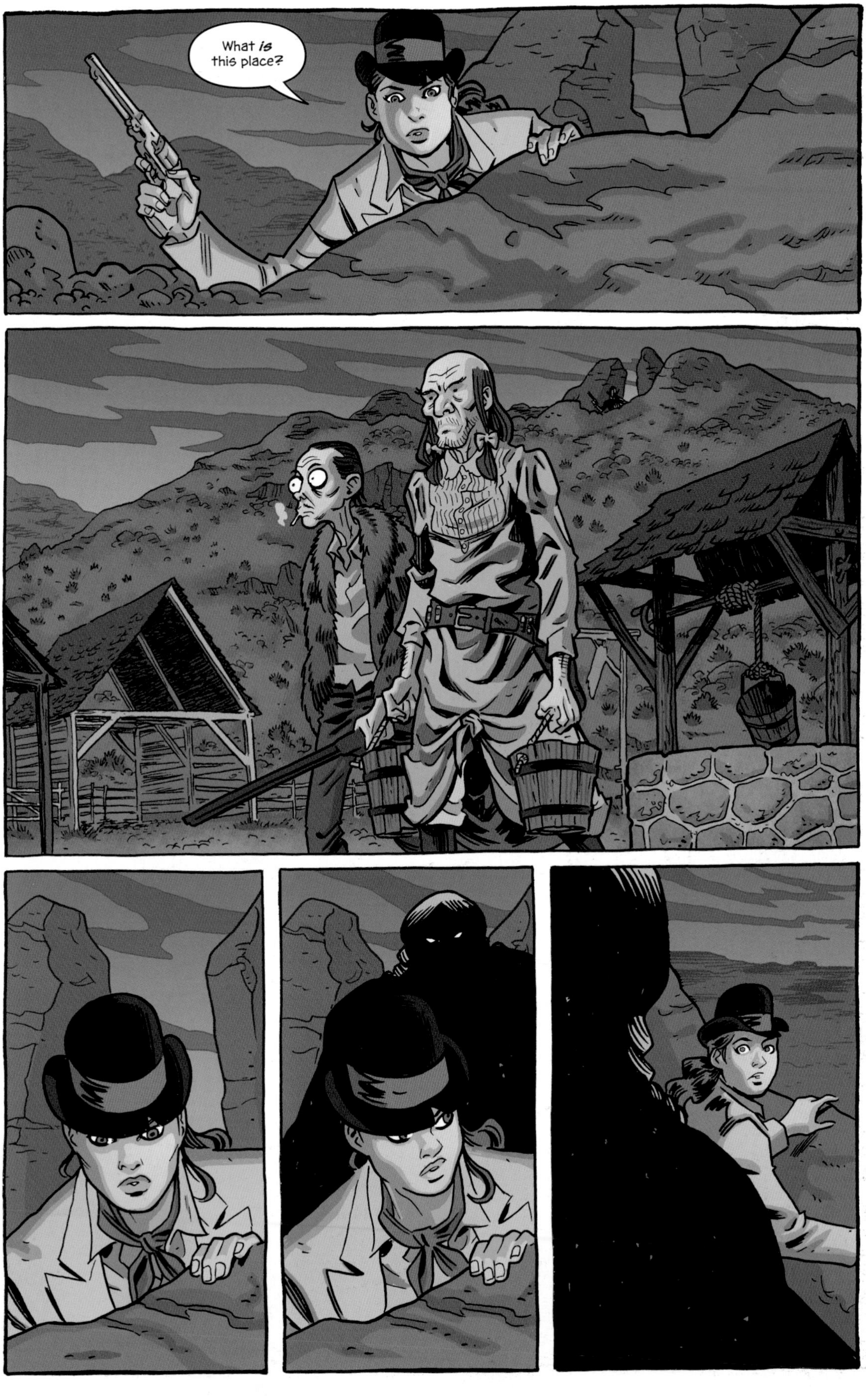
What *is* this place?

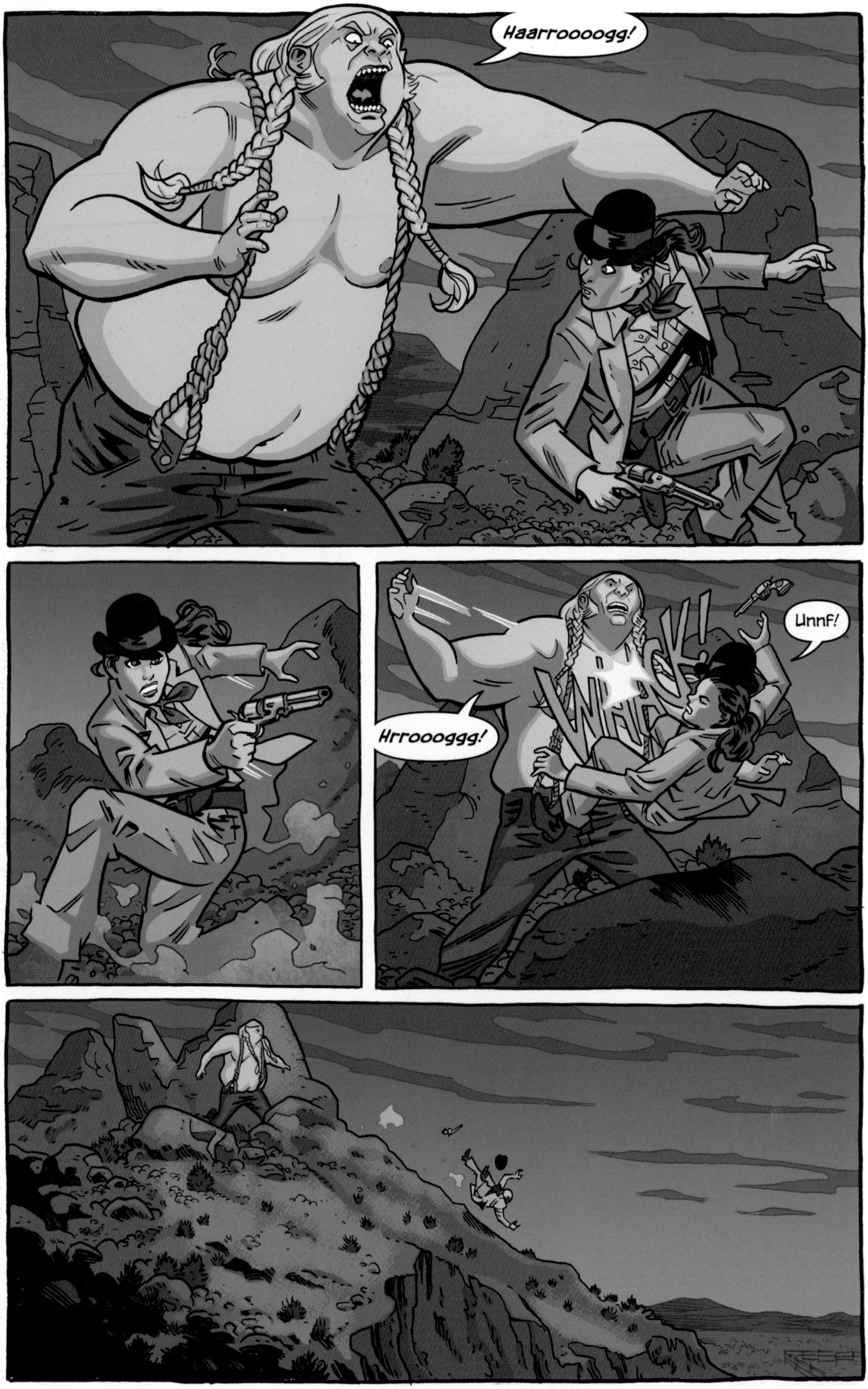
Haarroooogg!
Hrroooggg!
Unnf!

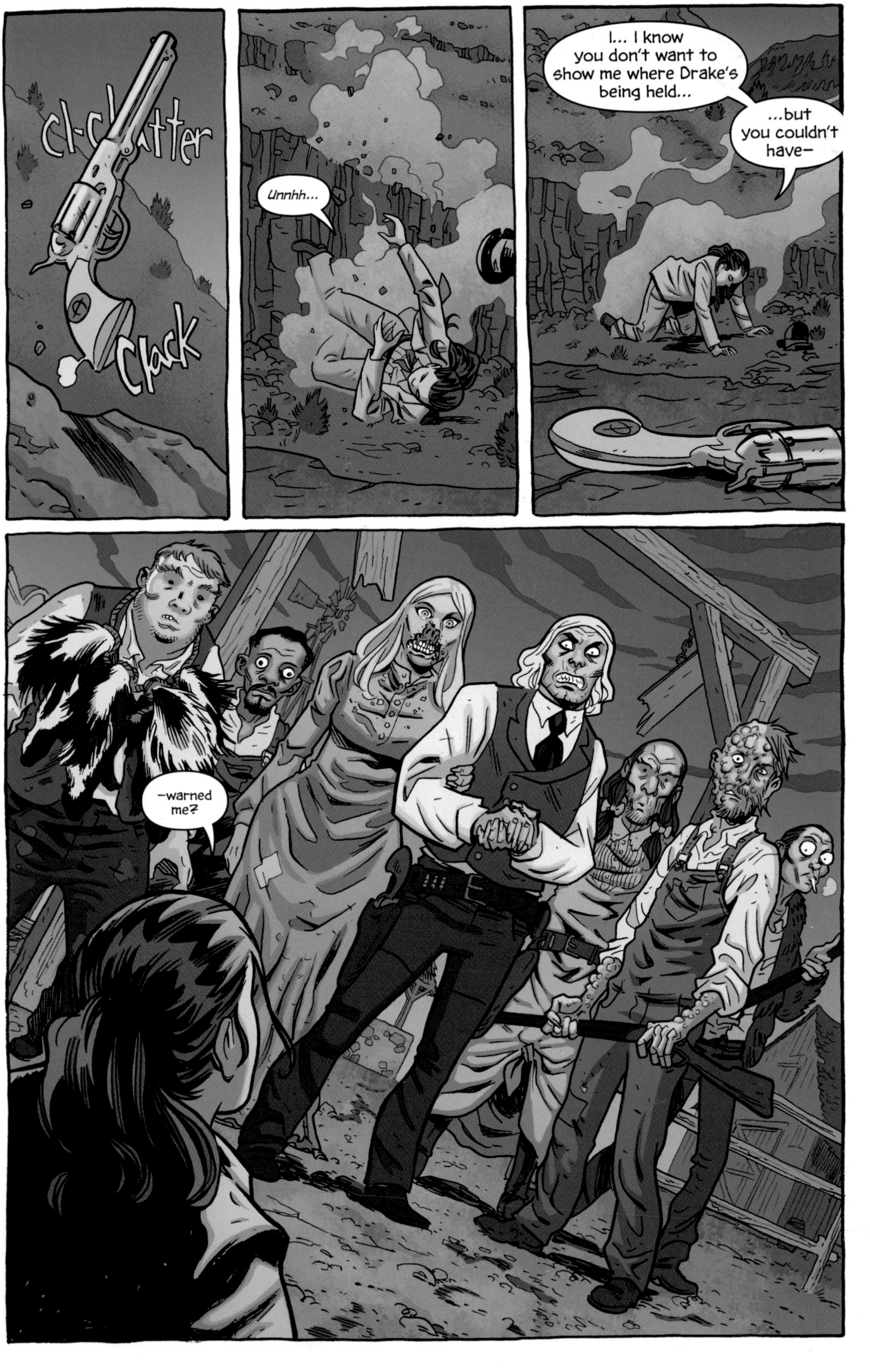
cl-clatter
clack
Unnhh...
I... I know you don't want to show me where Drake's being held...
...but you couldn't have–
–warned me?

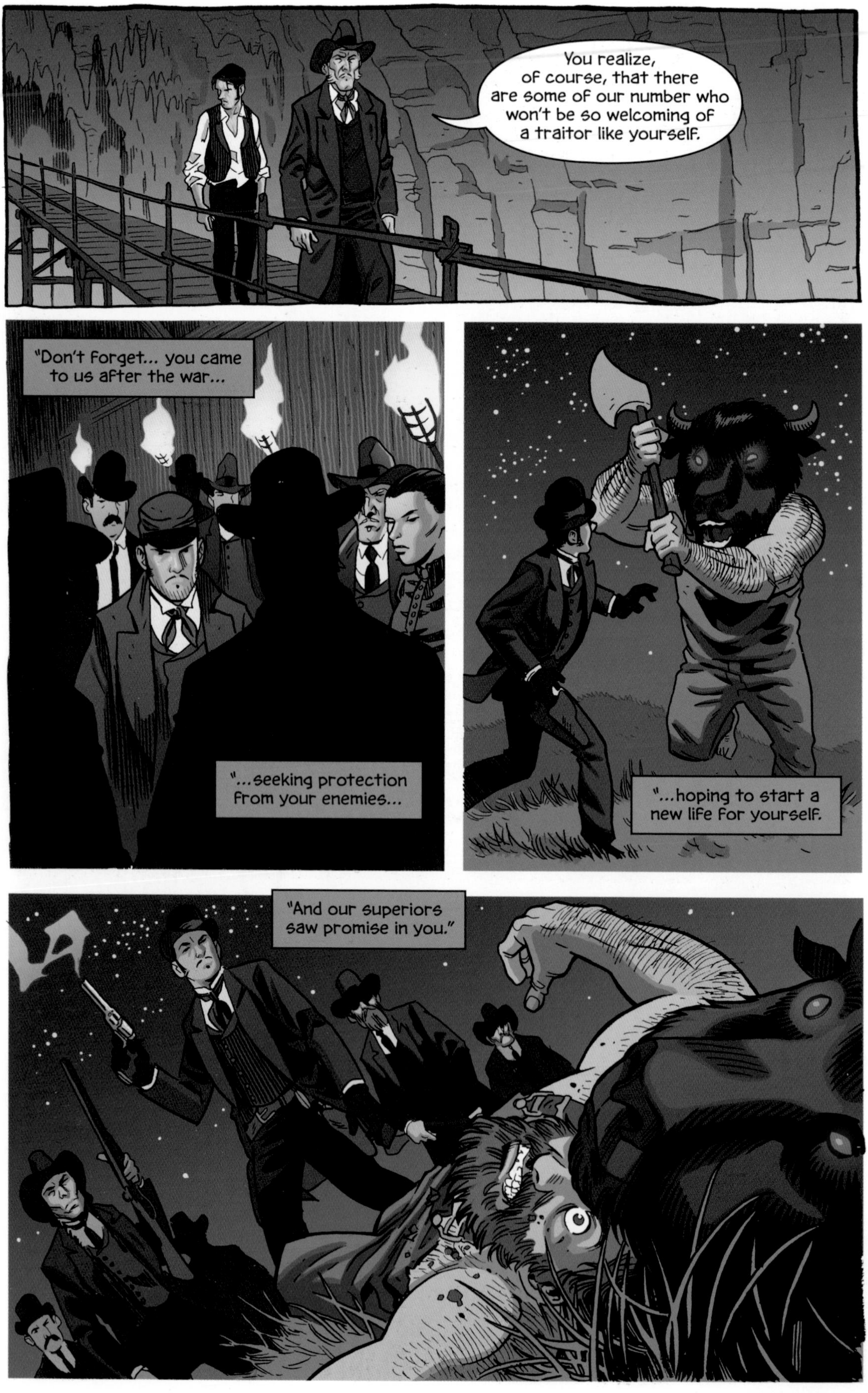
You realize, of course, that there are some of our number who won't be so welcoming of a traitor like yourself.
"Don't forget... you came to us after the war...
"...seeking protection from your enemies...
"...hoping to start a new life for yourself.
"And our superiors saw promise in you."

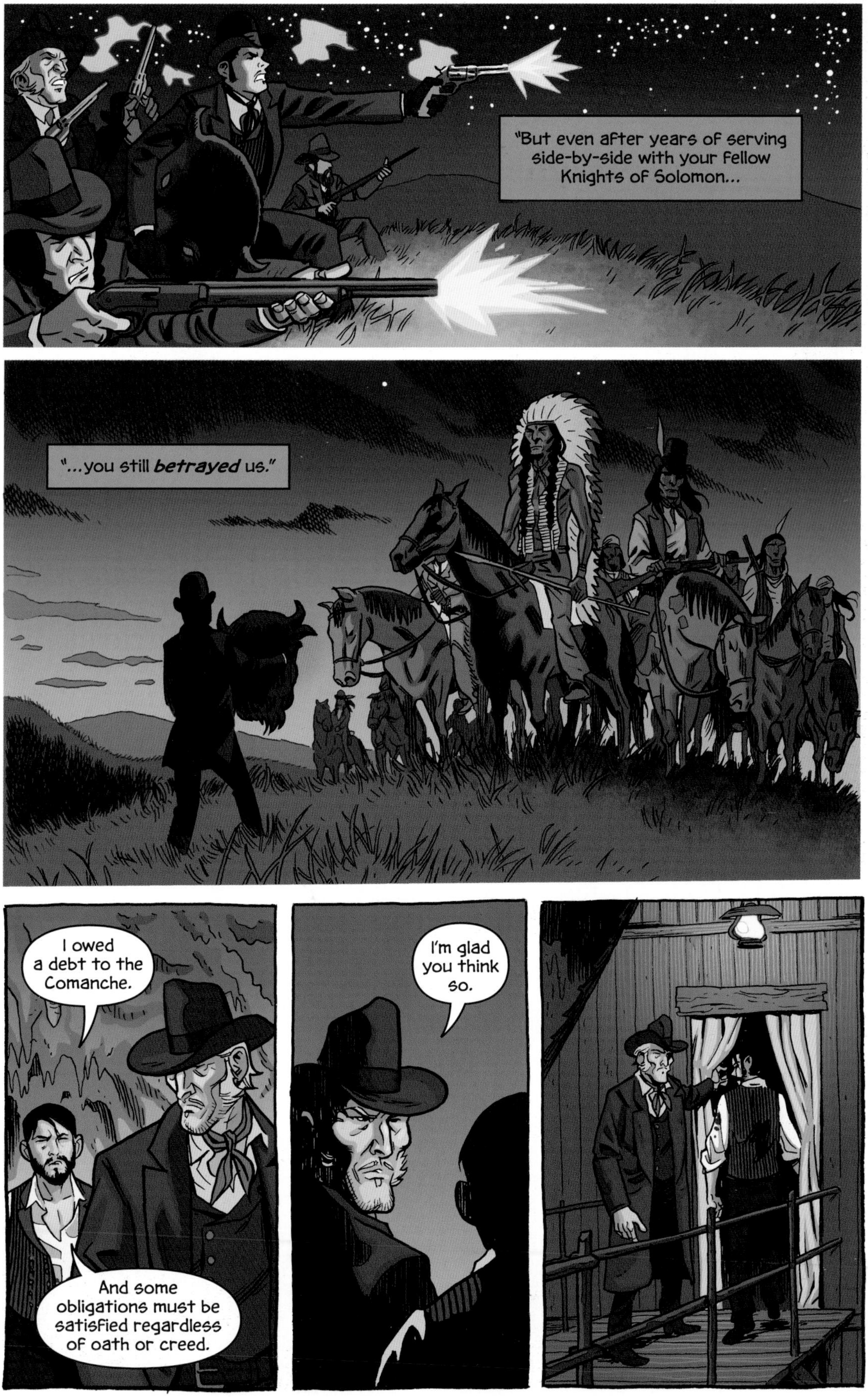
"But even after years of serving side-by-side with your fellow Knights of Solomon...
"...you still *betrayed* us."
I owed a debt to the Comanche.
And some obligations must be satisfied regardless of oath or creed.
I'm glad you think so.

I told you we had ways of warding ourselves from Ms. Montcrief's visions, didn't I?

I may have also mentioned that we have *seers* of our own.

You see, we're better prepared these days to root out duplicity should it surface within our ranks.

And *Jesup* here is very interested in what our robed friends have to say about your *intentions.*

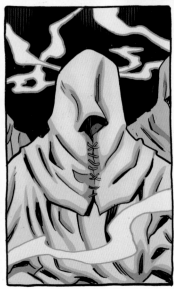

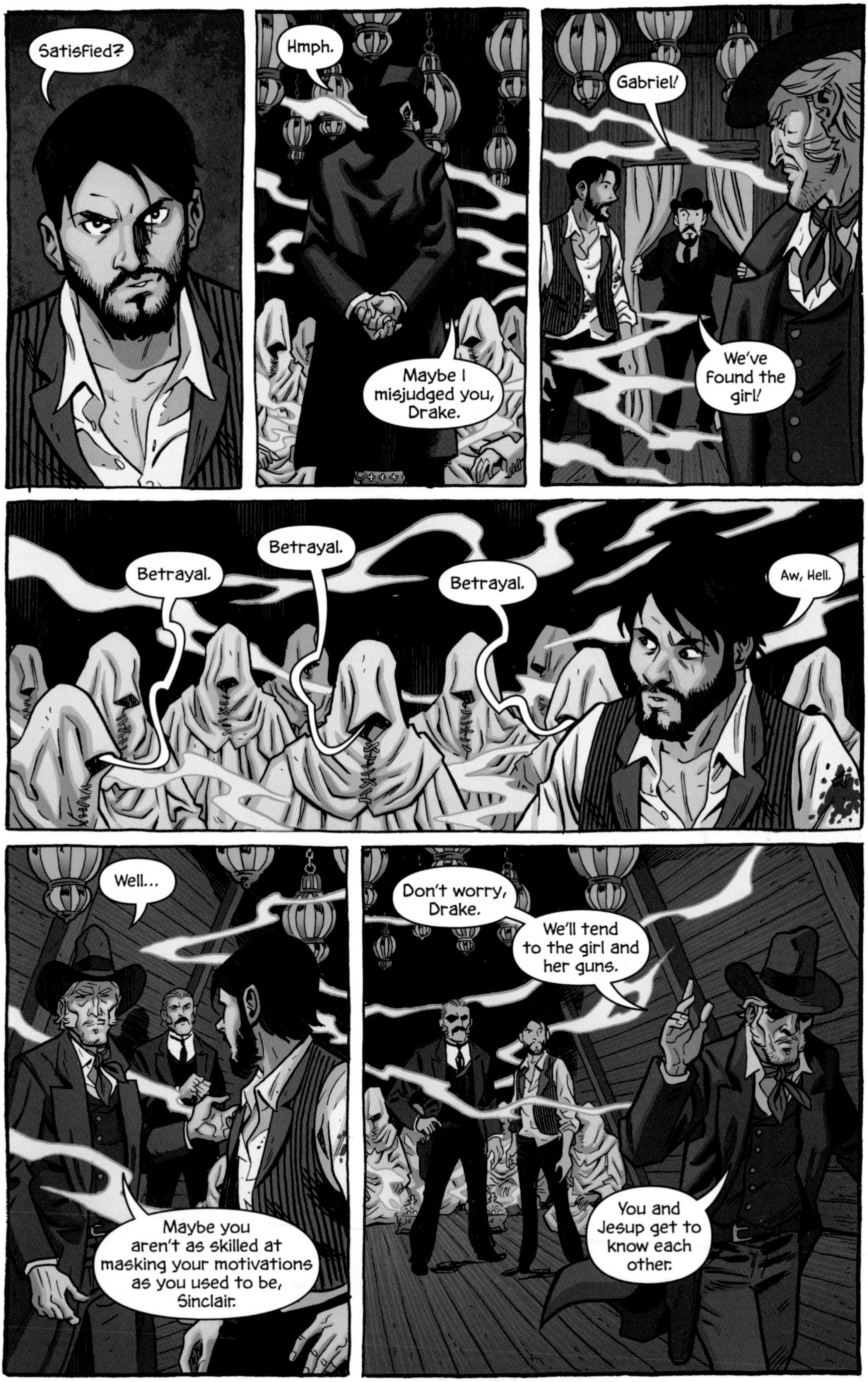
Satisfied?
Hmph.
Maybe I misjudged you, Drake.
Gabriel!
We've found the girl!
Betrayal.
Betrayal.
Betrayal.
Aw, Hell.
Well...
Maybe you aren't as skilled at masking your motivations as you used to be, Sinclair.
Don't worry, Drake.
We'll tend to the girl and her guns.
You and Jesup get to know each other.

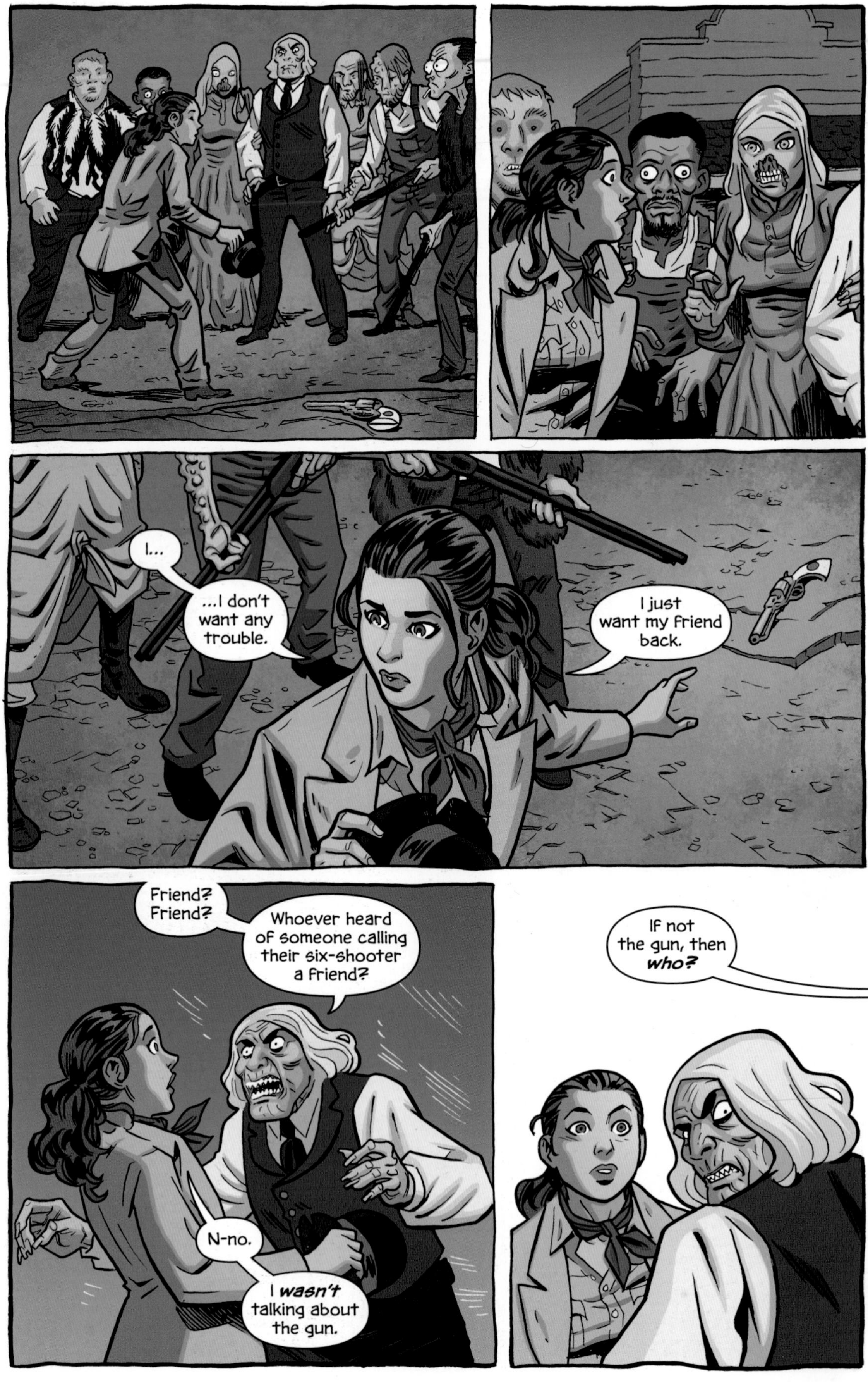
I...
...I don't want any trouble.
I just want my friend back.
Friend? Friend?
Whoever heard of someone calling their six-shooter a friend?
N-no.
I *wasn't* talking about the gun.
If not the gun, then *who?*

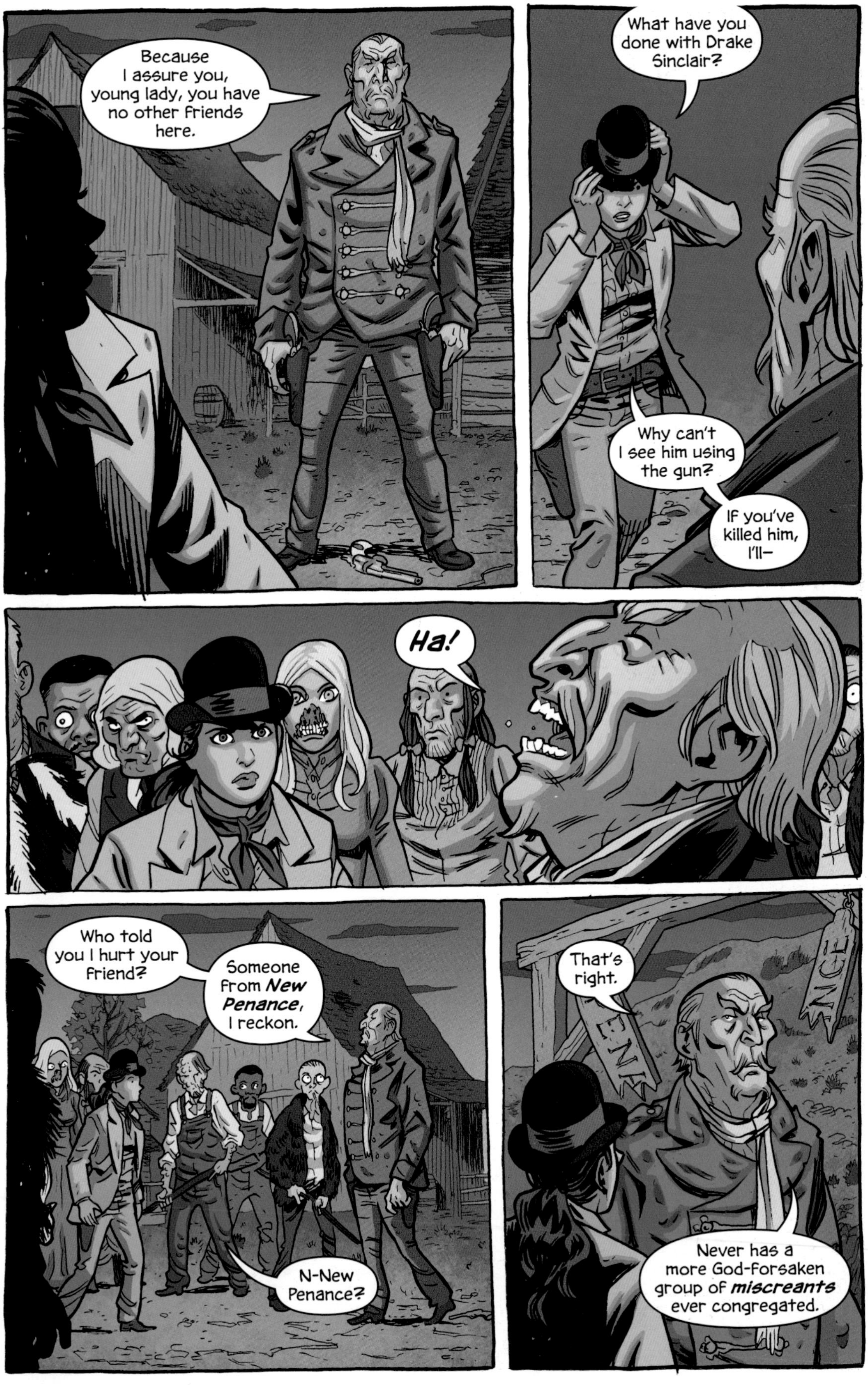
Because I assure you, young lady, you have no other friends here.
What have you done with Drake Sinclair?
Why can't I see him using the gun?
If you've killed him, I'll–
Ha!
Who told you I hurt your friend?
Someone from ***New Penance***, I reckon.
N-New Penance?
That's right.
Never has a more God-forsaken group of ***miscreants*** ever congregated.

They'd lie... cheat... and murder if given half the chance...

All so they could take what rightfully *belongs* to me and mine.

Who sent you? Maze?

I reckon he's getting right desperate if he sends a girl to do his business.

It's unfortunate, really. I've tried to be a reasonable man.

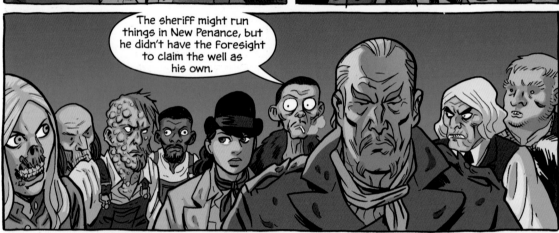

The sheriff might run things in New Penance, but he didn't have the foresight to claim the well as his own.

It's the water, isn't it?

The water changed the people in town... these people here....

It's poison, isn't it?

Poison?

No, not poison. It won't kill you.

Quite the opposite, in point of fact.

You drink enough of it, though, and you won't be able to live without it.

And now that New Penance has sent an assassin to kill me, they'll pay triple if they want so much as another sip.

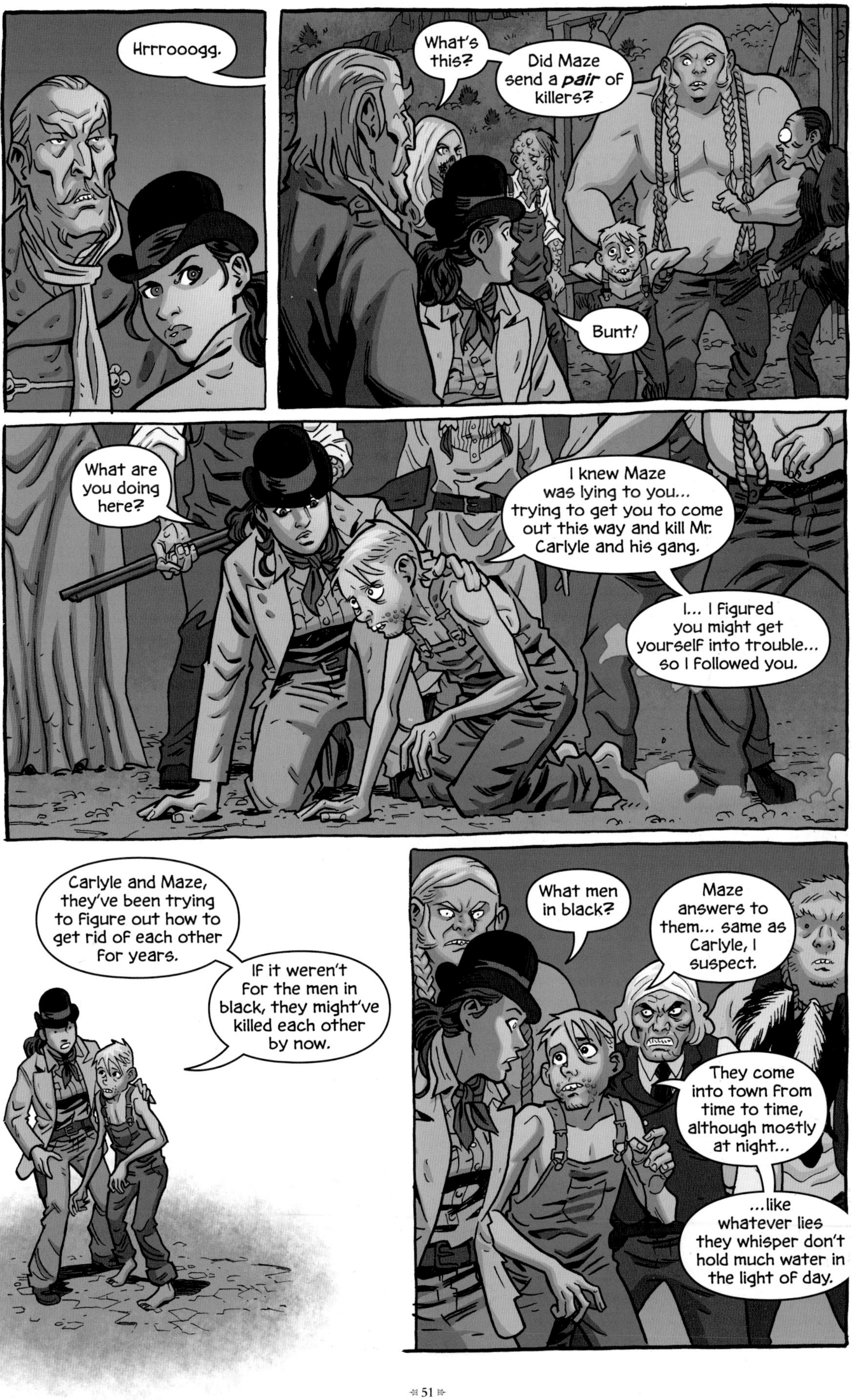
Hrrrooogg.
What's this?
Did Maze send a *pair* of killers?
Bunt!
What are you doing here?
I knew Maze was lying to you... trying to get you to come out this way and kill Mr. Carlyle and his gang.
I... I figured you might get yourself into trouble... so I followed you.
Carlyle and Maze, they've been trying to figure out how to get rid of each other for years.
If it weren't for the men in black, they might've killed each other by now.
What men in black?
Maze answers to them... same as Carlyle, I suspect.
They come into town from time to time, although mostly at night...
...like whatever lies they whisper don't hold much water in the light of day.

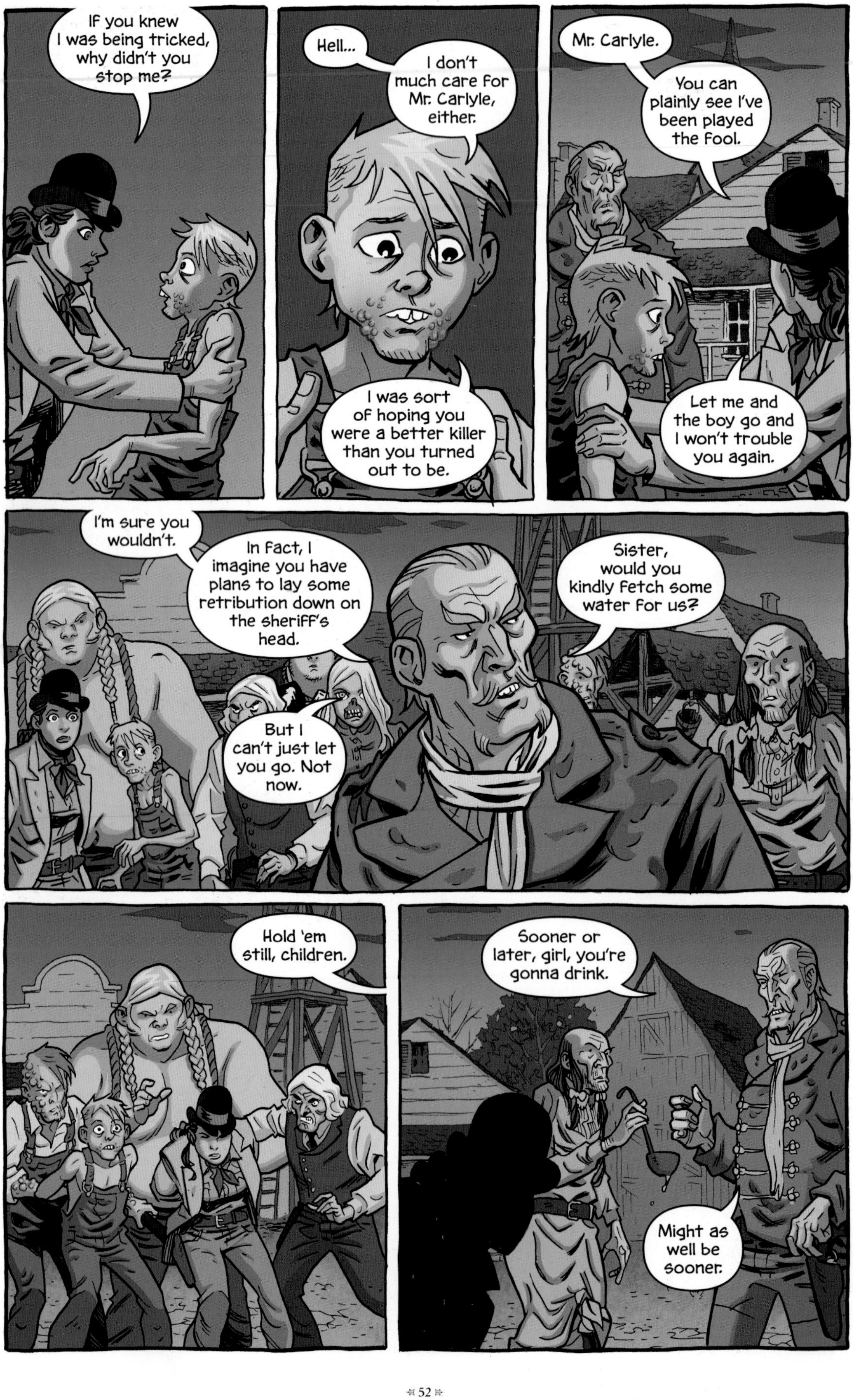
If you knew I was being tricked, why didn't you stop me?
Hell...
I don't much care for Mr. Carlyle, either.
I was sort of hoping you were a better killer than you turned out to be.
Mr. Carlyle.
You can plainly see I've been played the fool.
Let me and the boy go and I won't trouble you again.
I'm sure you wouldn't.
In fact, I imagine you have plans to lay some retribution down on the sheriff's head.
But I can't just let you go. Not now.
Sister, would you kindly fetch some water for us?
Hold 'em still, children.
Sooner or later, girl, you're gonna drink.
Might as well be sooner.

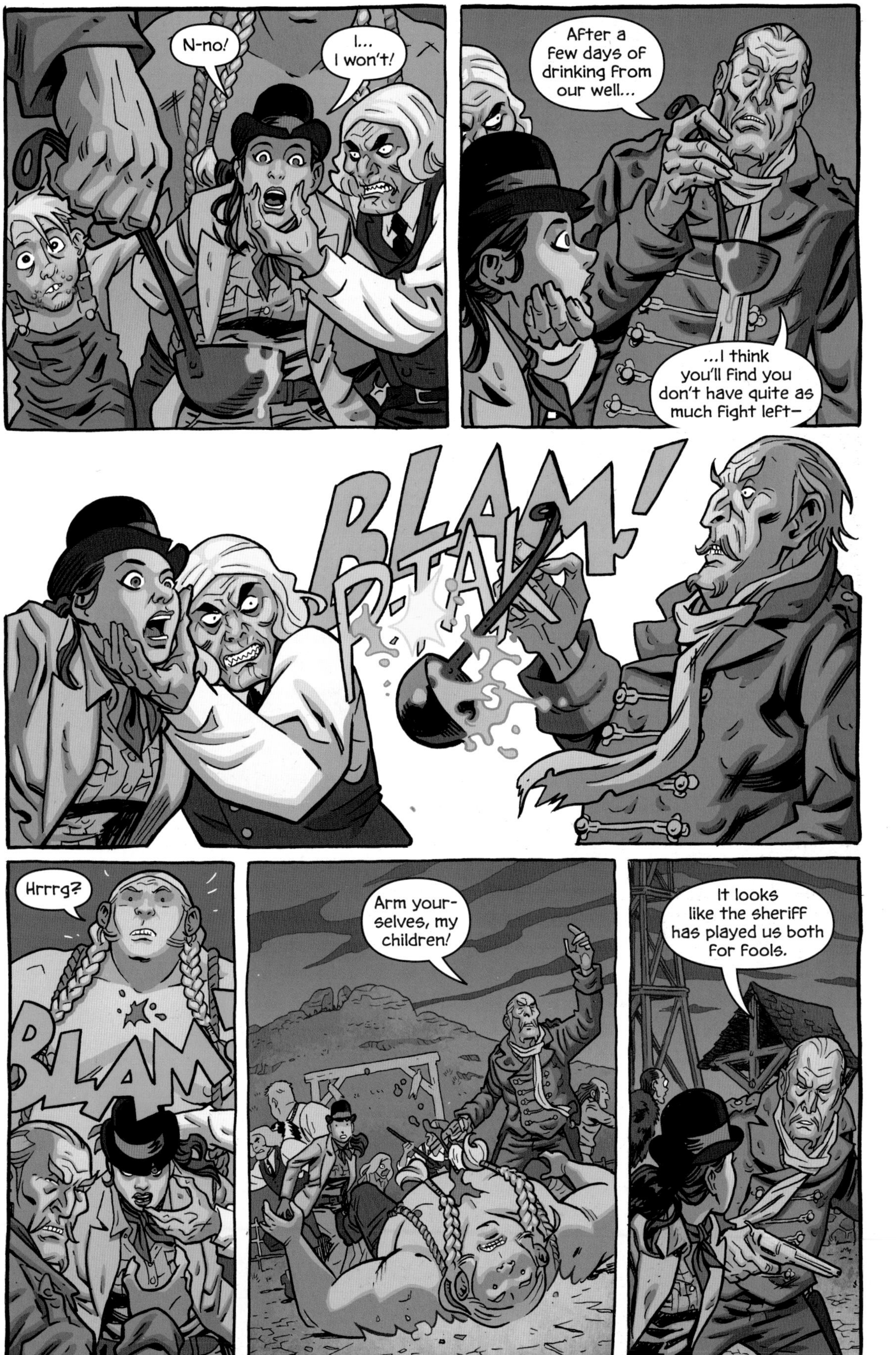
N-no!
I... I won't!
After a few days of drinking from our well...
...I think you'll find you don't have quite as much fight left—
BLAM!
P-TANK
Hrrrg?
BLAM
Arm your-selves, my children!
It looks like the sheriff has played us both for fools.

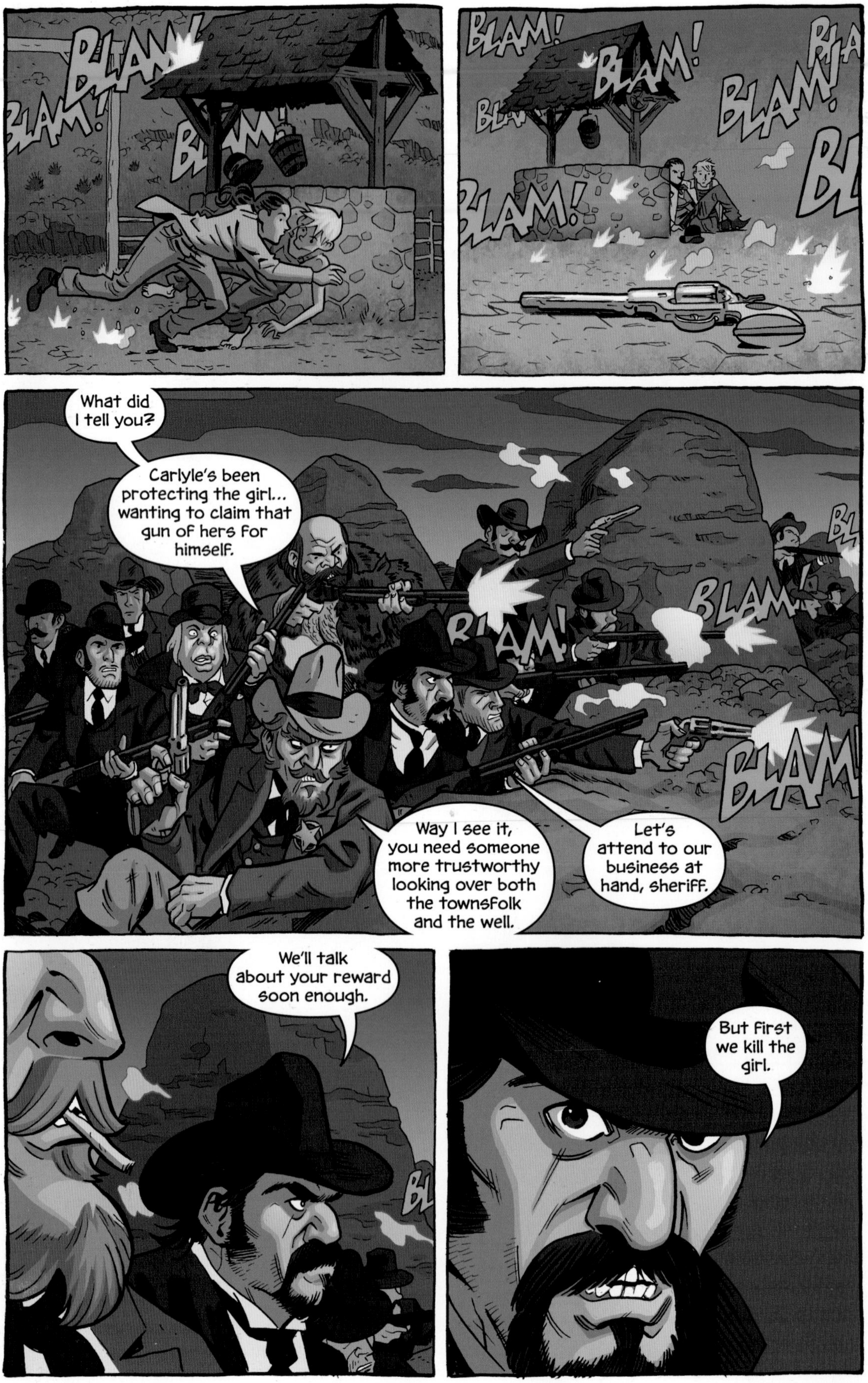
BLAM!
BLAM!
BLAM!
BLAM!
BLAM!
BLAM!
BLAM!
BLAM!
What did I tell you?
Carlyle's been protecting the girl... wanting to claim that gun of hers for himself.
BLAM!
BLAM!
Way I see it, you need someone more trustworthy looking over both the townsfolk and the well.
Let's attend to our business at hand, sheriff.
We'll talk about your reward soon enough.
But first we kill the girl.

CHAPTER THREE

BLAM!
B-BLAM!
You might have come out here to kill me, girl...
BLAM!
BLAM!
KAPOW!
B-BLAM!
BLAM!
B-BLAM!
...but I reckon Sheriff Maze is gonna put us *both* in the dirt before he's done!
What do we do? What do we do?
BLAM!
Just keep your head down.
BLAM!
I'll think of *something*.
BLAM!

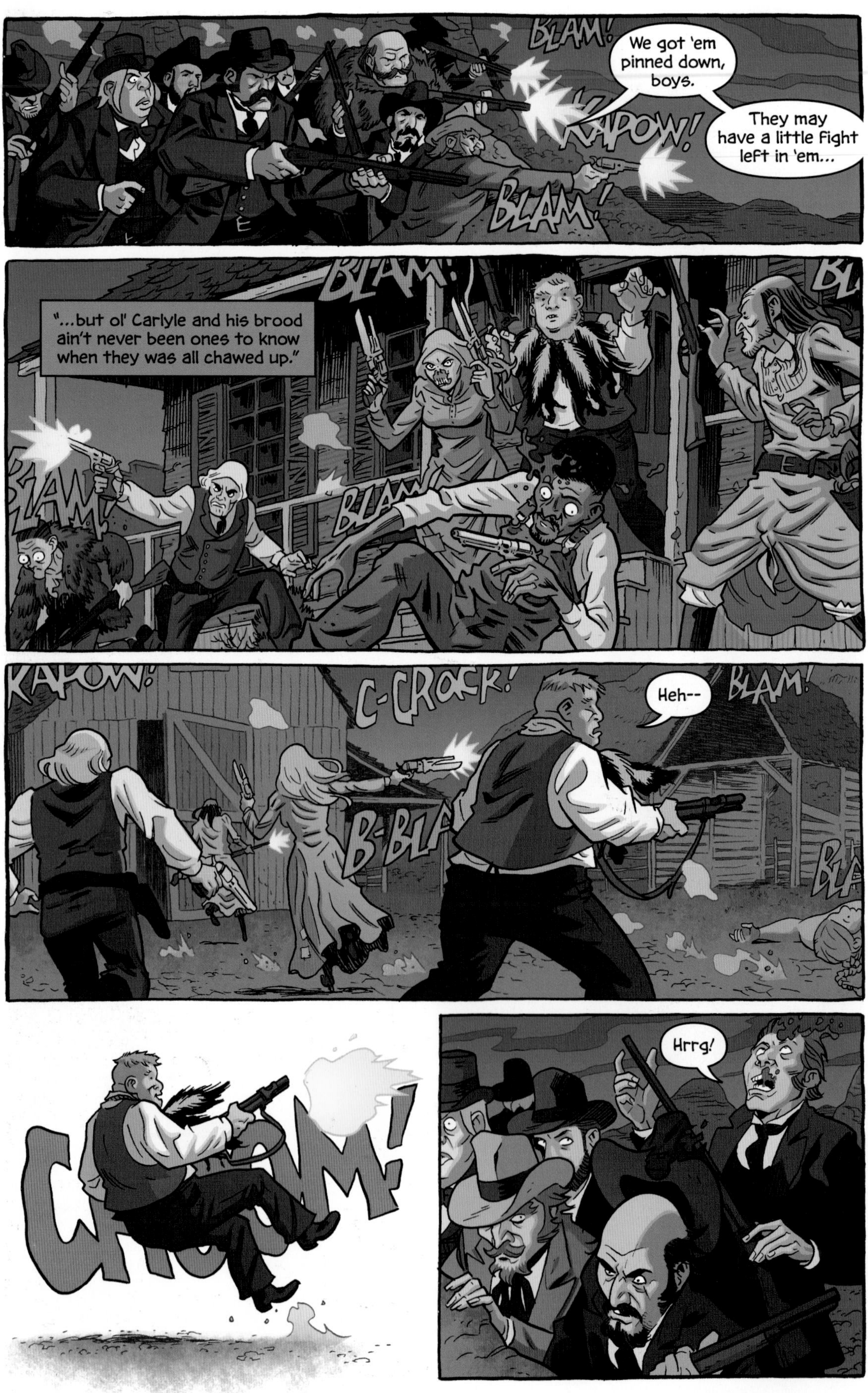
BLAM!
We got 'em pinned down, boys.
They may have a little fight left in 'em...
KAPOW!
BLAM!
BLAM!
"...but ol' Carlyle and his brood ain't never been ones to know when they was all chawed up."
BLAM!
KAPOW!
C-CROCK!
Heh--
BLAM!
Hrrg!

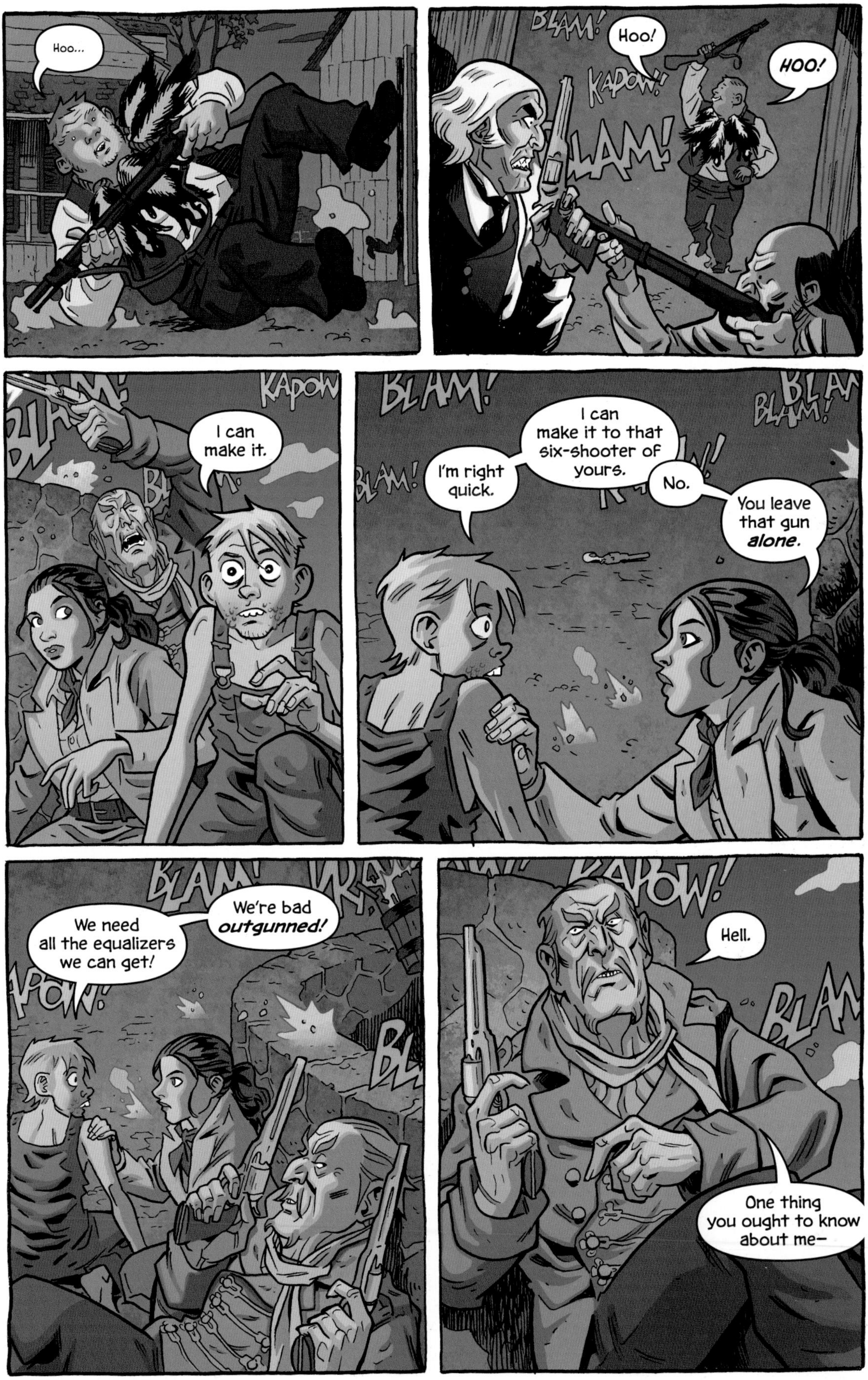
Hoo...
BLAM!
Hoo!
KAPOW!!
HOO!
BLAM!
KAPOW
I can make it.
BLAM!
I'm right quick.
I can make it to that six-shooter of yours.
BLAM!
No.
You leave that gun *alone*.
BLAM!
We need all the equalizers we can get!
We're bad *outgunned!*
KAPOW!
Hell.
One thing you ought to know about me—

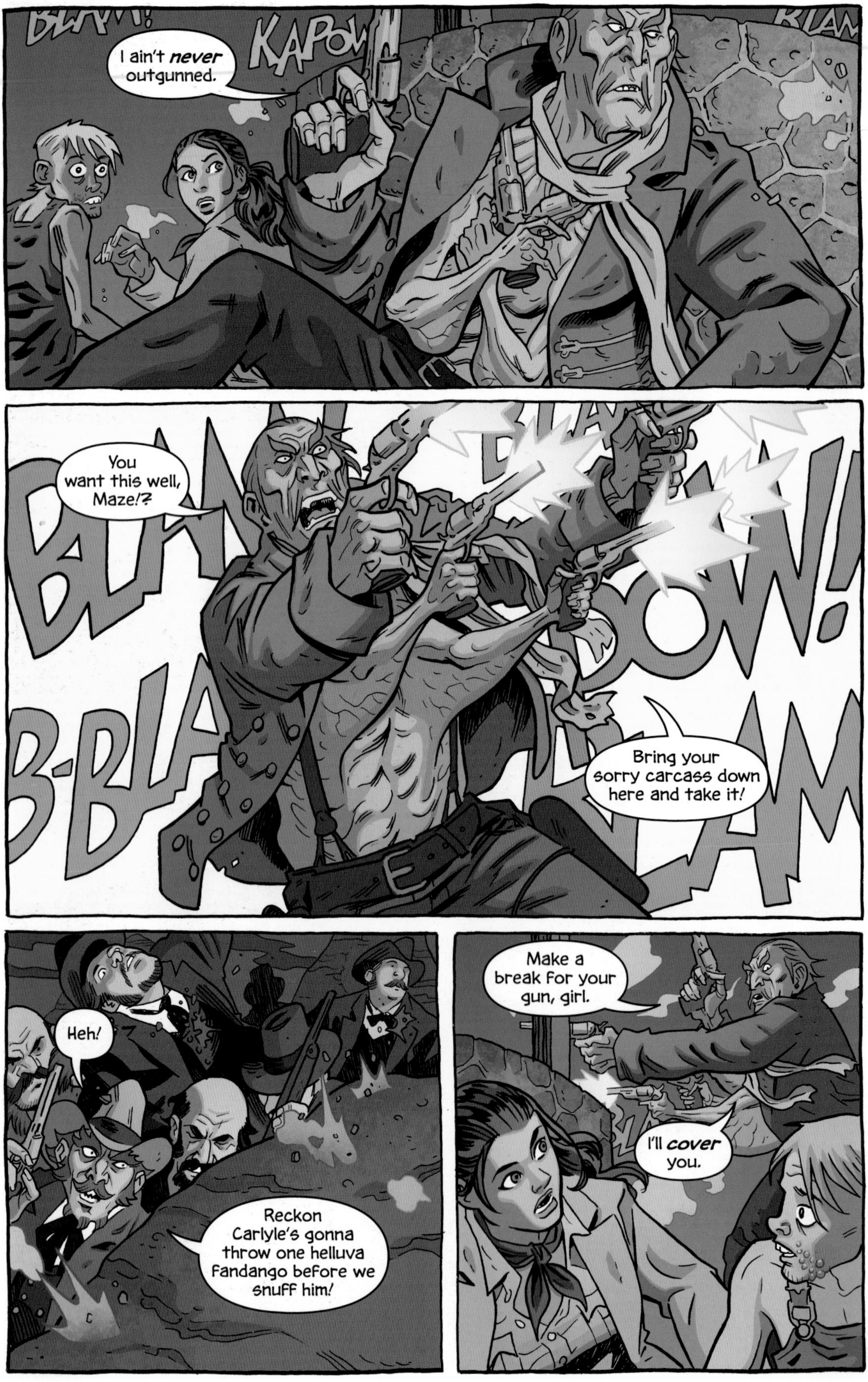

I ain't ***never*** outgunned.
You want this well, Maze!?
Bring your sorry carcass down here and take it!
Heh!
Reckon Carlyle's gonna throw one helluva fandango before we snuff him!
Make a break for your gun, girl.
I'll ***cover*** you.

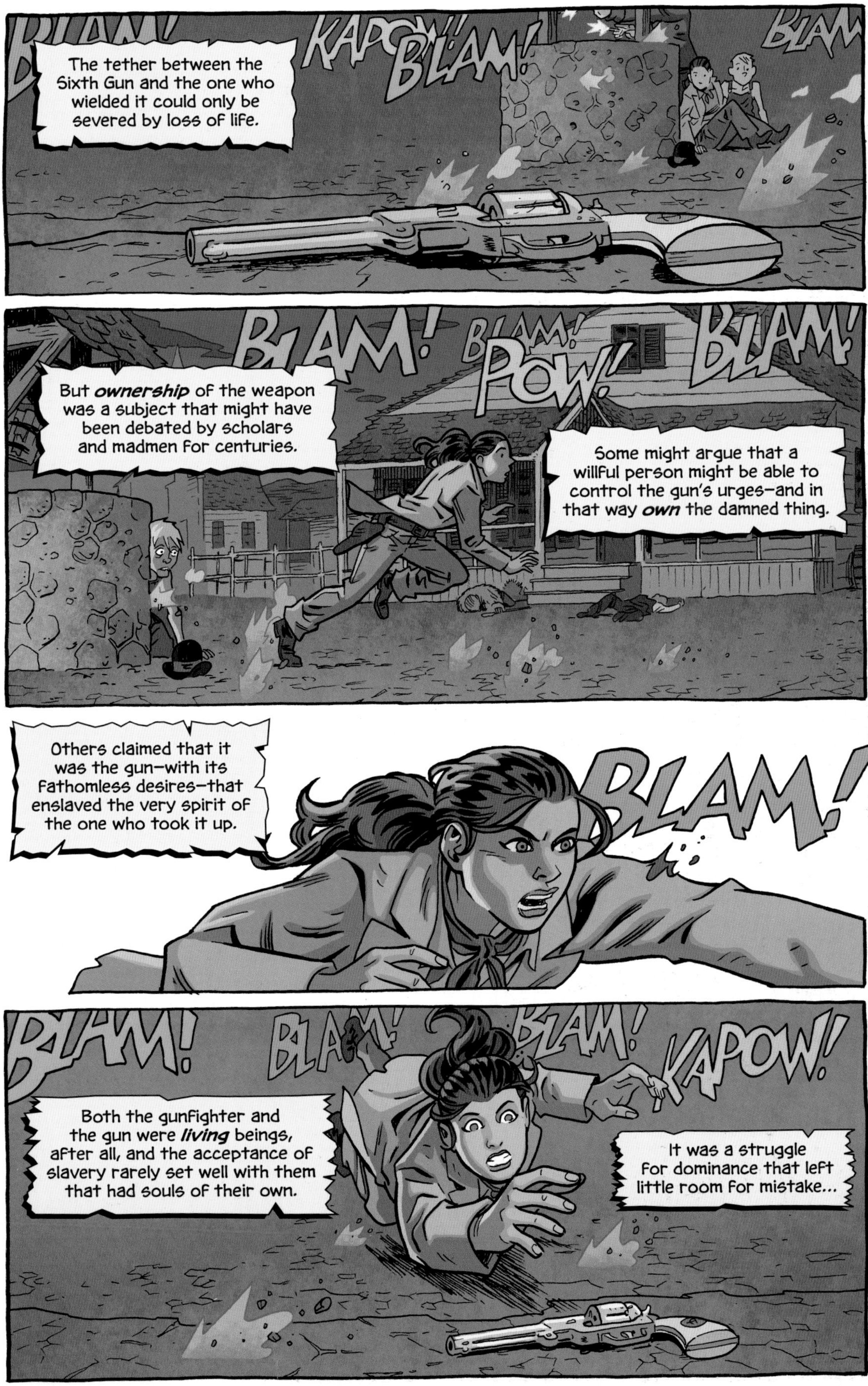
KAPOW!!
BLAM!
The tether between the Sixth Gun and the one who wielded it could only be severed by loss of life.
BLAM!
BLAM!
POW!
BLAM!
But *ownership* of the weapon was a subject that might have been debated by scholars and madmen for centuries.
Some might argue that a willful person might be able to control the gun's urges—and in that way *own* the damned thing.
Others claimed that it was the gun—with its fathomless desires—that enslaved the very spirit of the one who took it up.
BLAM!
BLAM!
BLAM!
BLAM!
KAPOW!
Both the gunfighter and the gun were *living* beings, after all, and the acceptance of slavery rarely set well with them that had souls of their own.
It was a struggle for dominance that left little room for mistake...

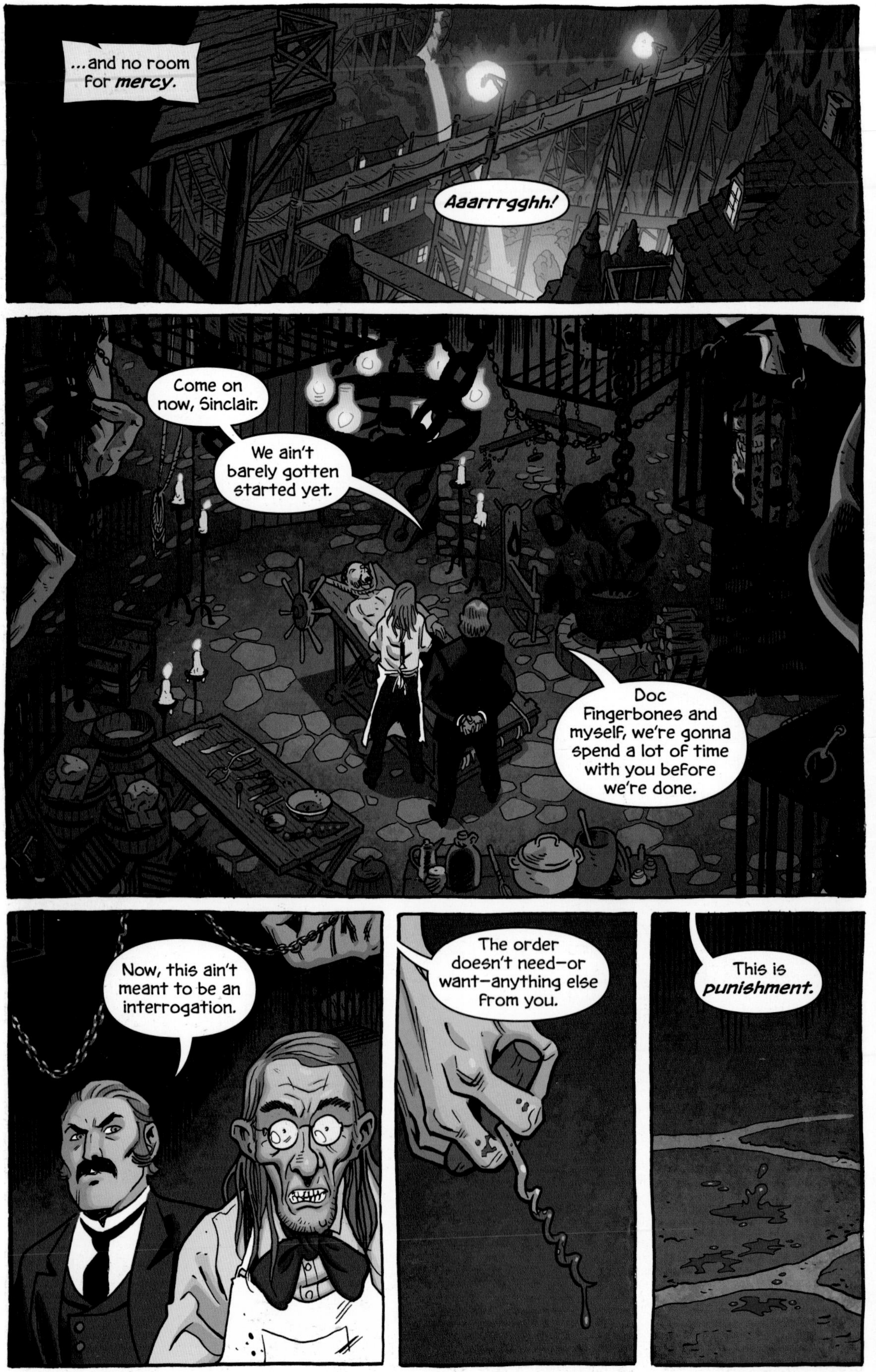
...and no room for *mercy*.
Aaarrrgghh!
Come on now, Sinclair.
We ain't barely gotten started yet.
Doc Fingerbones and myself, we're gonna spend a lot of time with you before we're done.
Now, this ain't meant to be an interrogation.
The order doesn't need—or want—anything else from you.
This is *punishment*.

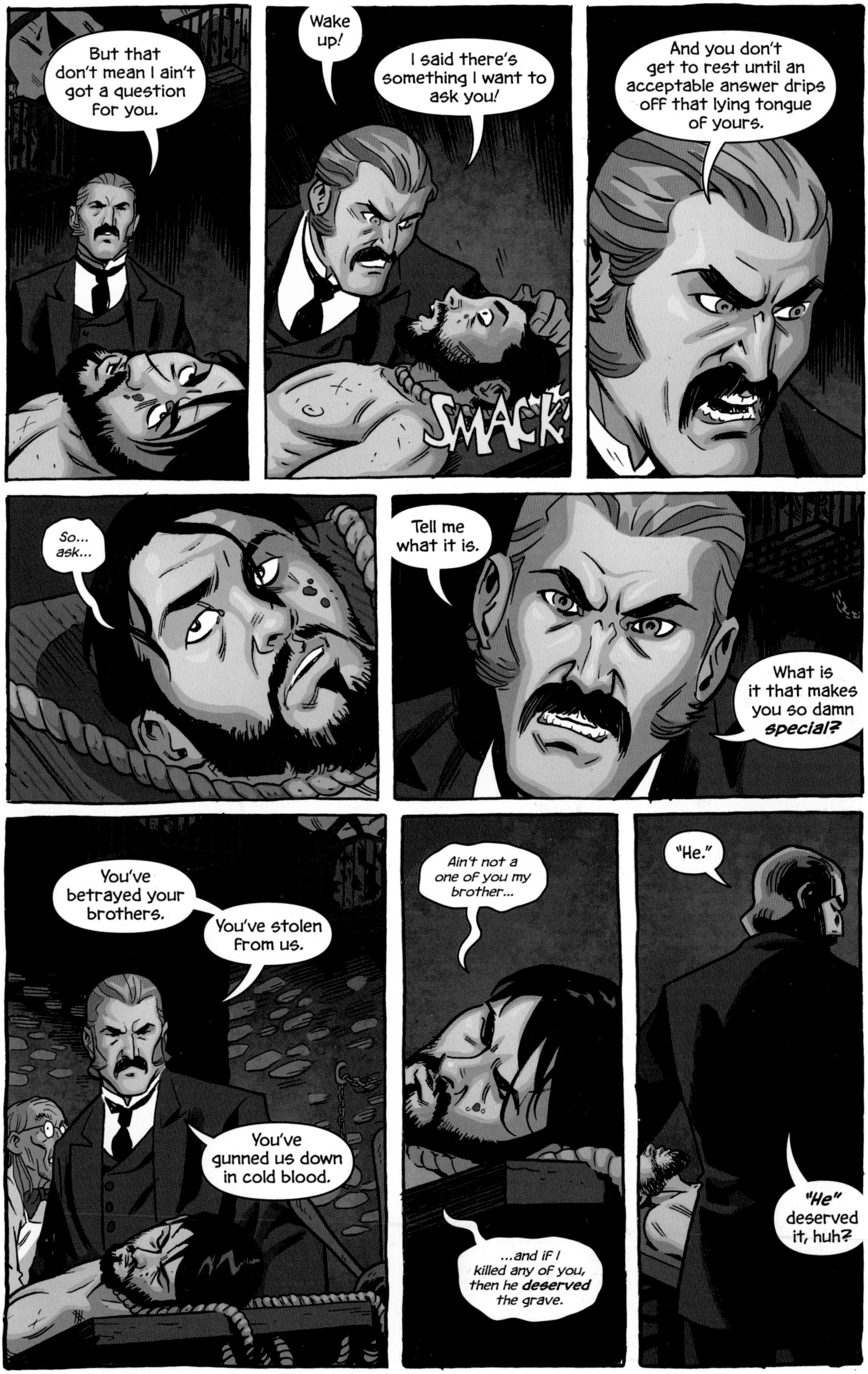
But that don't mean I ain't got a question for you.
Wake up!
I said there's something I want to ask you!
SMACK!
And you don't get to rest until an acceptable answer drips off that lying tongue of yours.
So... ask...
Tell me what it is.
What is it that makes you so damn *special?*
You've betrayed your brothers.
You've stolen from us.
You've gunned us down in cold blood.
Ain't not a one of you my brother...
*...and if I killed any of you, then he **deserved** the grave.*
"He."
"He" deserved it, huh?

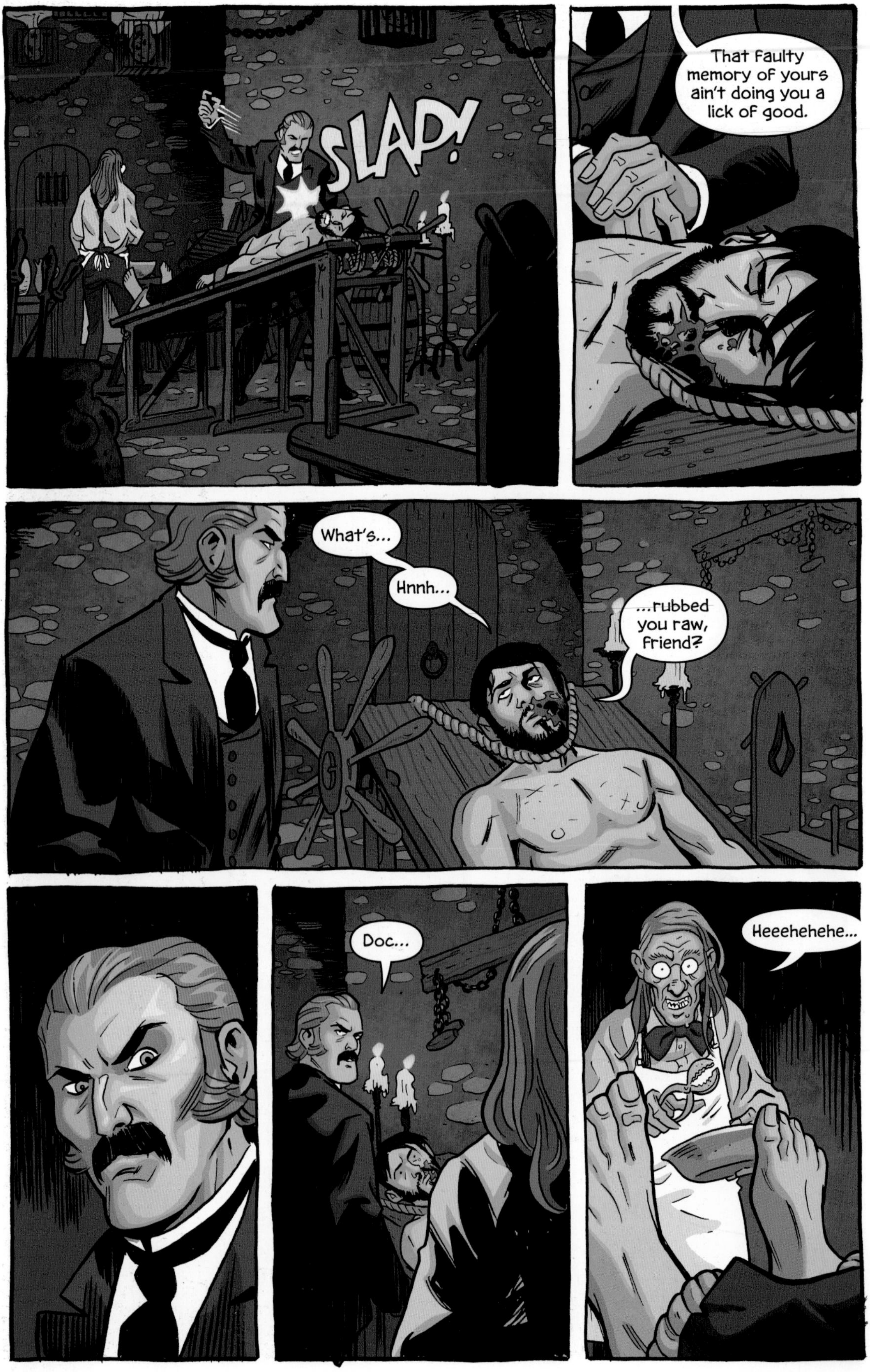
SLAP!
That faulty memory of yours ain't doing you a lick of good.
What's...
Hnnh...
...rubbed you raw, friend?
Doc...
Heeehehehe...

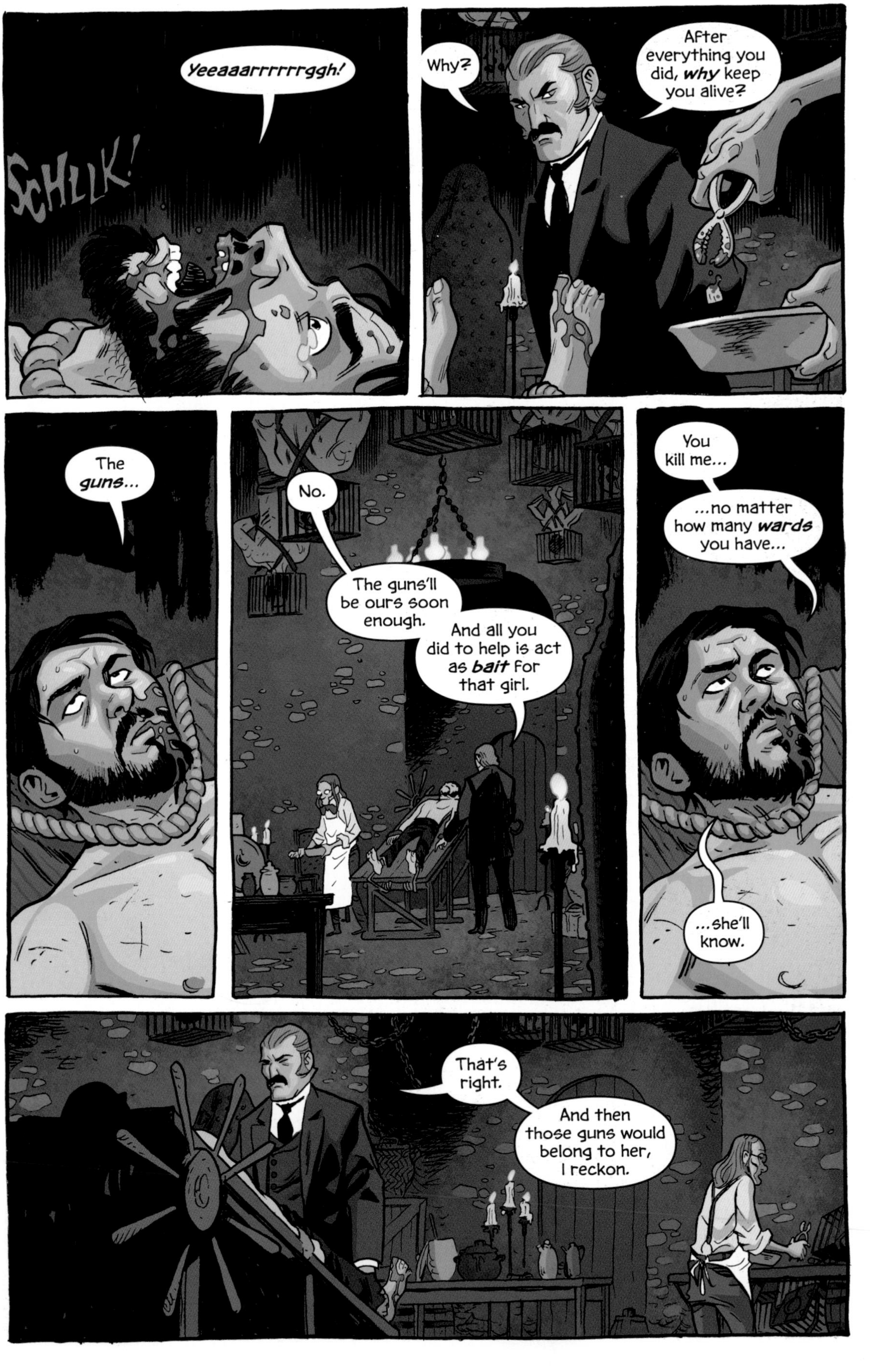
Yeeaaarrrrrrggh!
SCHLLK!
Why?
After everything you did, why keep you alive?
The guns...
No.
The guns'll be ours soon enough.
And all you did to help is act as bait for that girl.
You kill me...
...no matter how many wards you have...
...she'll know.
That's right.
And then those guns would belong to her, I reckon.

Do you think that scares me, though?

There's got to be more to it than that, don't you think?

Killing that girl... that ain't *nothing*.

Hell it ain't.

I just can't figure why'd they let you live.

The Six are as good as ours.

We're sitting right on top of a seal...

...and we've got the *sacrifice* ready.

Sacrifice?

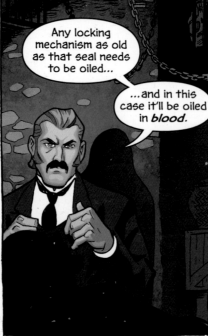

Any locking mechanism as old as that seal needs to be oiled...

...and in this case it'll be oiled in *blood*.

"I'm sure you can appreciate what we've done, Sinclair.

"Out here in the middle of nowhere, and we've bound an entire town to this place."

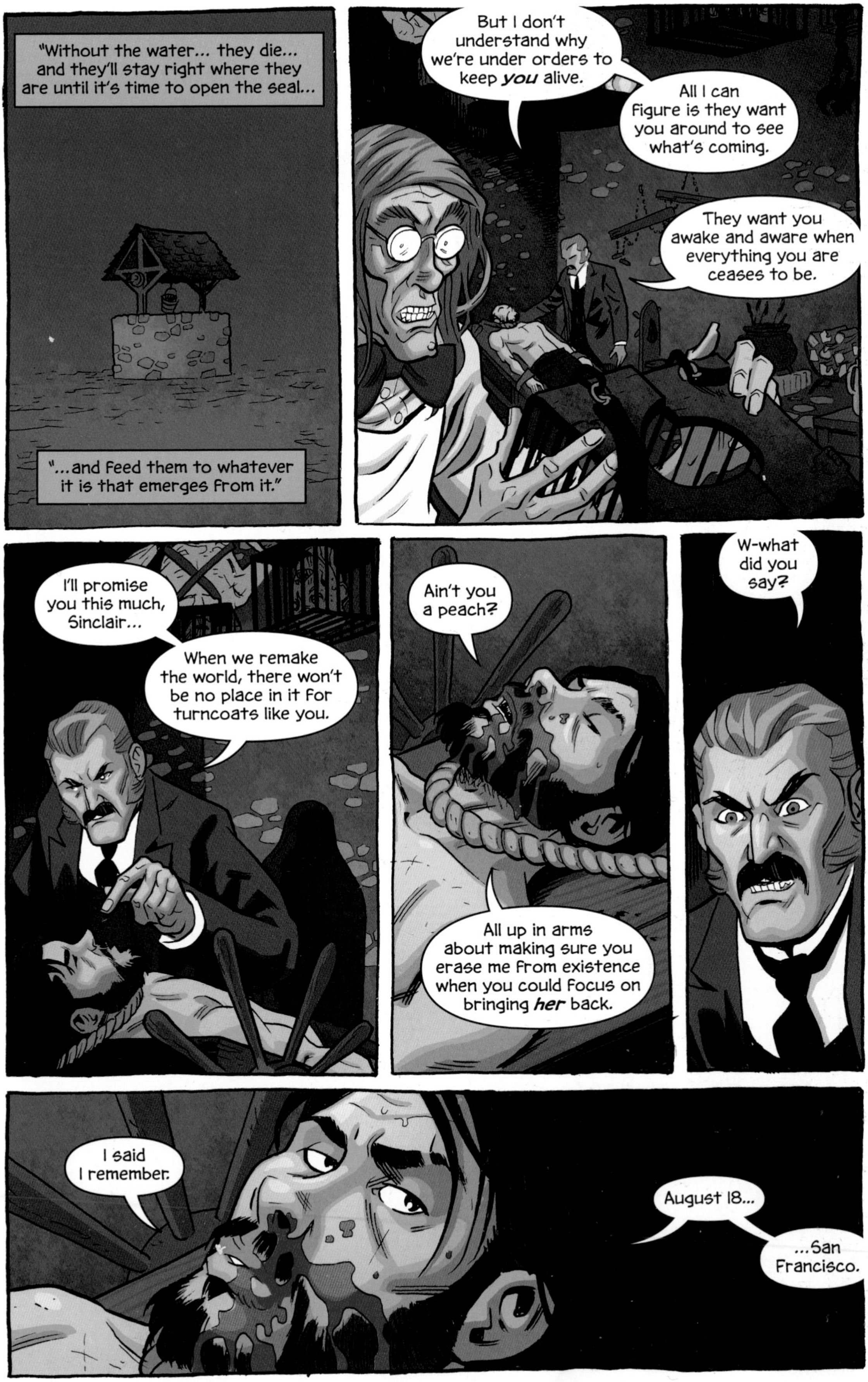
"Without the water... they die... and they'll stay right where they are until it's time to open the seal...
"...and feed them to whatever it is that emerges from it."
But I don't understand why we're under orders to keep *you* alive.
All I can figure is they want you around to see what's coming.
They want you awake and aware when everything you are ceases to be.
I'll promise you this much, Sinclair...
When we remake the world, there won't be no place in it for turncoats like you.
Ain't you a peach?
All up in arms about making sure you erase me from existence when you could focus on bringing *her* back.
W-what did you say?
I said I remember.
August 18...
...San Francisco.

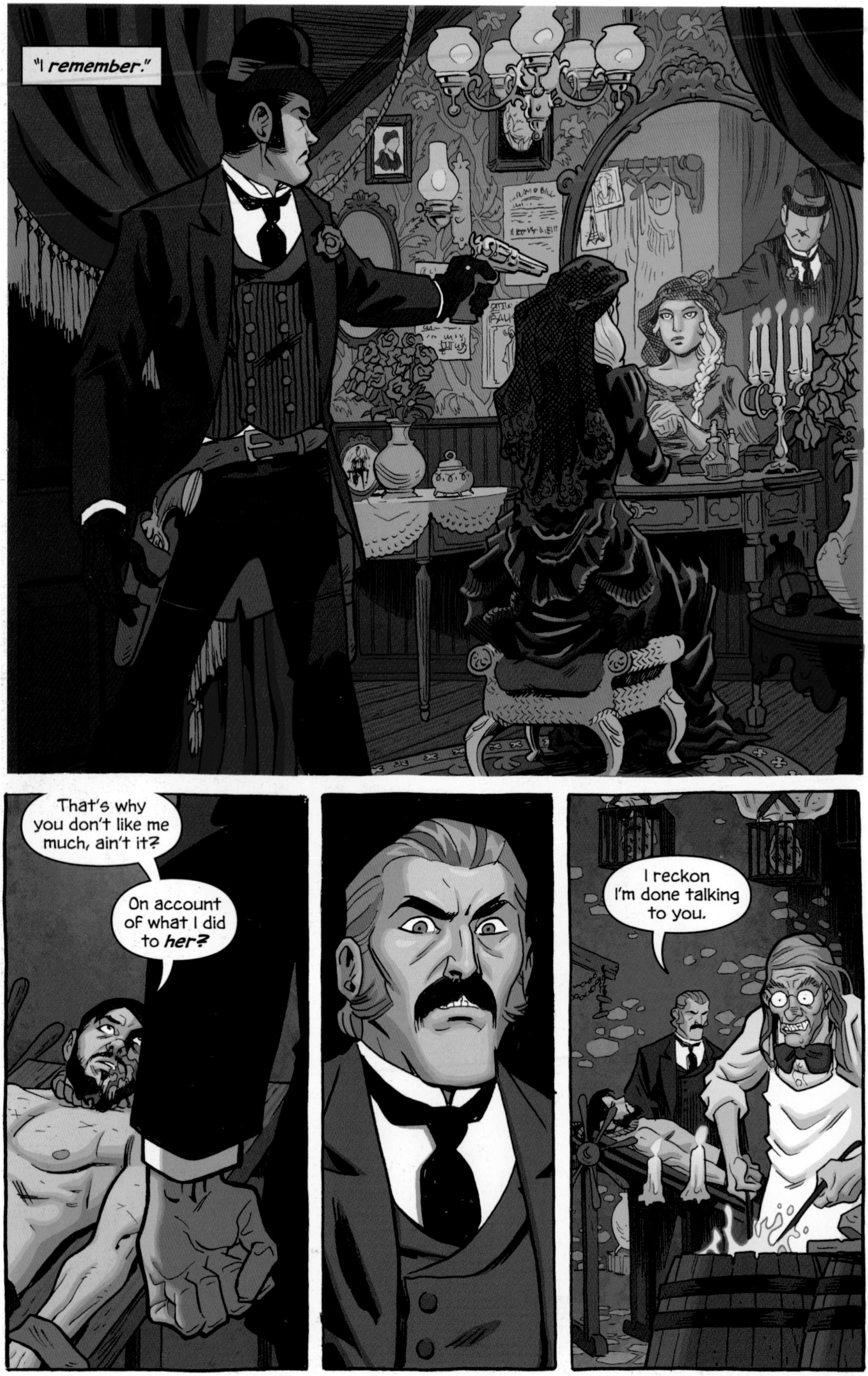
"I *remember.*"
That's why you don't like me much, ain't it?
On account of what I did to ***her?***
I reckon I'm done talking to you.

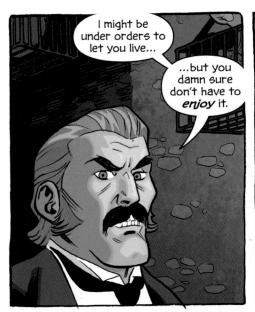

I might be under orders to let you live...

...but you damn sure don't have to *enjoy* it.

Hehehehe...

Of all the things the Knights of Solomon have collected over the years, this here's my *favorite*.

Lessee if you like it just as much as I do.

Oh, Hell...

SKKK-HHH

SSSSSSKKK

No gunfight is as cut and dry as it might seem.

BLAM!   KAPOW!

BLAM!   TK KAPOW!

BLAM!

B-RLAM!

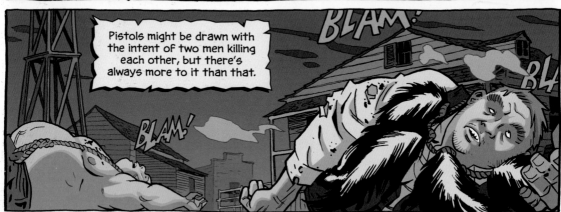

Pistols might be drawn with the intent of two men killing each other, but there's always more to it than that.

BLAM!

BLAM!

BL

The fight might be about family, or honor, or betrayal, or love.

POW!

BLAM!

BLAM!

Almost always there's a struggle with one's own *fear*.

Stick your ugly head up, Maze!

I'm gonna give you one last chance, Carlyle, for old times' sake!

Light out right now—but leave the girl behind—and I promise not to shoot you in the back!

I'll give you a couple of seconds to think that over!

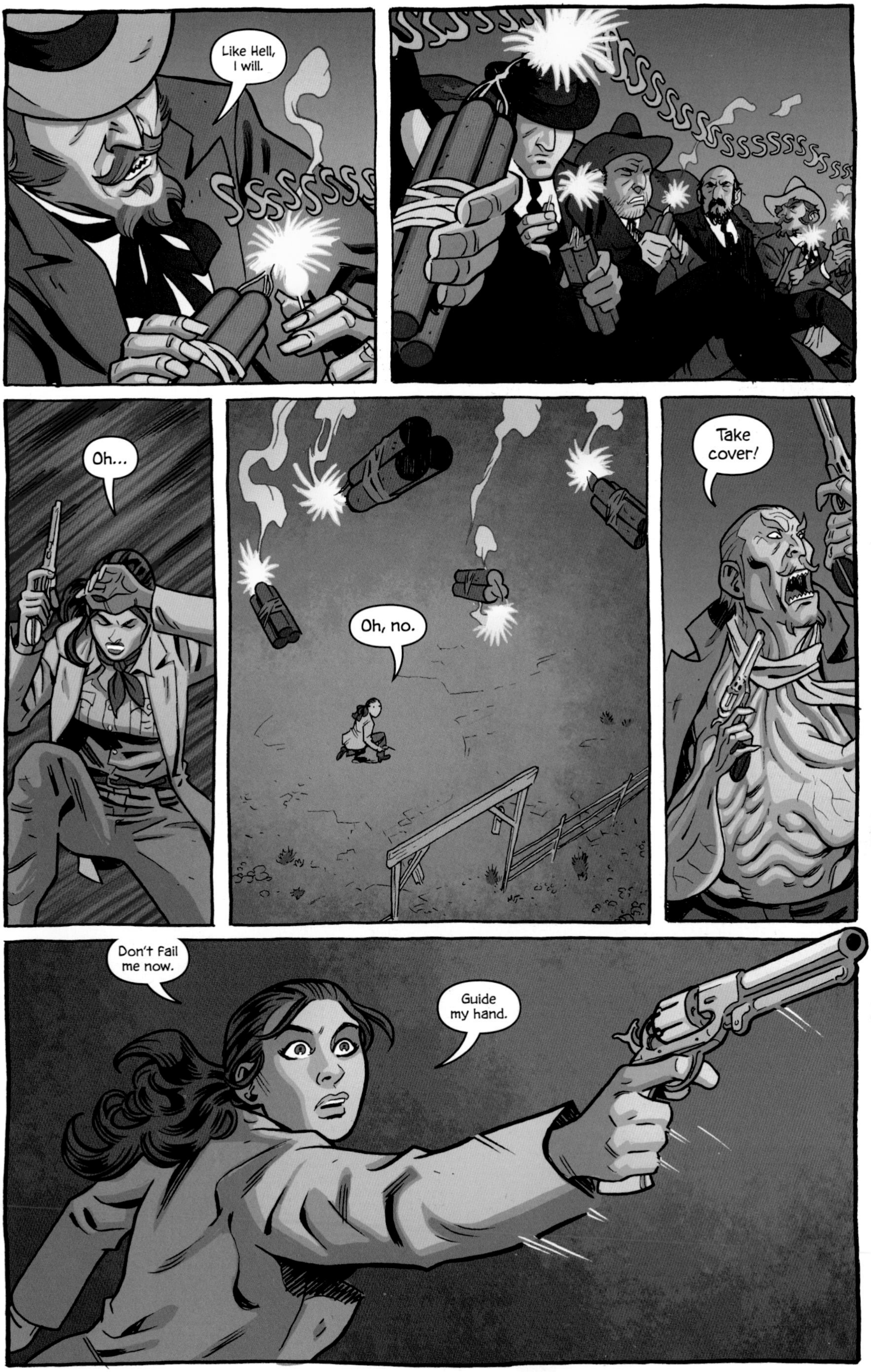
Like Hell, I will.
SSSSSSSS
SSSSSSSSSSSSSSSSSSSSSSSSS
Oh...
Oh, no.
Take cover!
Don't fail me now.
Guide my hand.

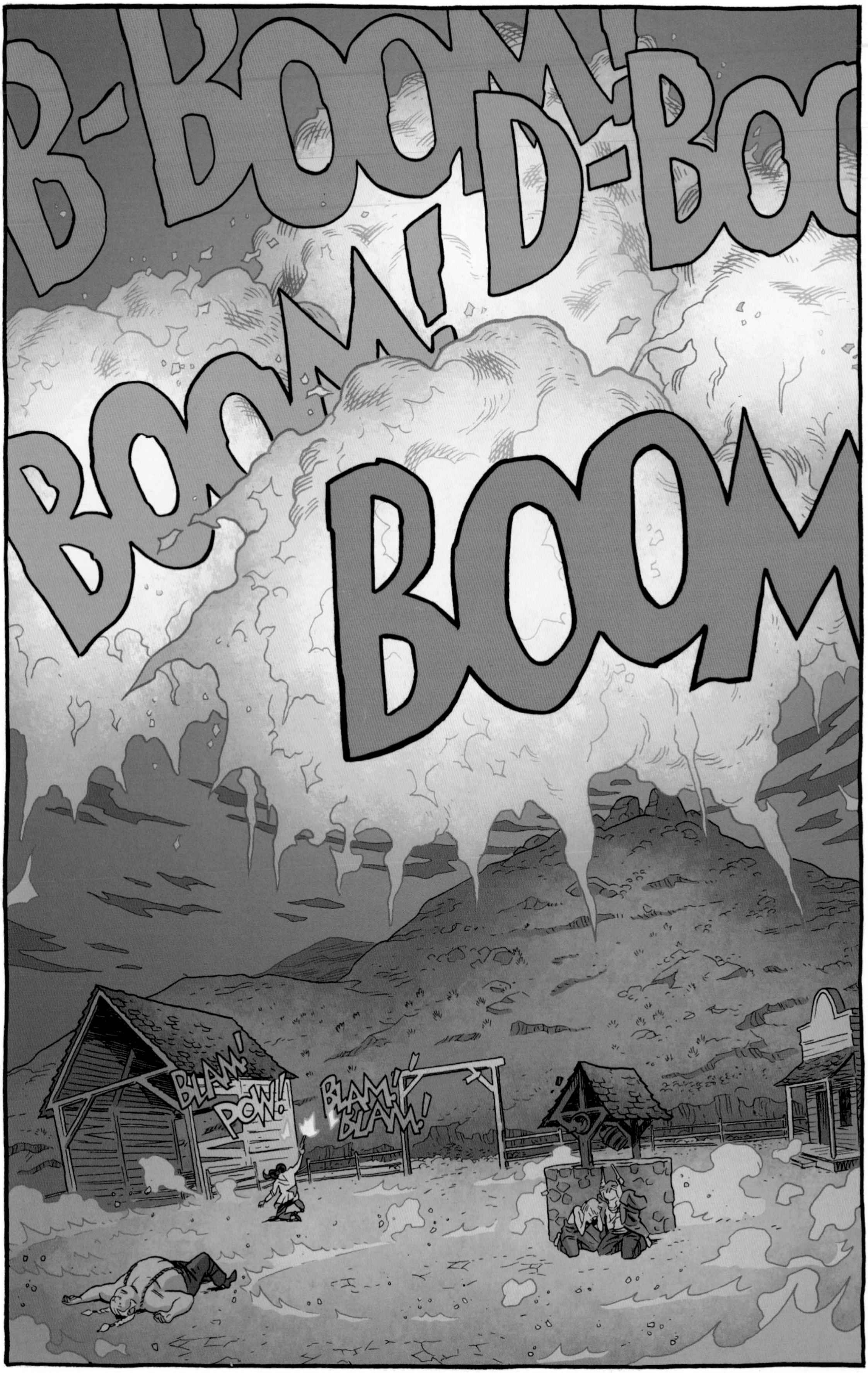

B-BOOM!
D-BOO
BOOM!
BOOM
BLAM!
POW!!
BLAM!
BLAM!

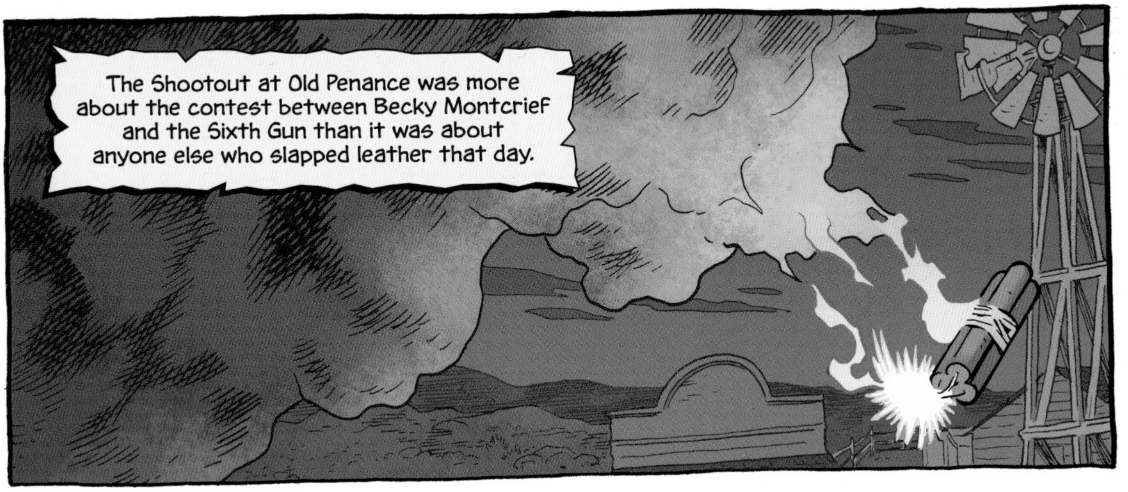
The Shootout at Old Penance was more about the contest between Becky Montcrief and the Sixth Gun than it was about anyone else who slapped leather that day.

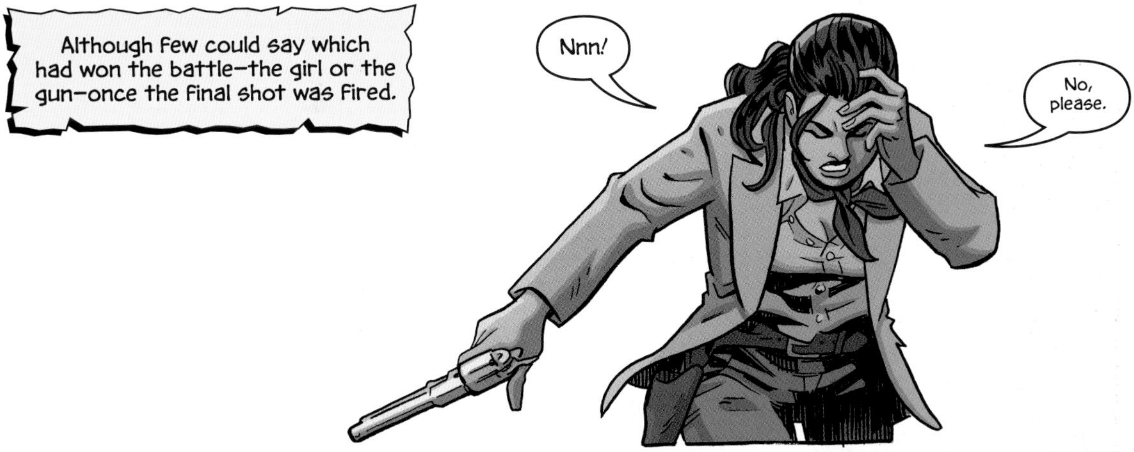
Although few could say which had won the battle—the girl or the gun—once the final shot was fired.
Nnn!
No, please.

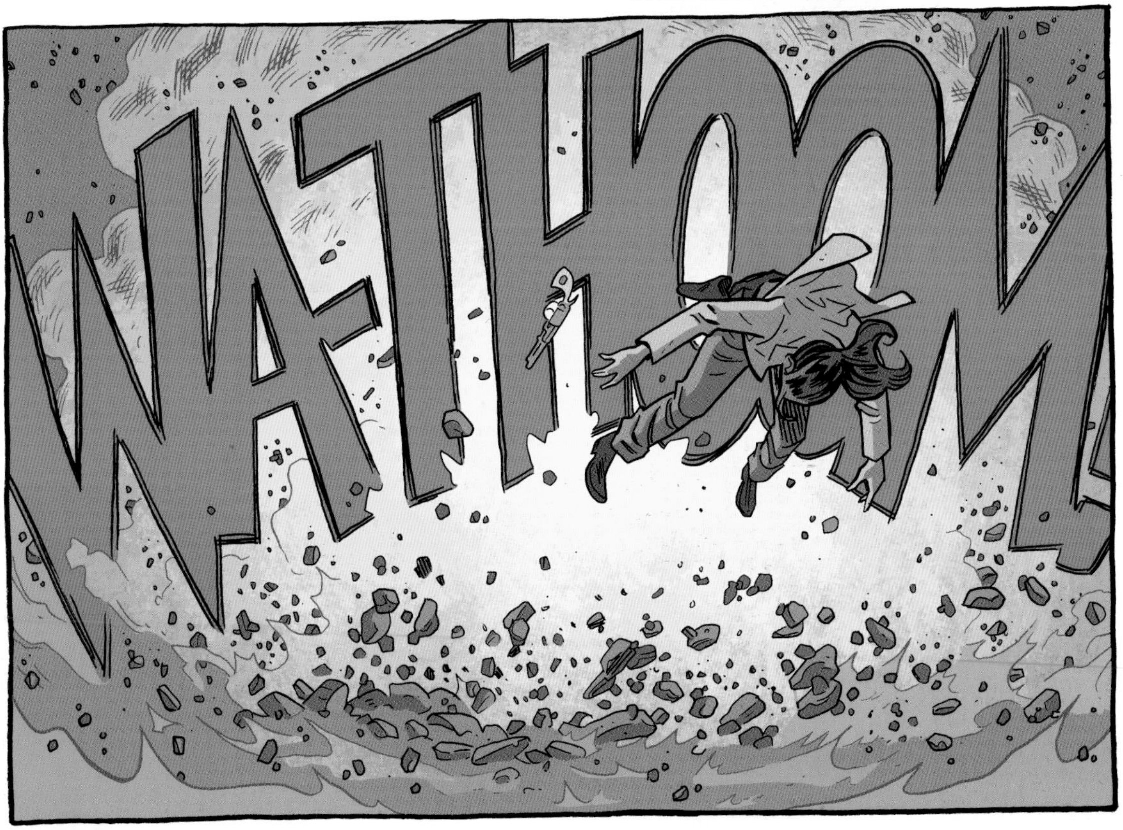
WATHOOM

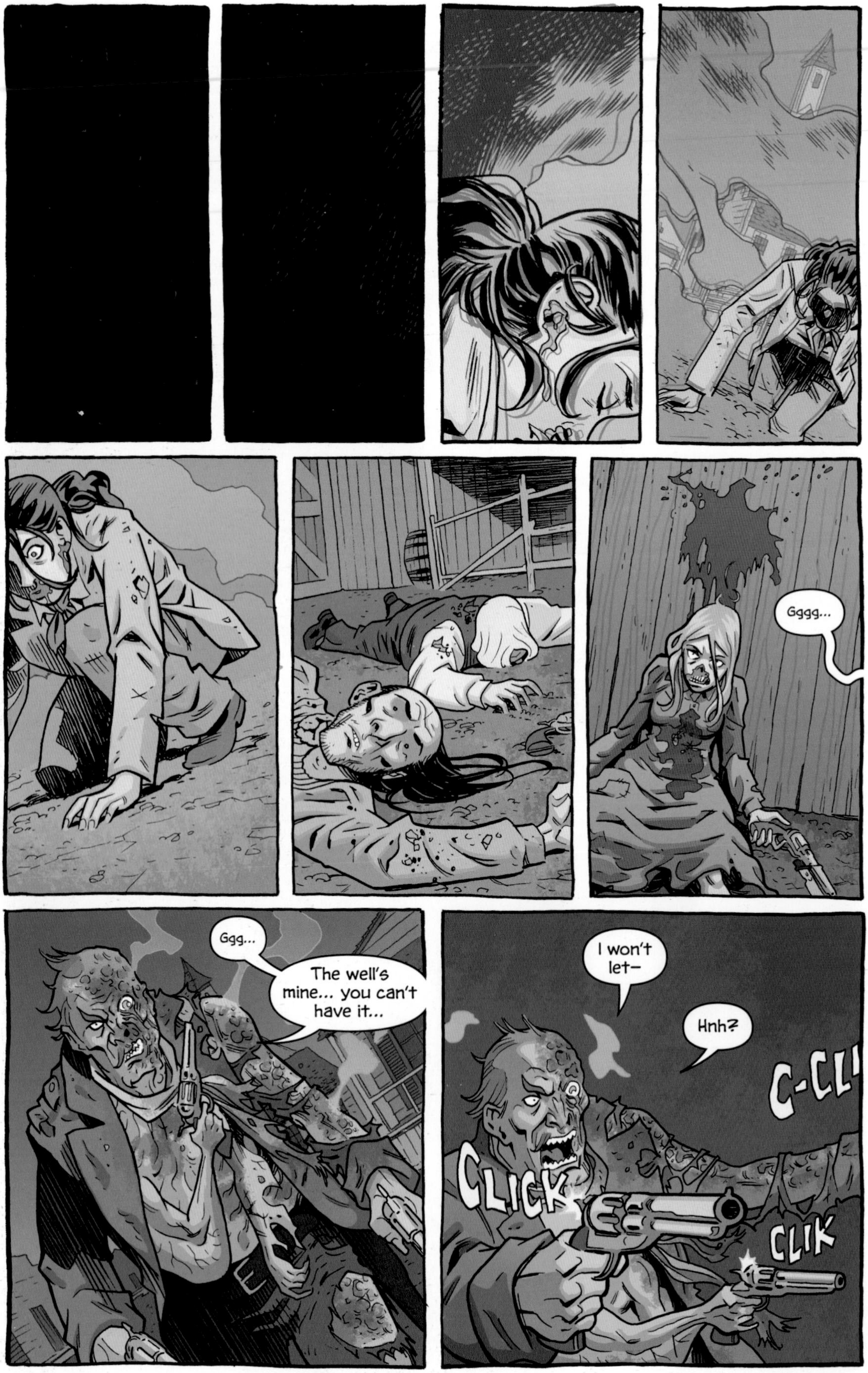
Gggg...
Ggg...
The well's mine... you can't have it...
I won't let–
Hnh?
C-CLI
CLICK
CLIK

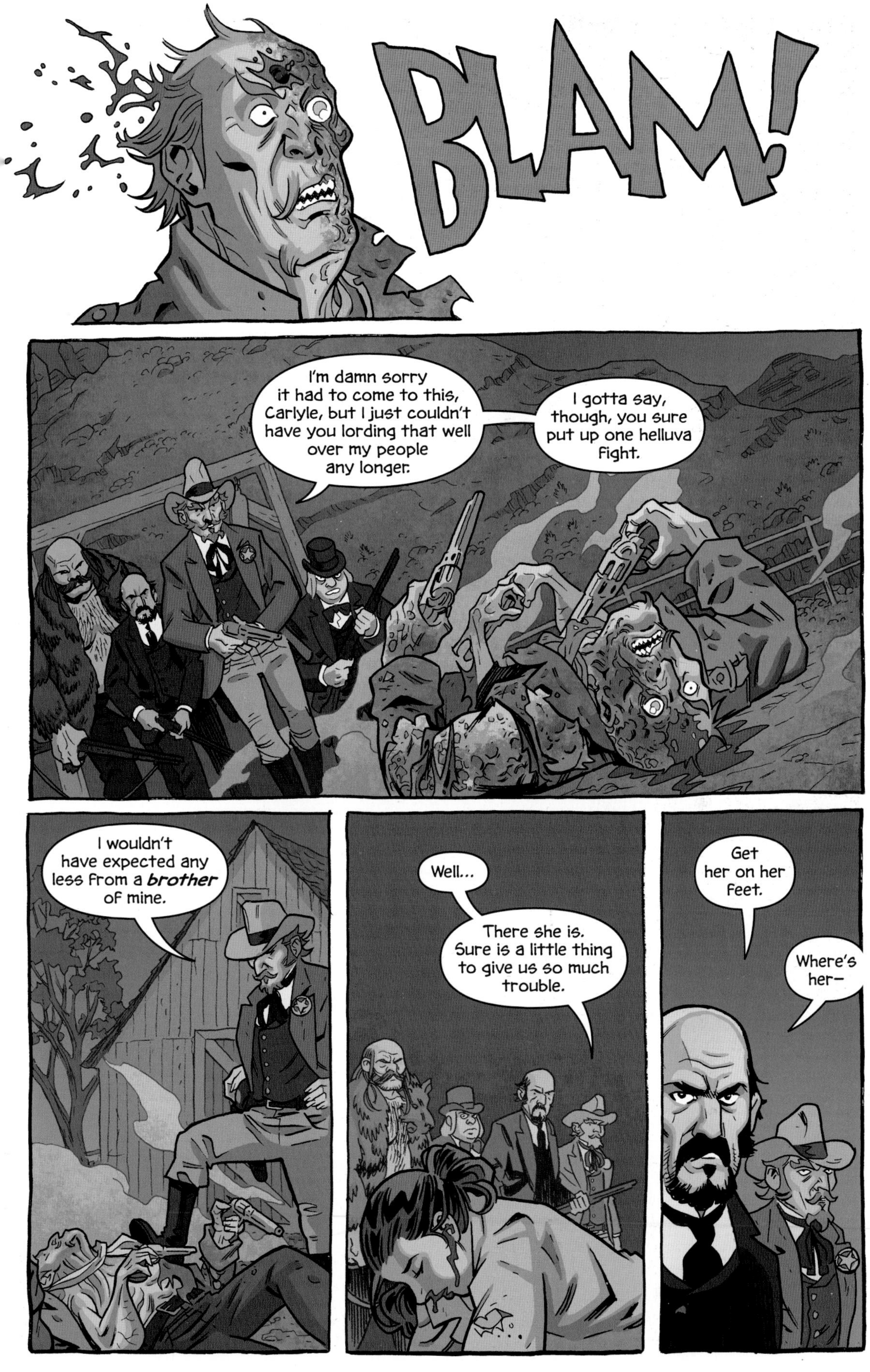
BLAM!
I'm damn sorry it had to come to this, Carlyle, but I just couldn't have you lording that well over my people any longer.
I gotta say, though, you sure put up one helluva fight.
I wouldn't have expected any less from a **brother** of mine.
Well...
There she is. Sure is a little thing to give us so much trouble.
Get her on her feet.
Where's her—

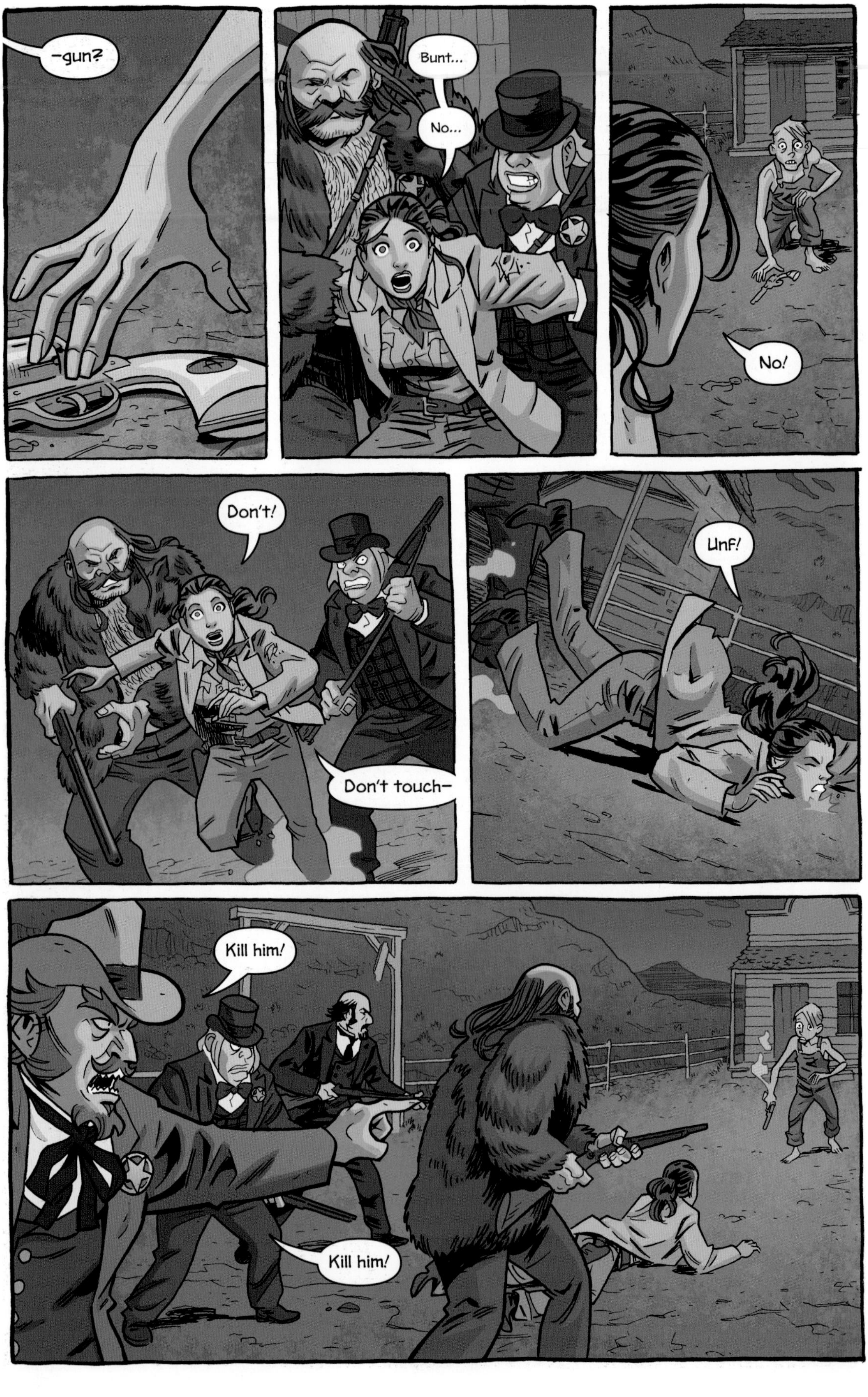
-gun?
Bunt...
No...
No!
Don't!
Don't touch-
Unf!
Kill him!
Kill him!

Uuhh...

BLAM!

BLAMBLAM!

B BL

Uuhh...

Uhhhhhhhh....

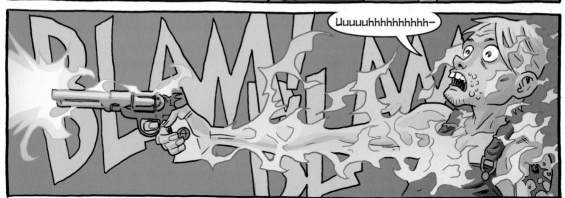

Uuuuuhhhhhhhhh–

BLAM BLAM

BLAM B-BLAM

BLAM BLAM

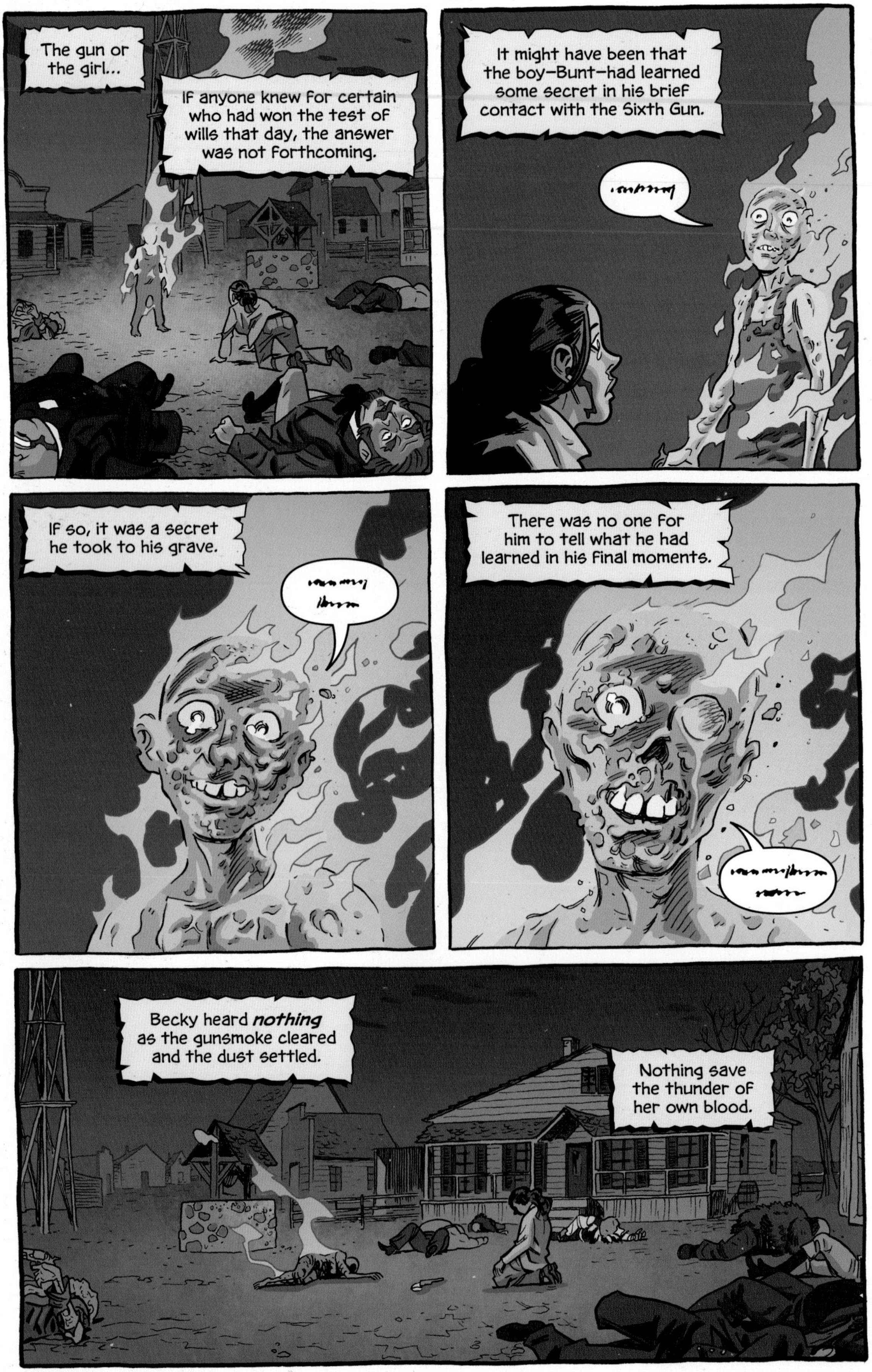
The gun or the girl...
If anyone knew for certain who had won the test of wills that day, the answer was not forthcoming.
It might have been that the boy—Bunt—had learned some secret in his brief contact with the Sixth Gun.
If so, it was a secret he took to his grave.
There was no one for him to tell what he had learned in his final moments.
Becky heard ***nothing*** as the gunsmoke cleared and the dust settled.
Nothing save the thunder of her own blood.

CHAPTER
FOUR

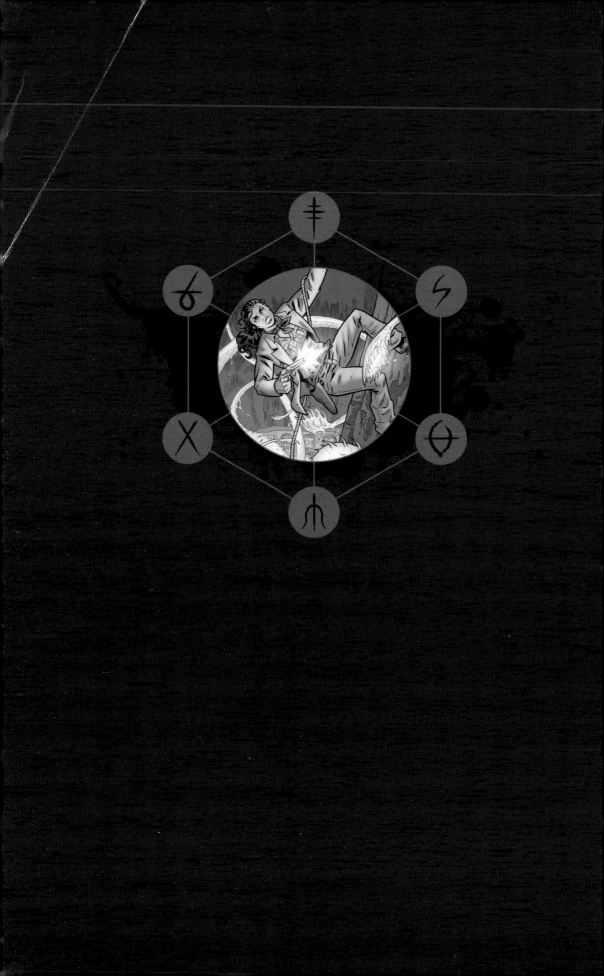

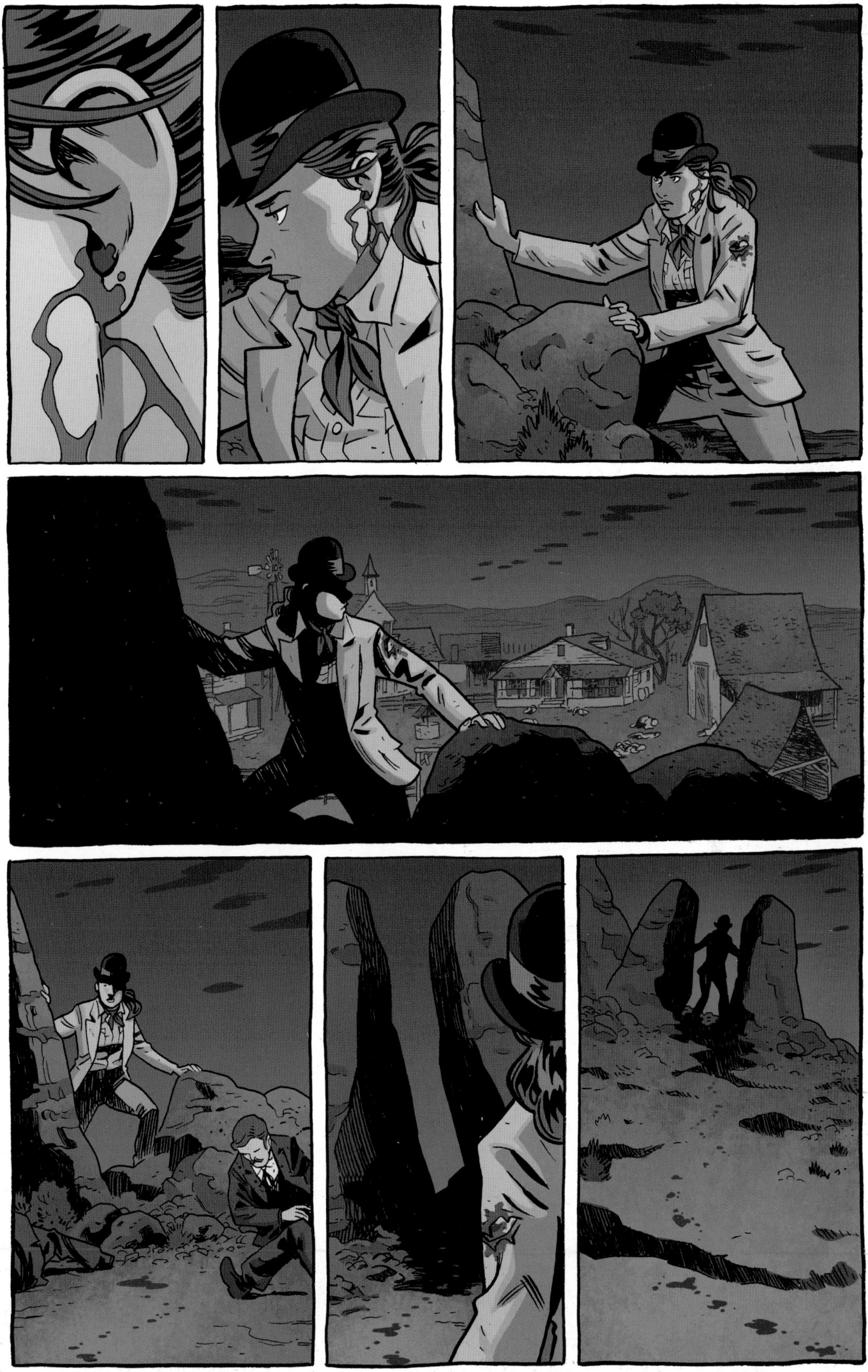

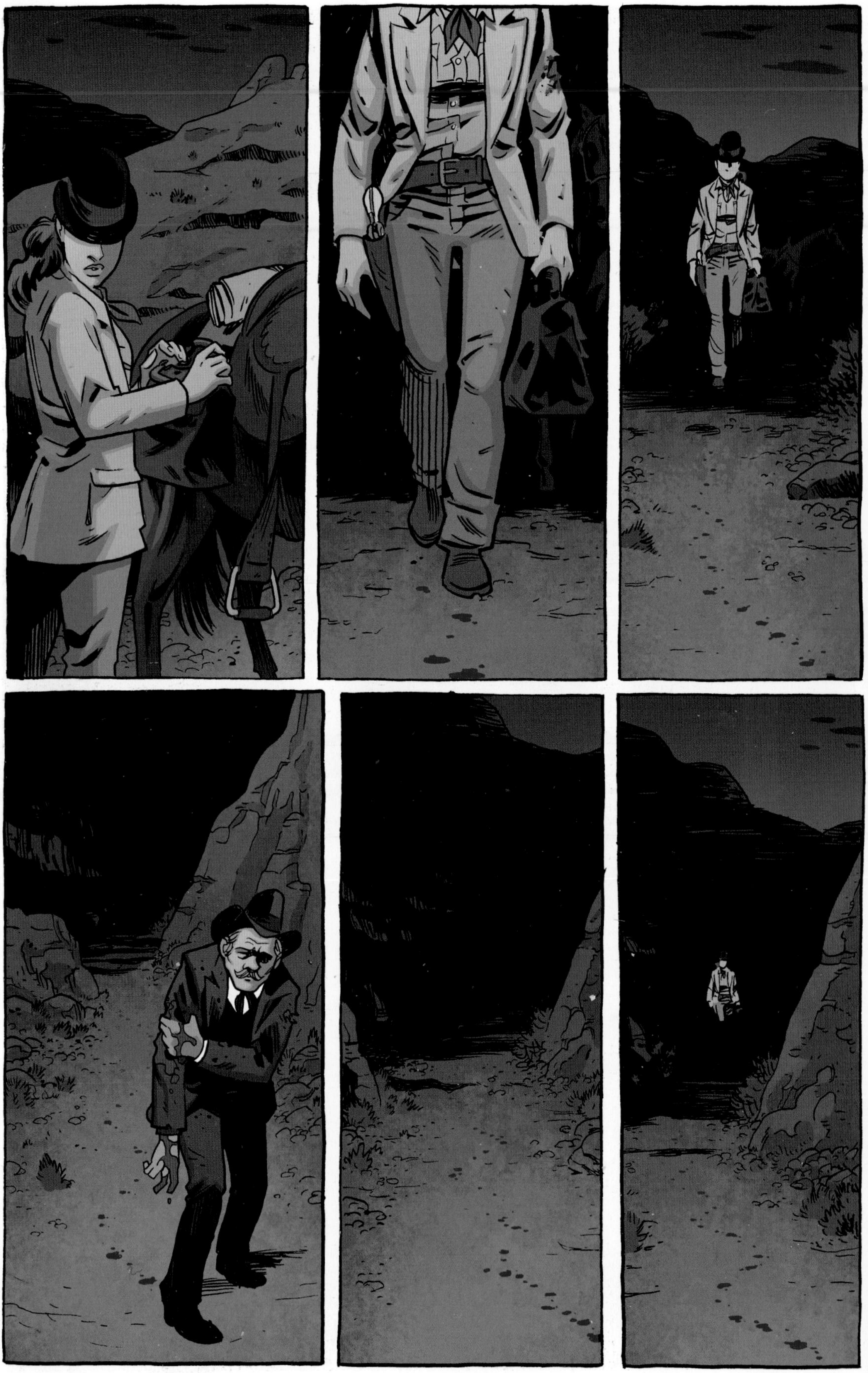

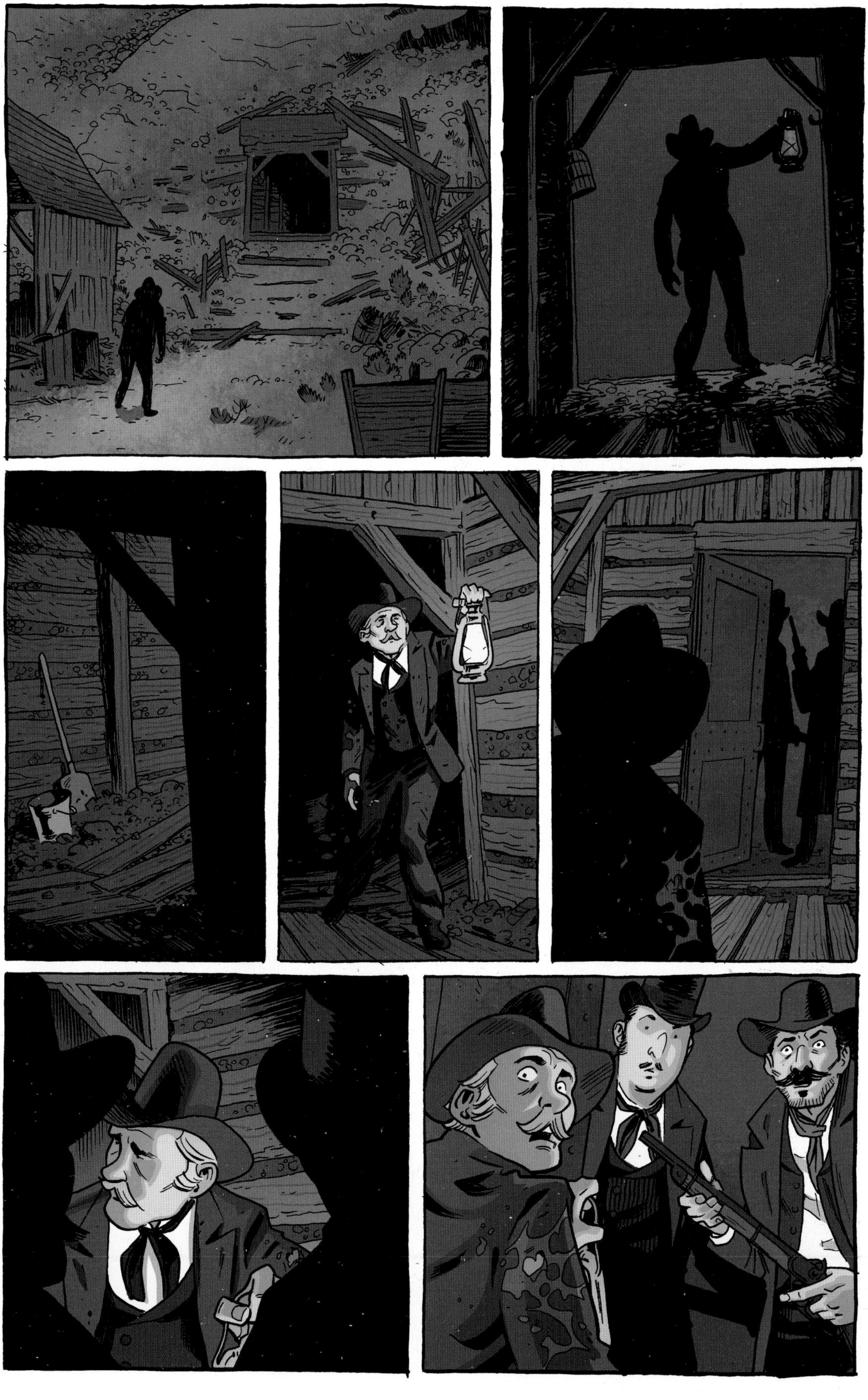

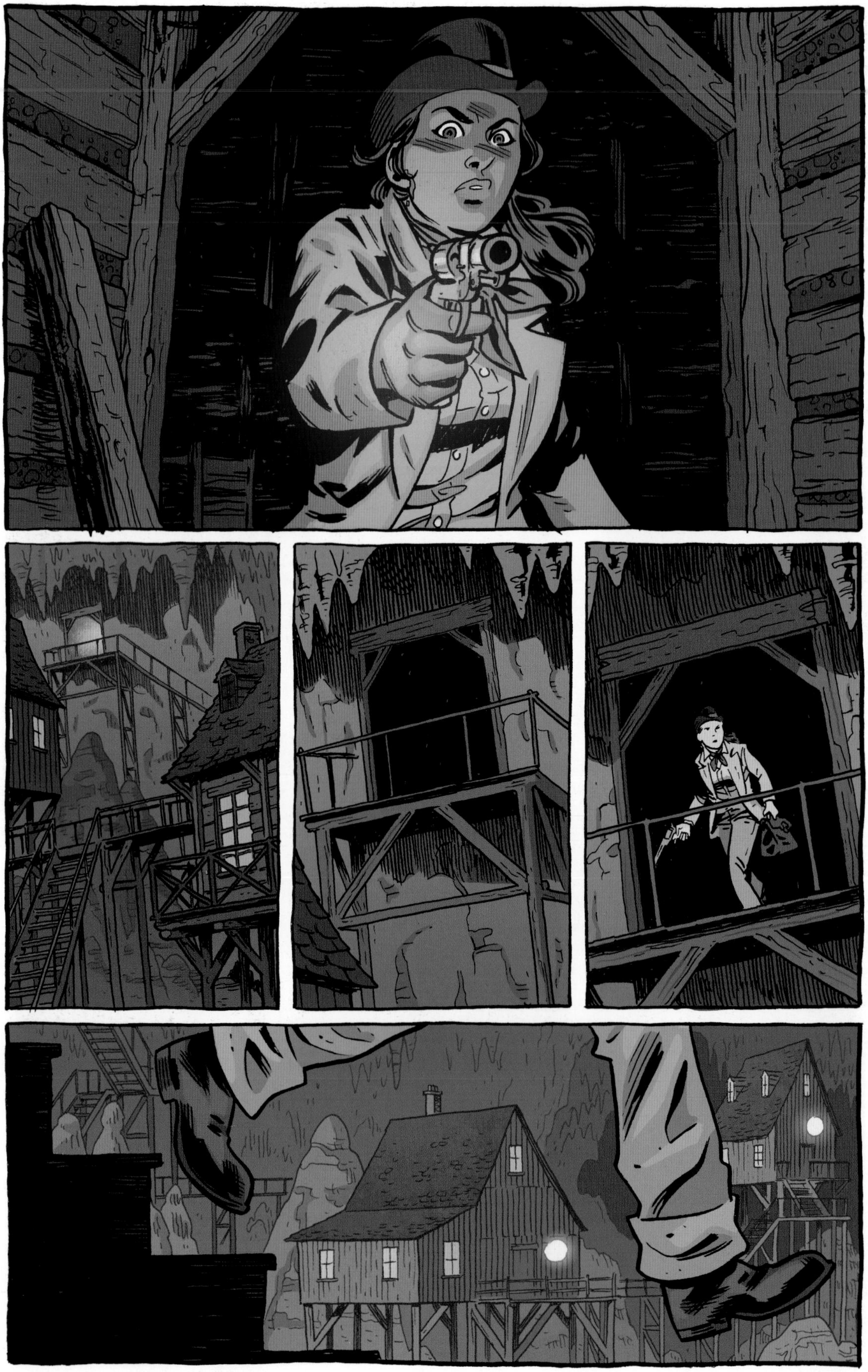

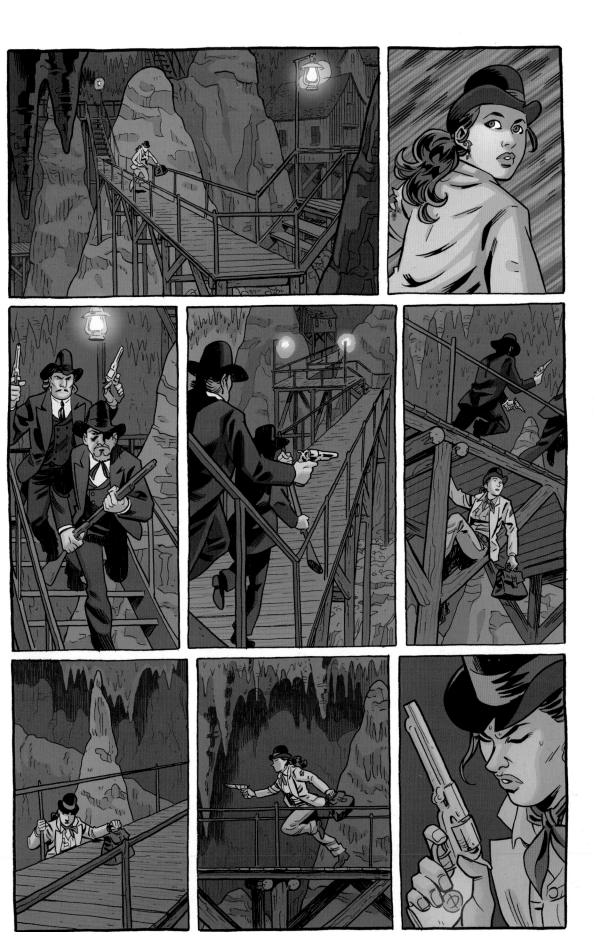

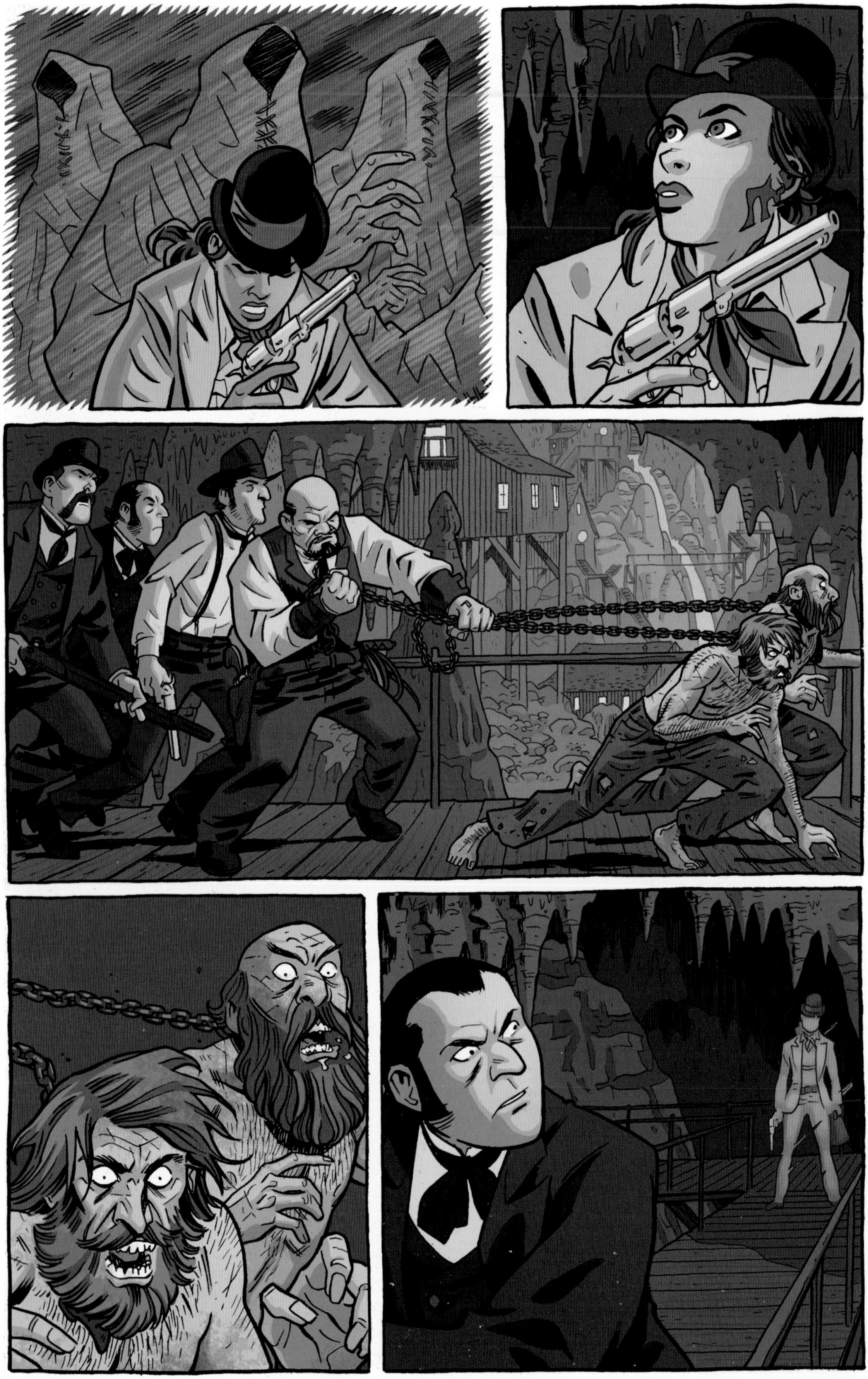

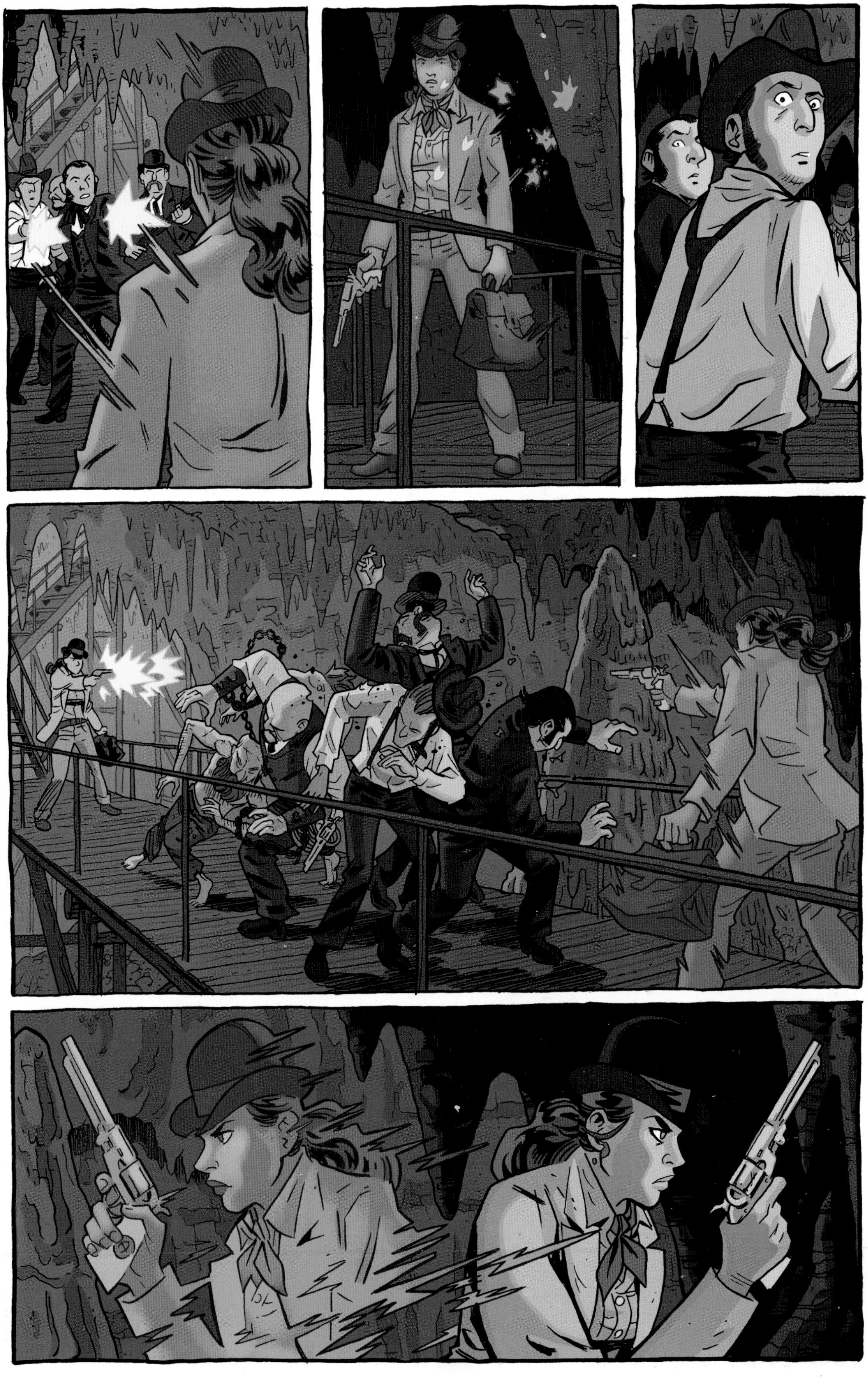

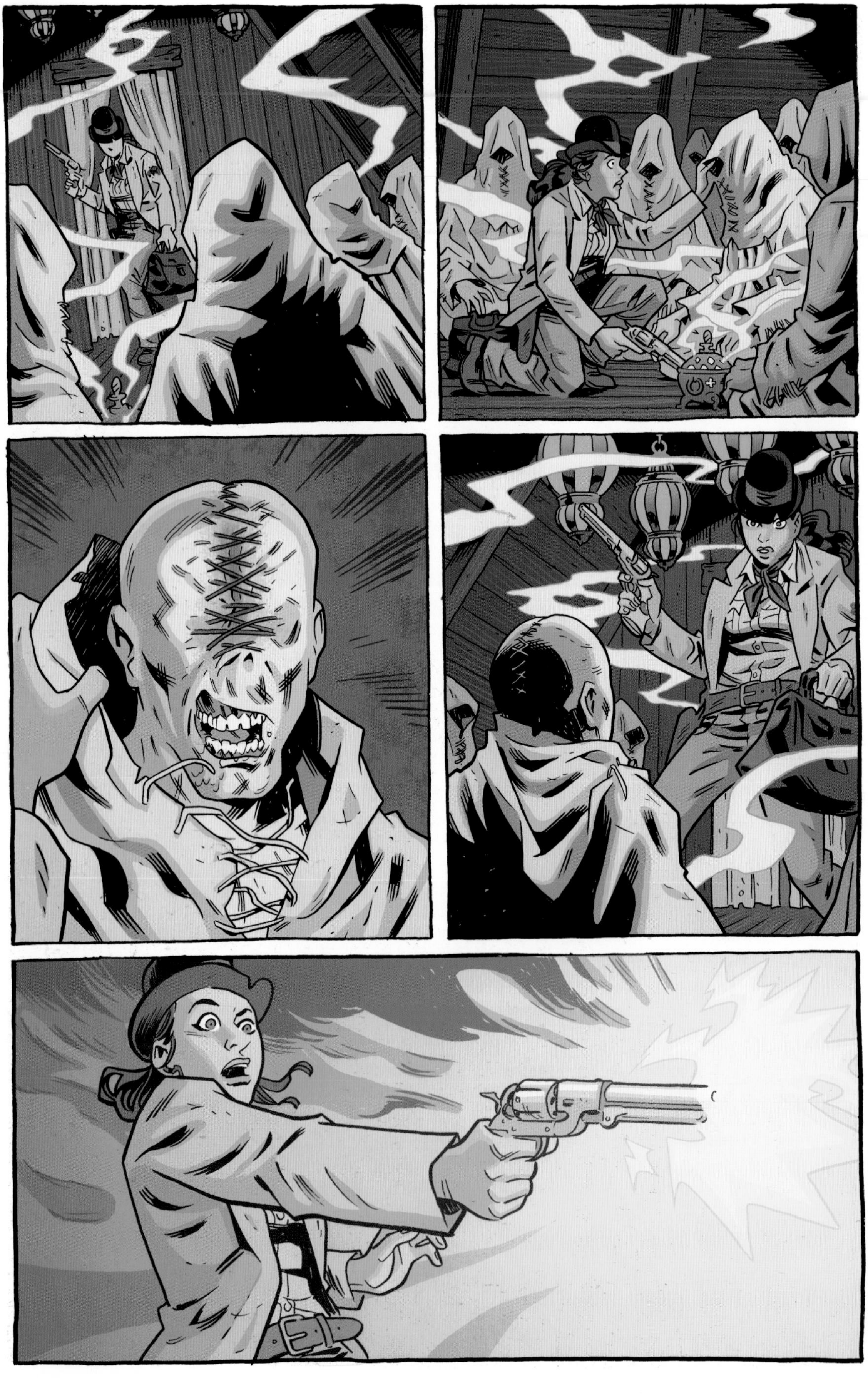

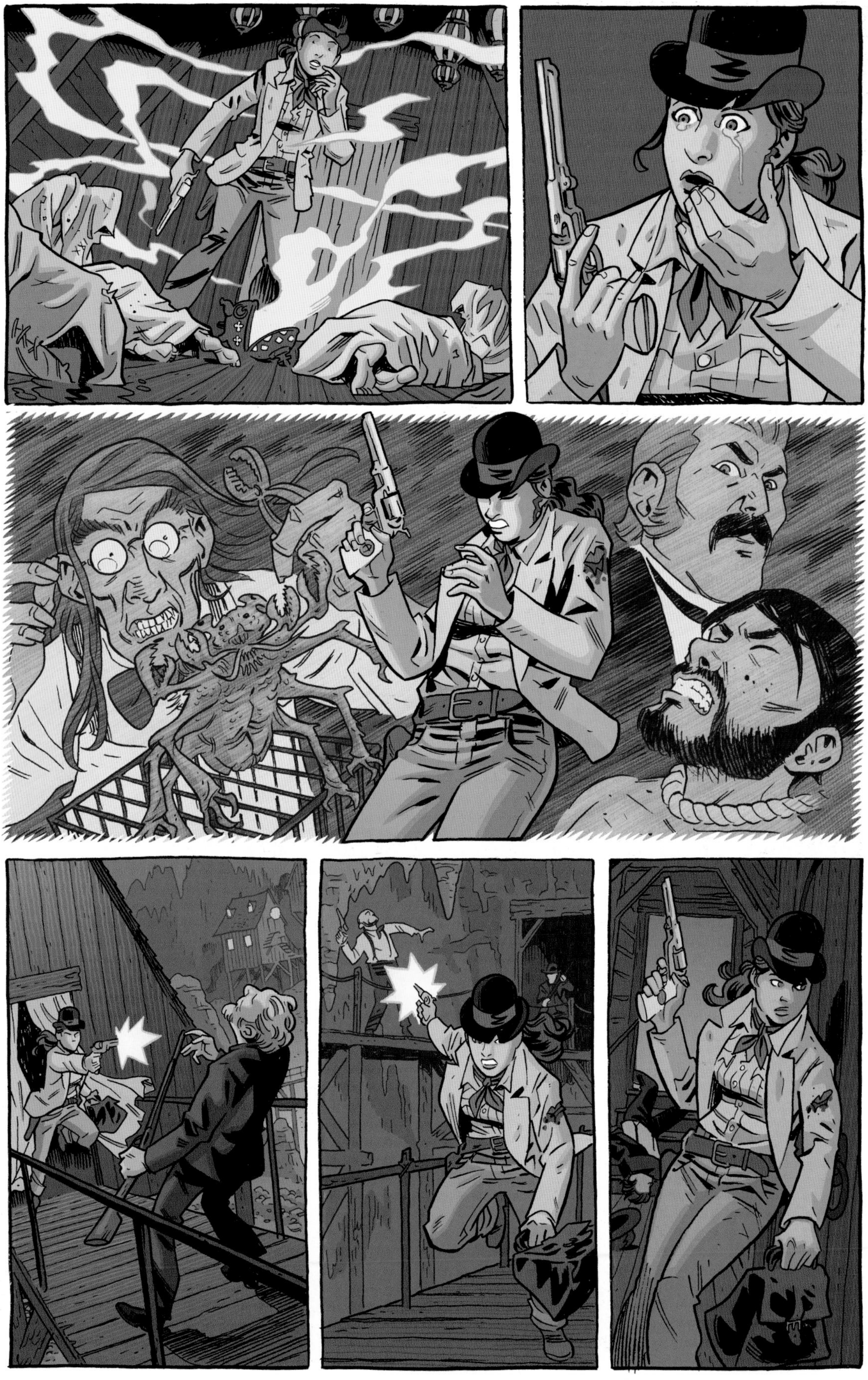

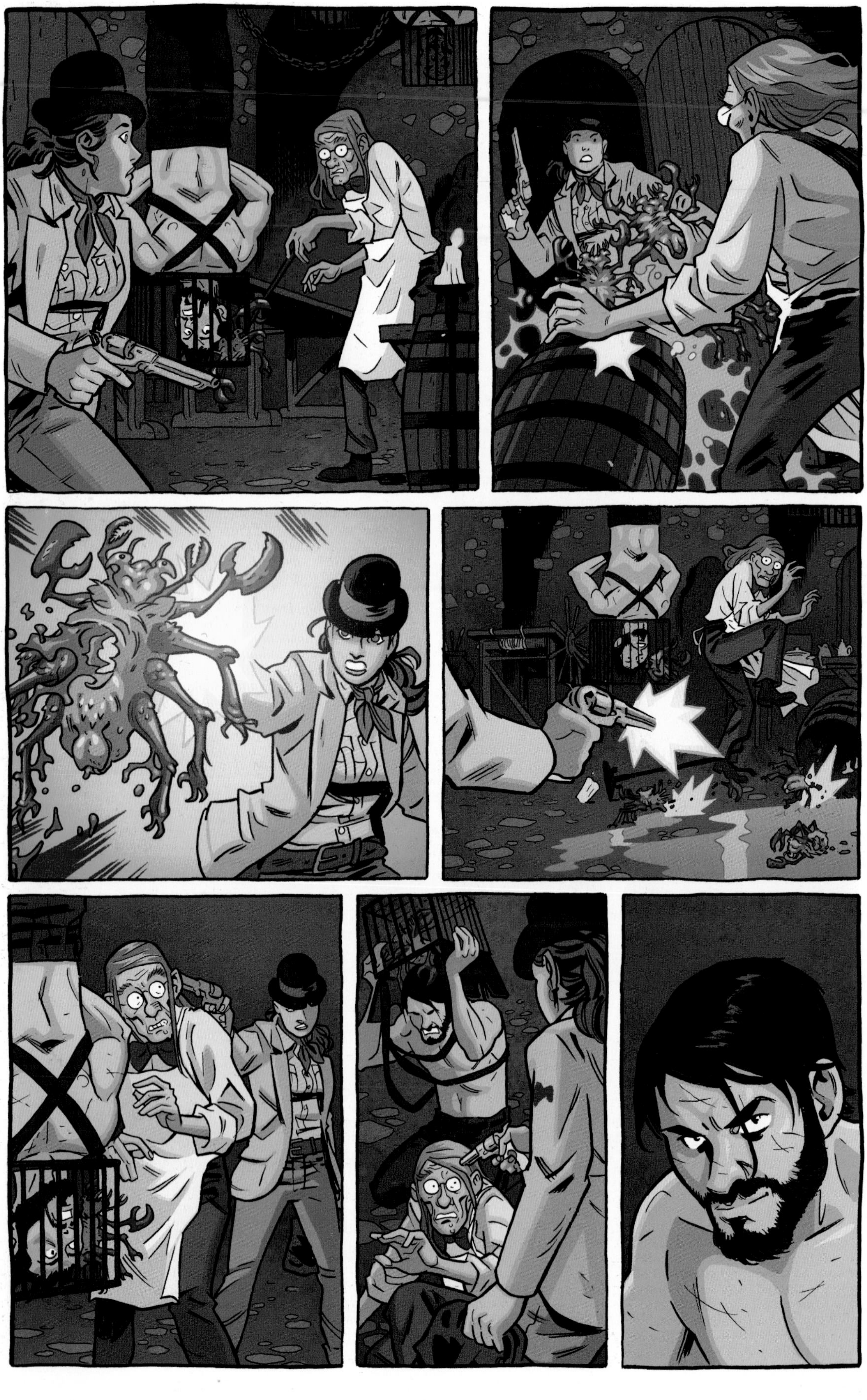

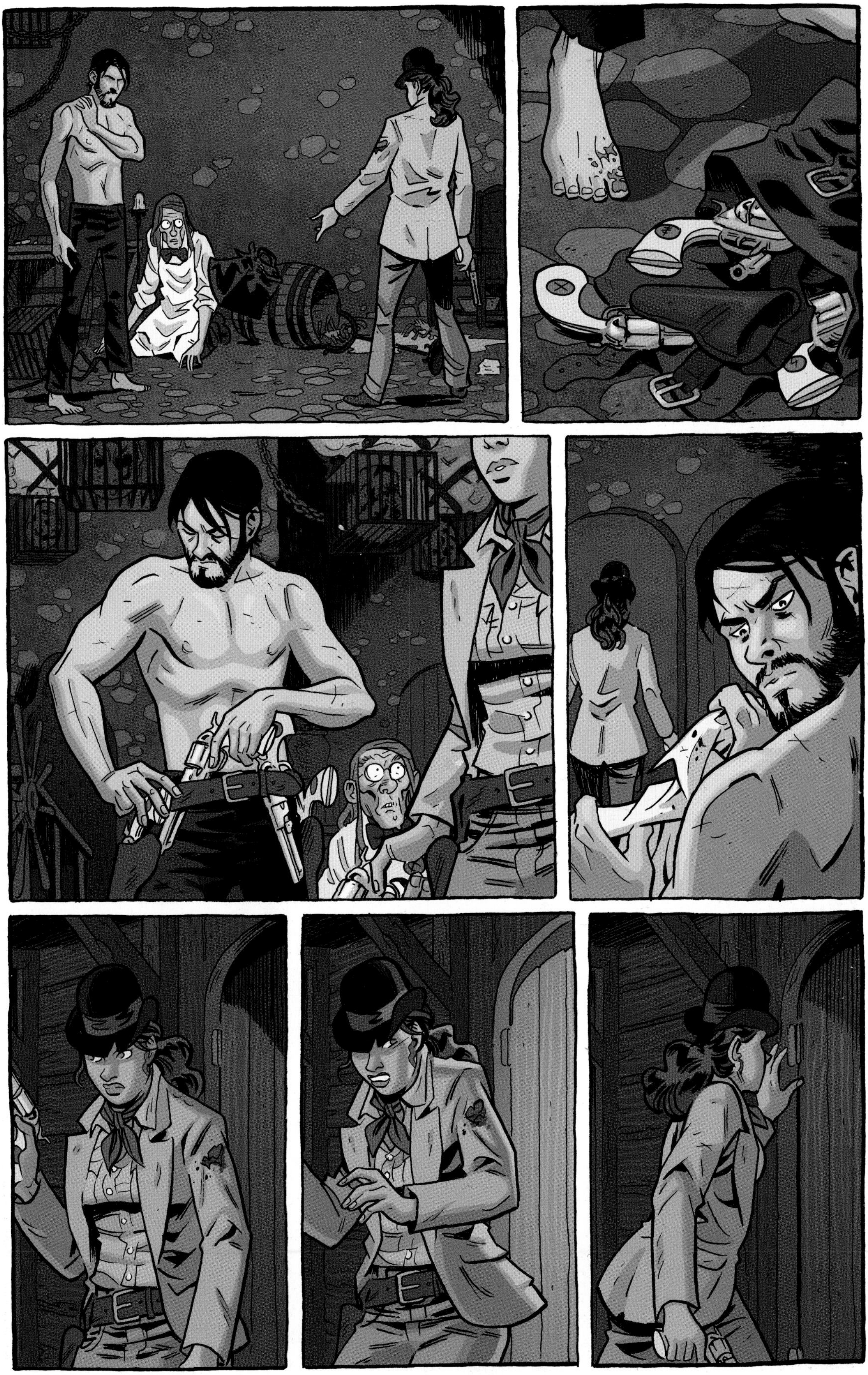

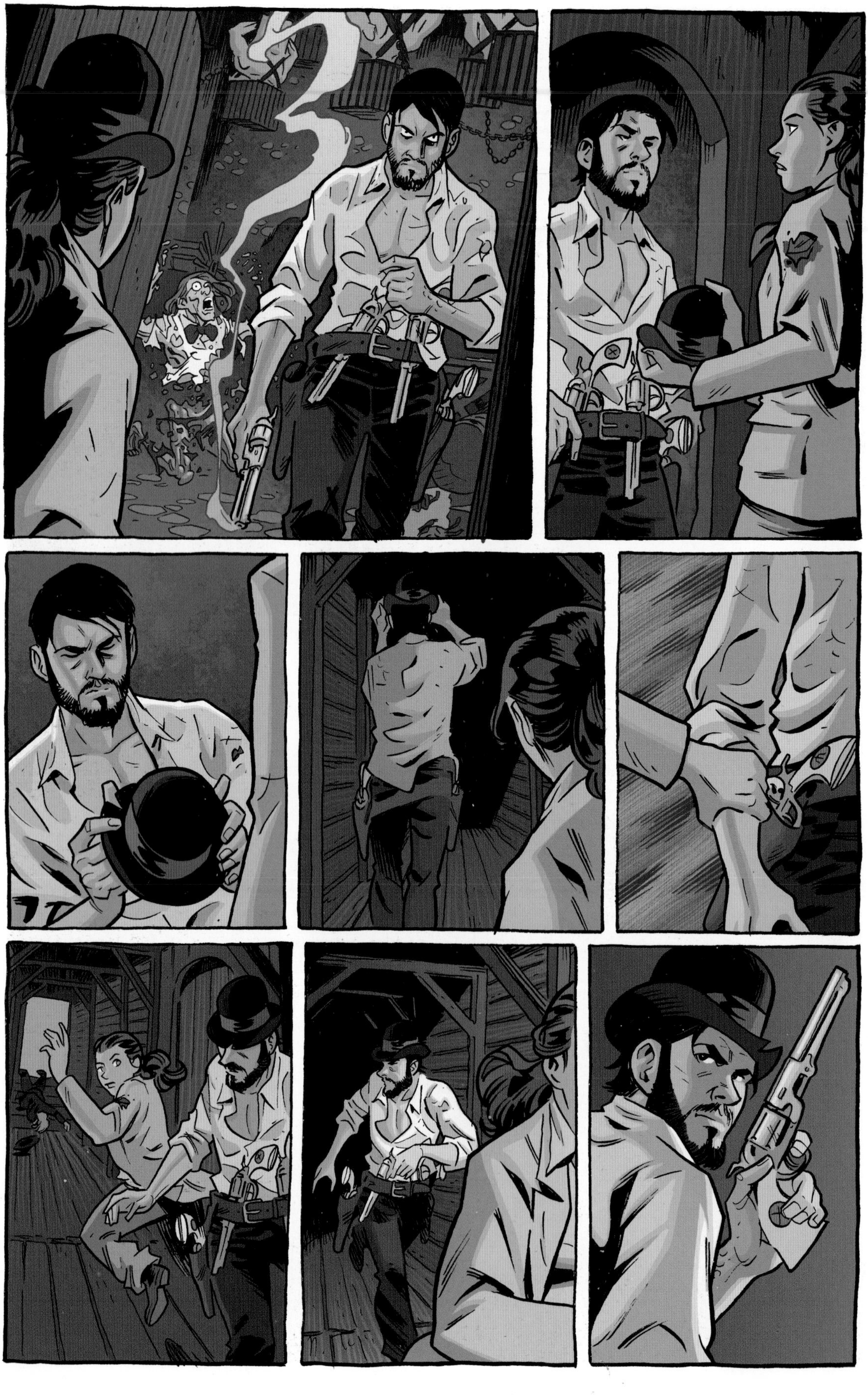

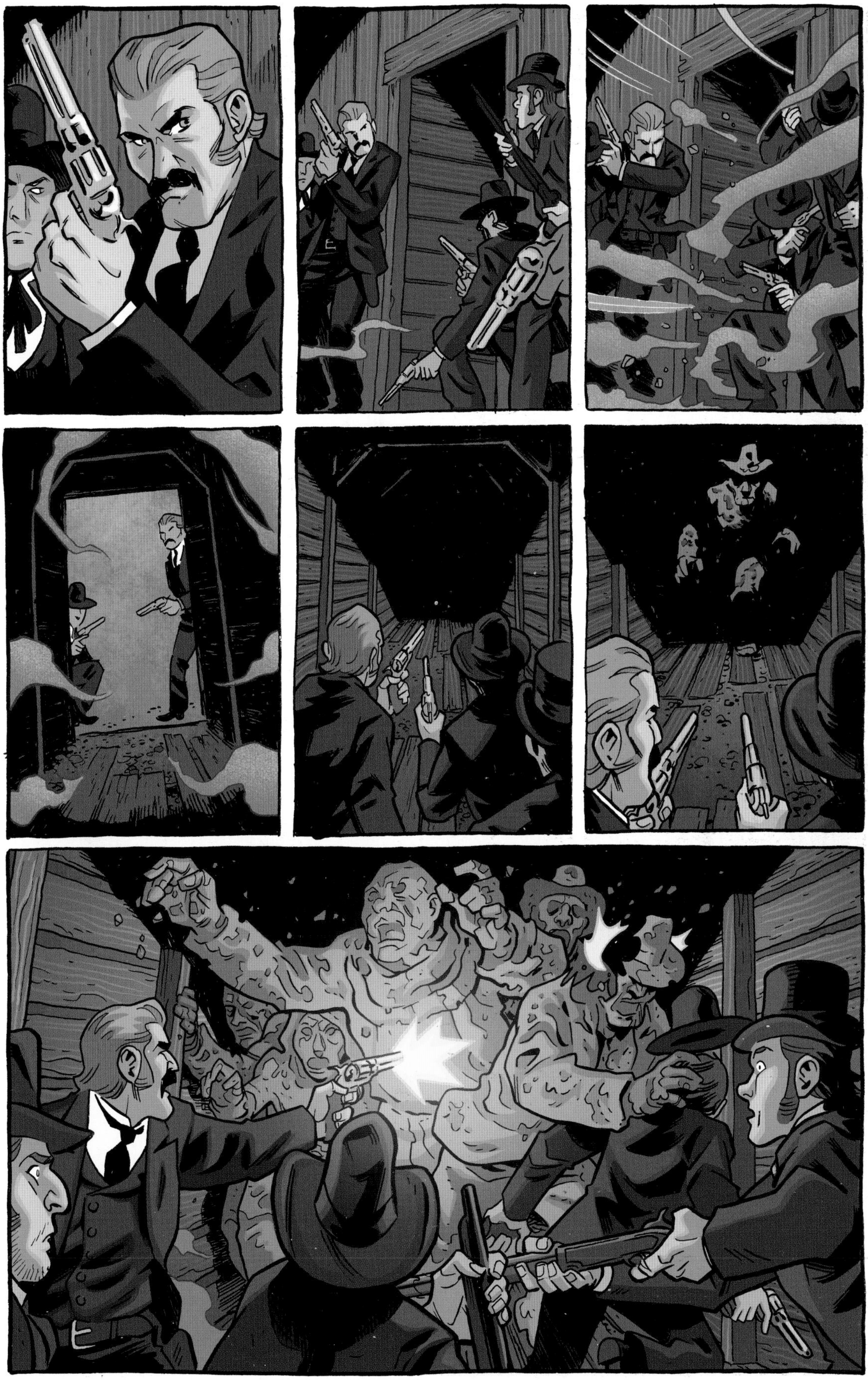

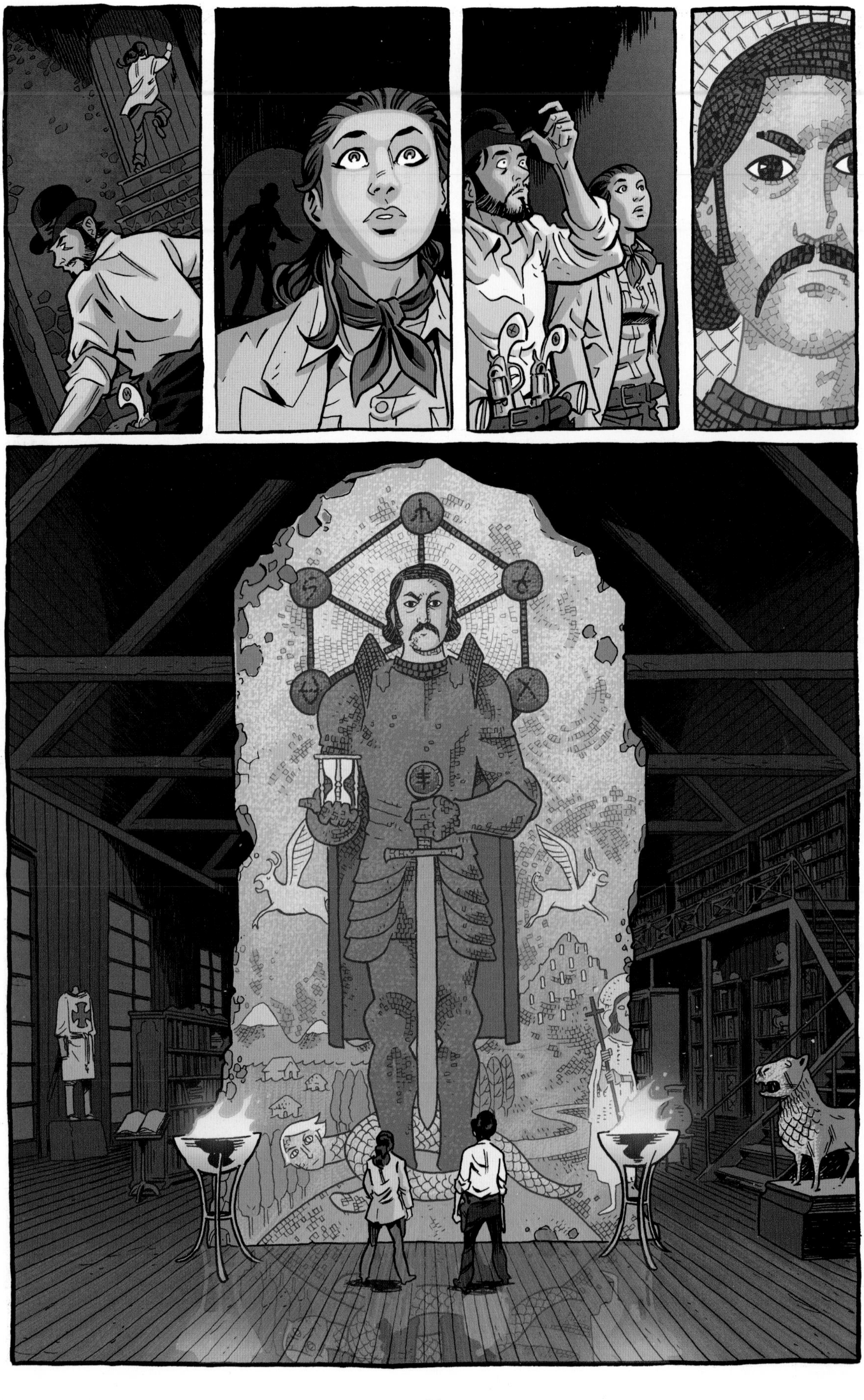

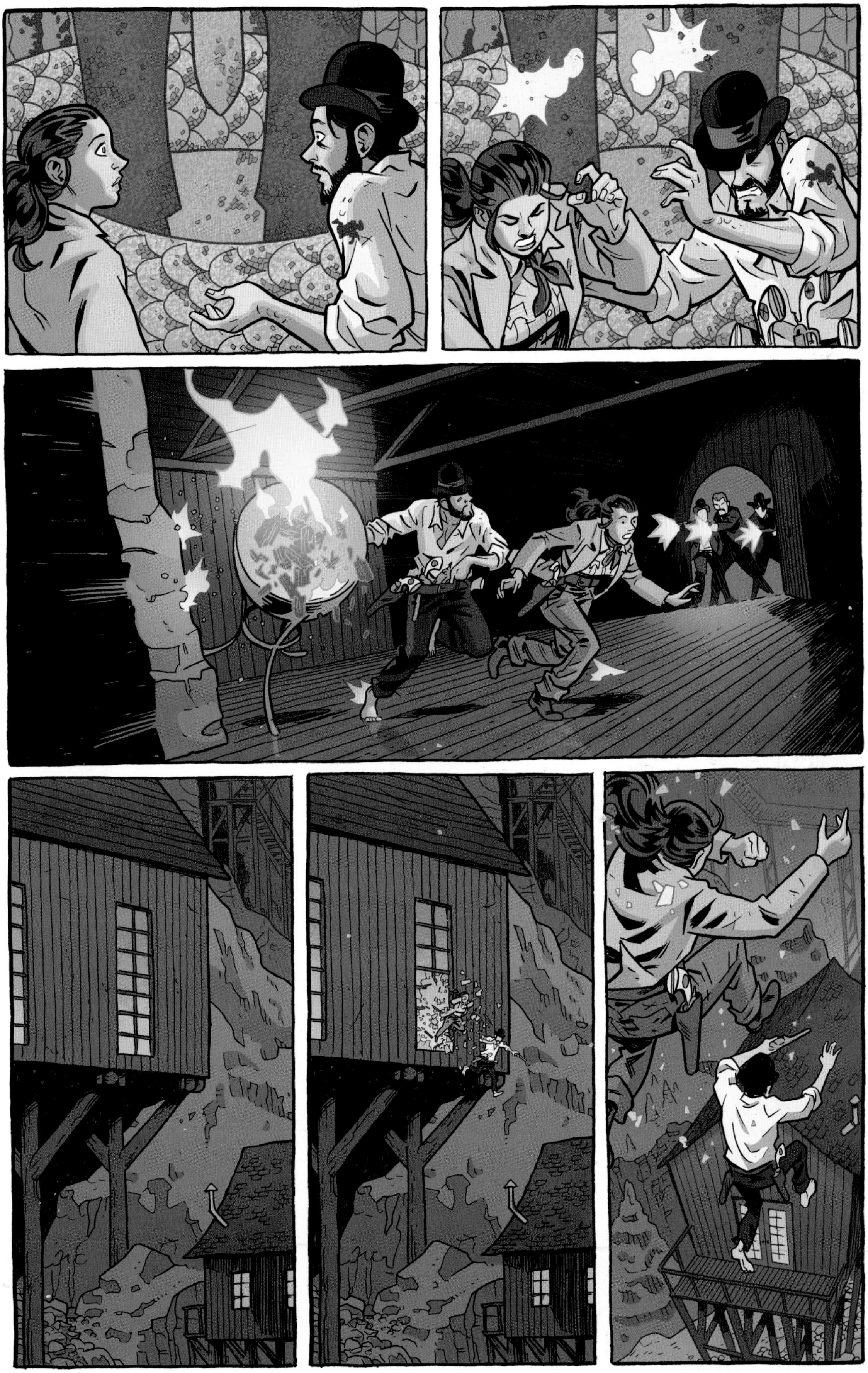

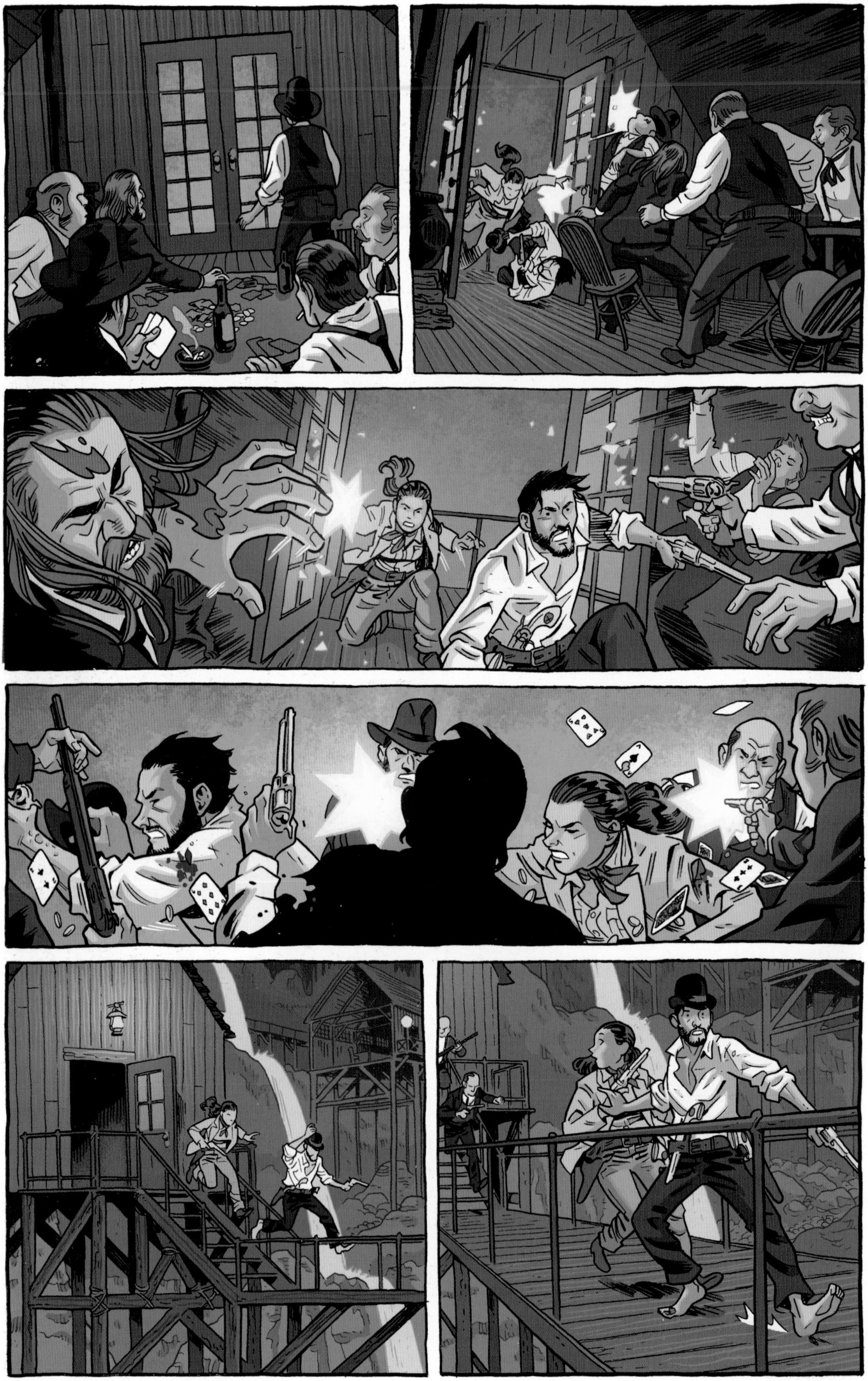

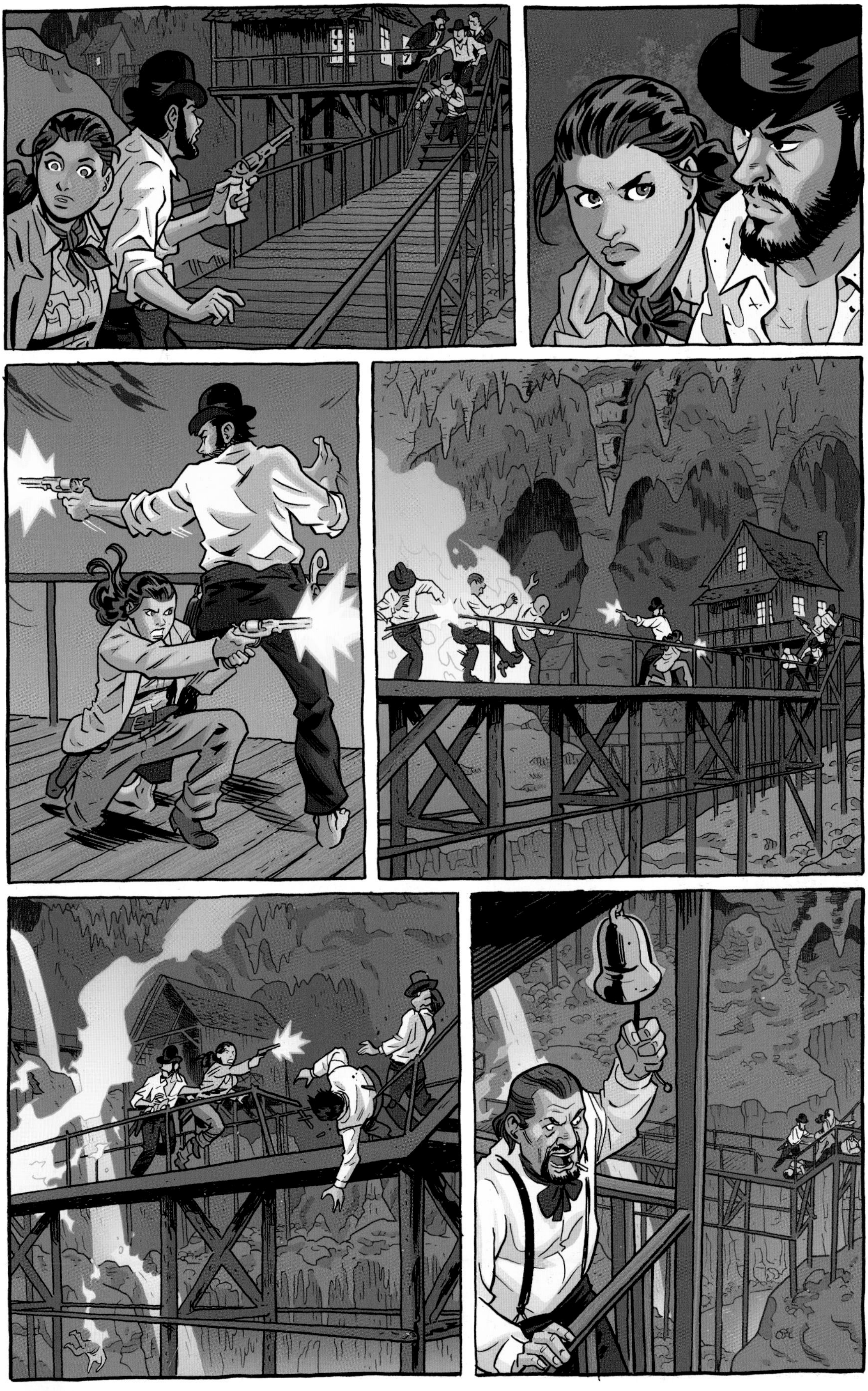

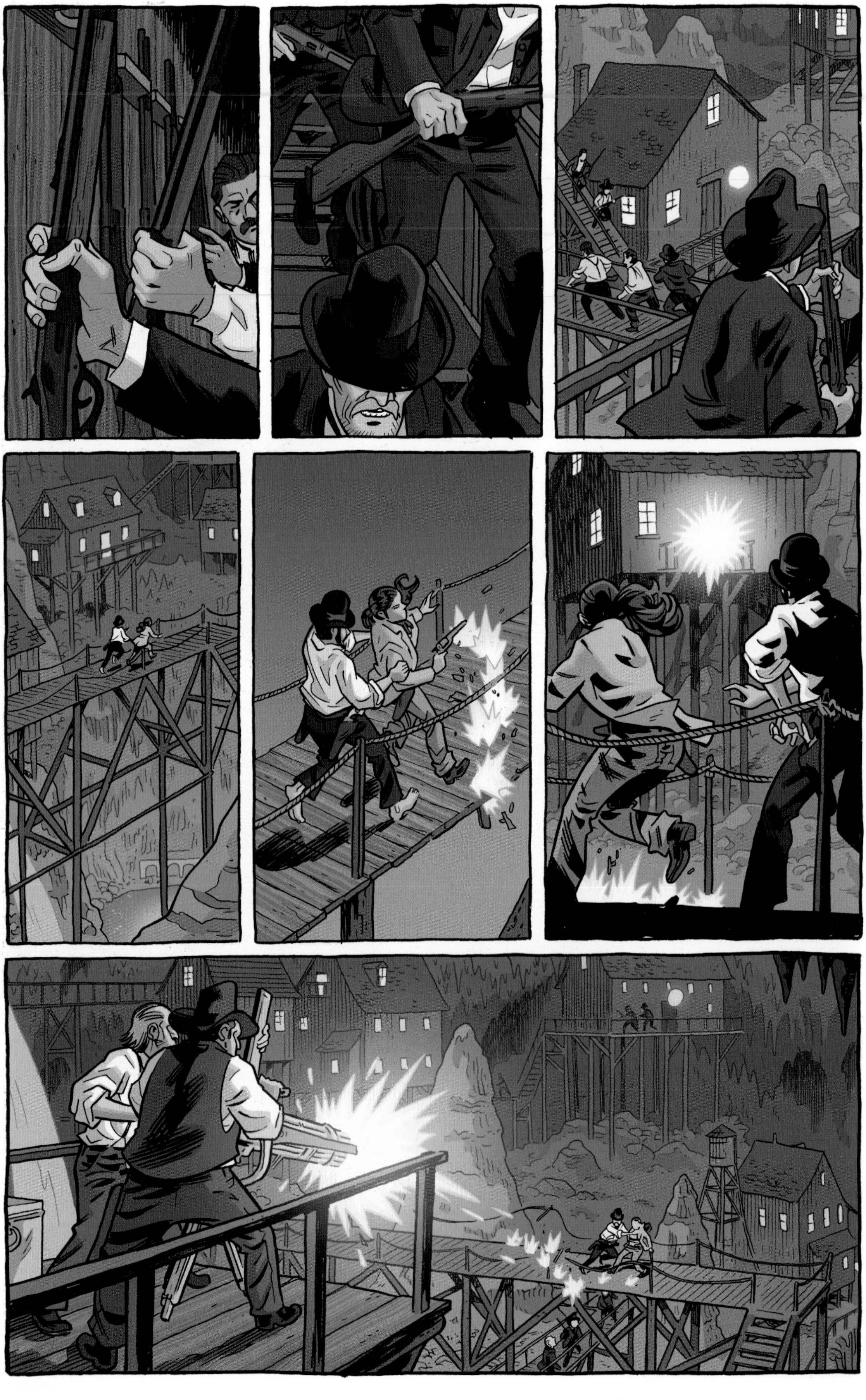

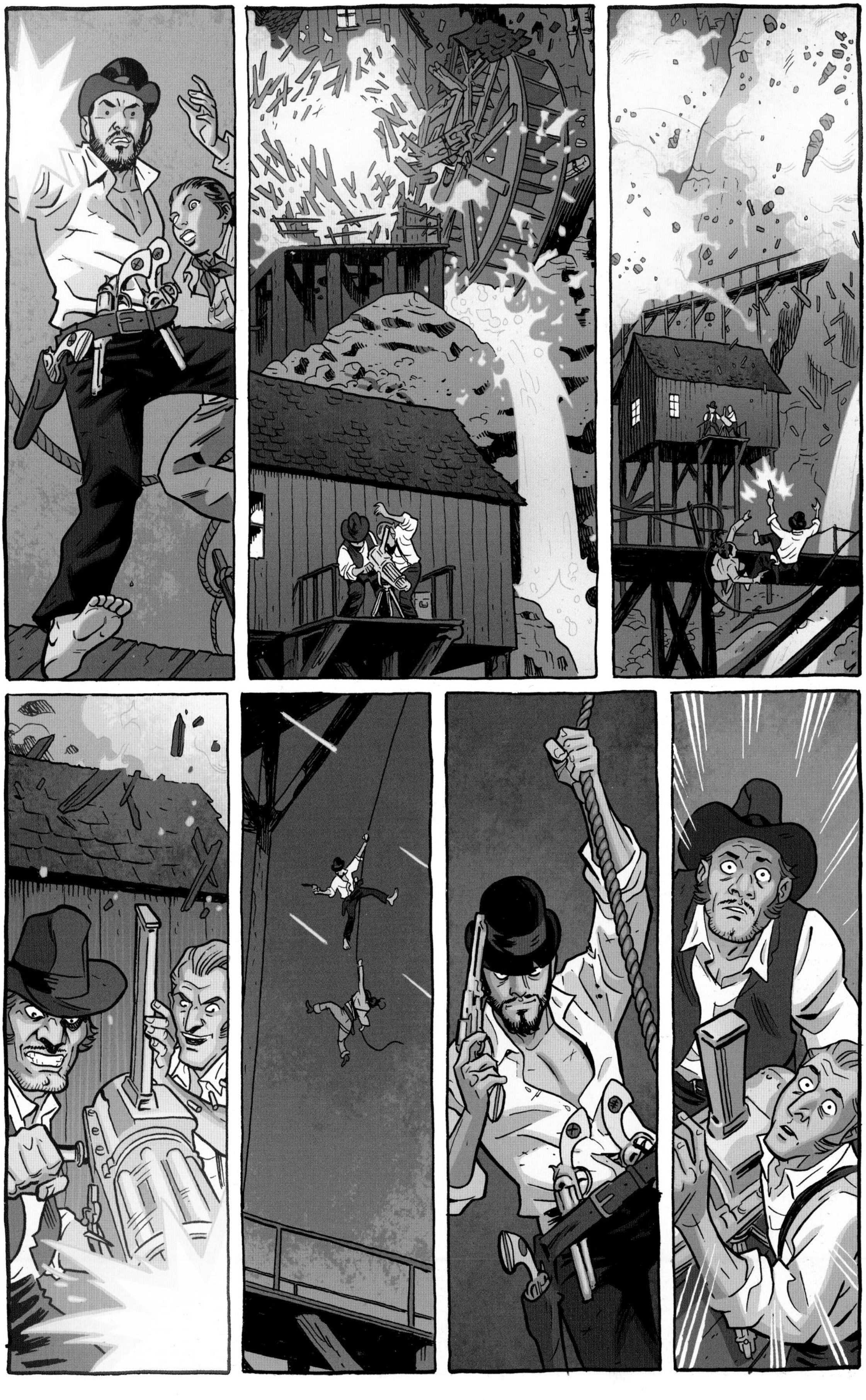

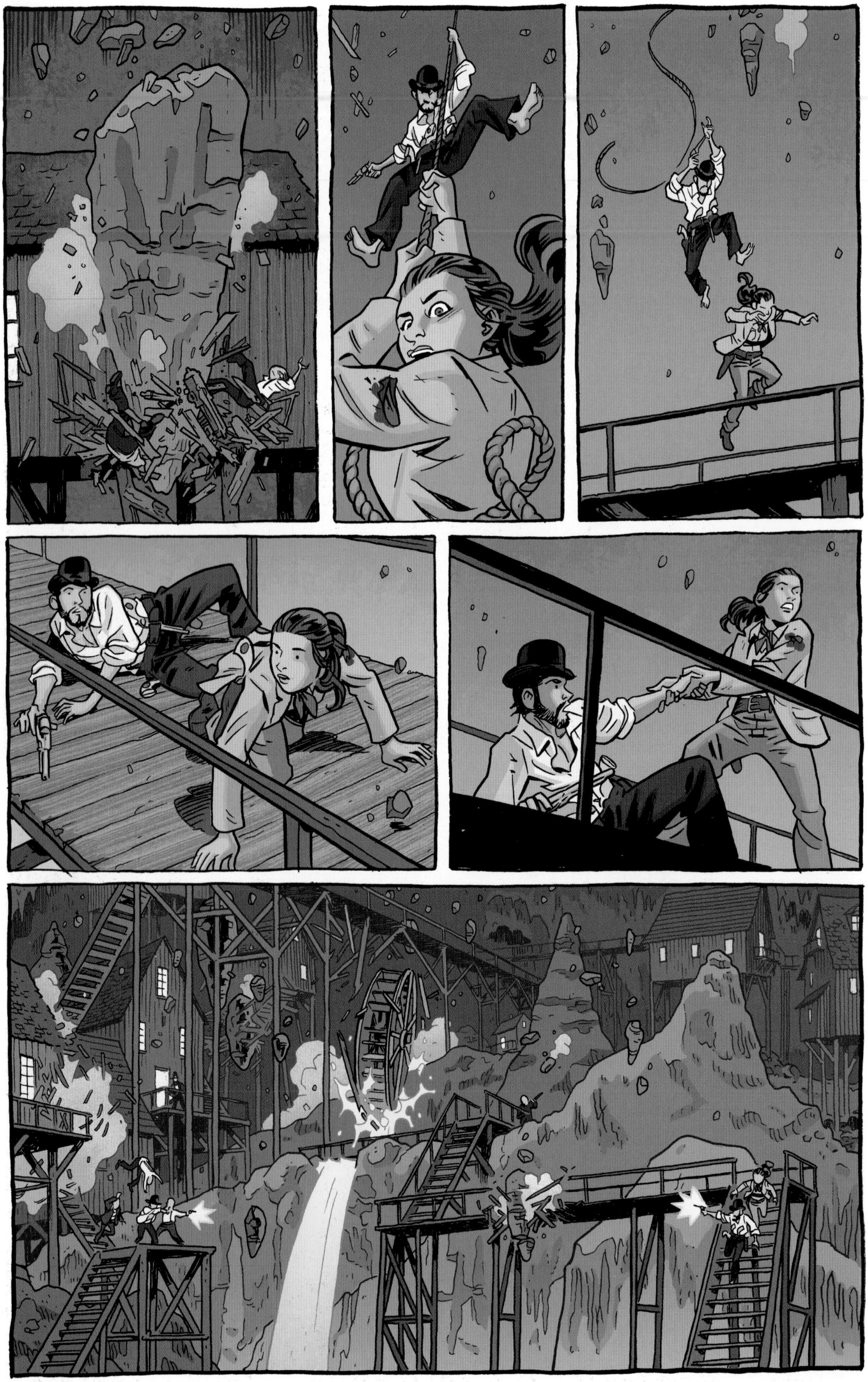

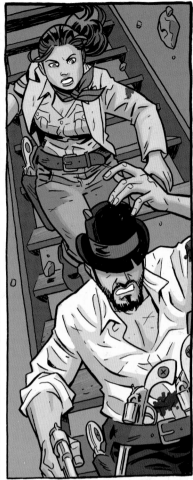

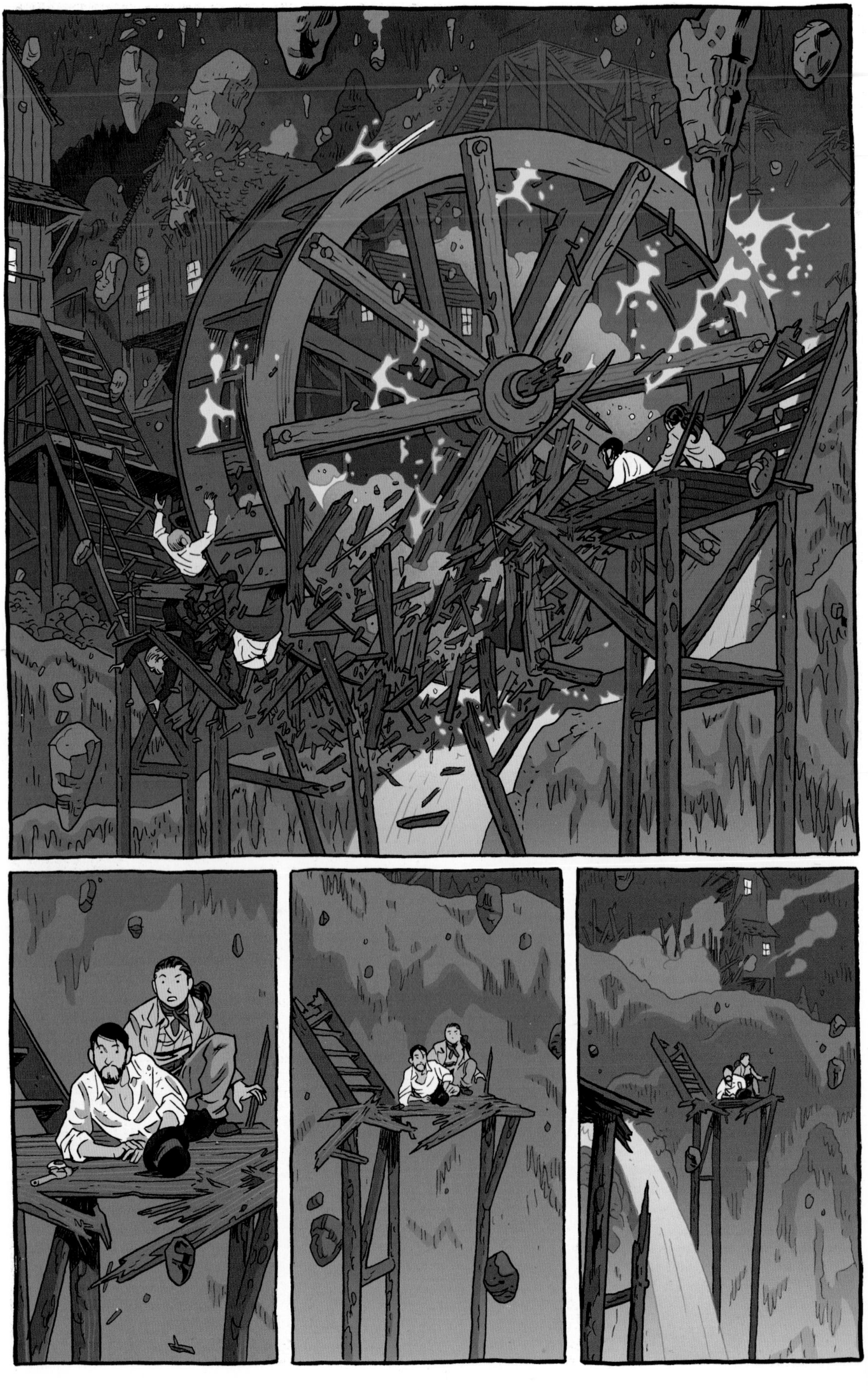

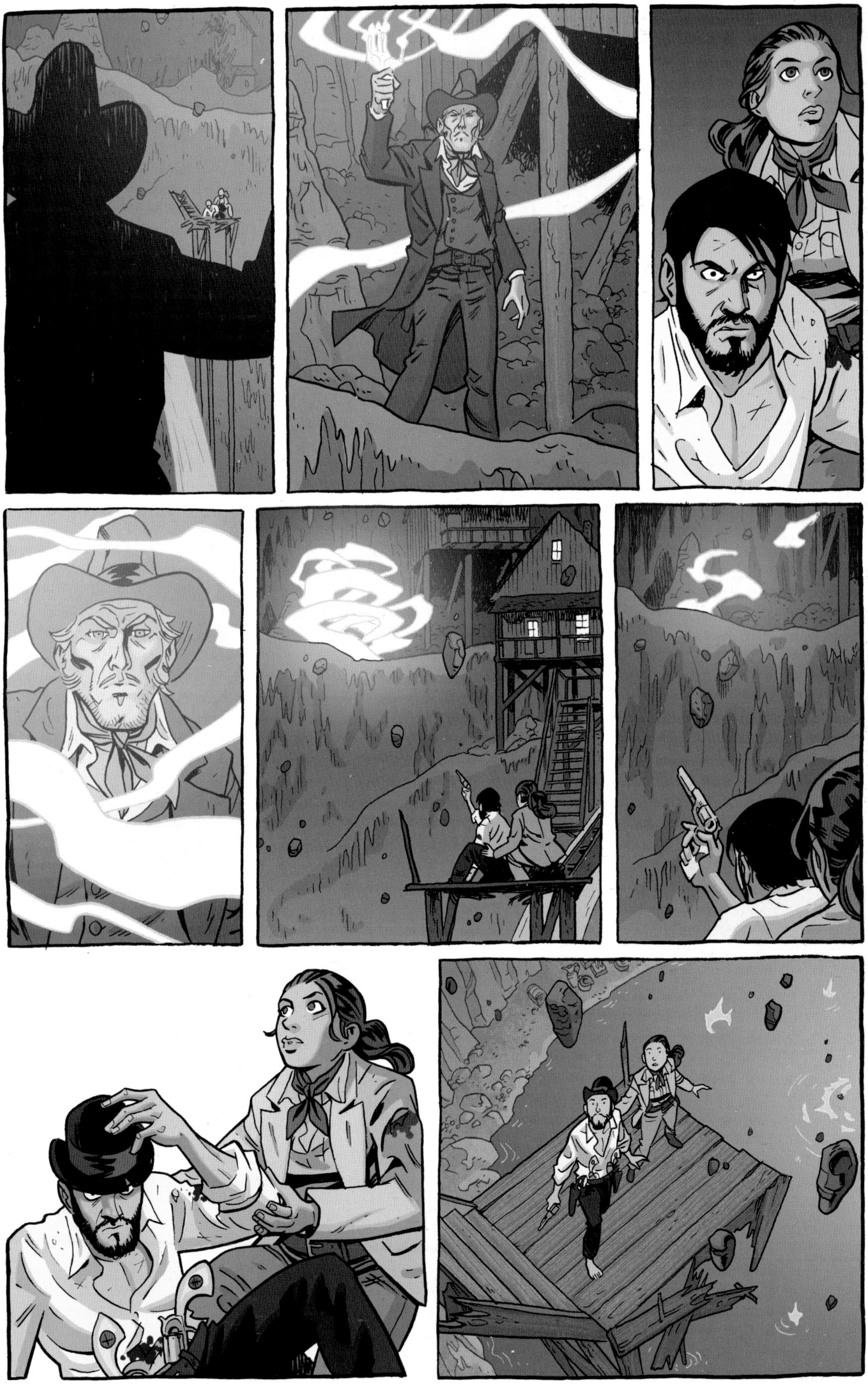

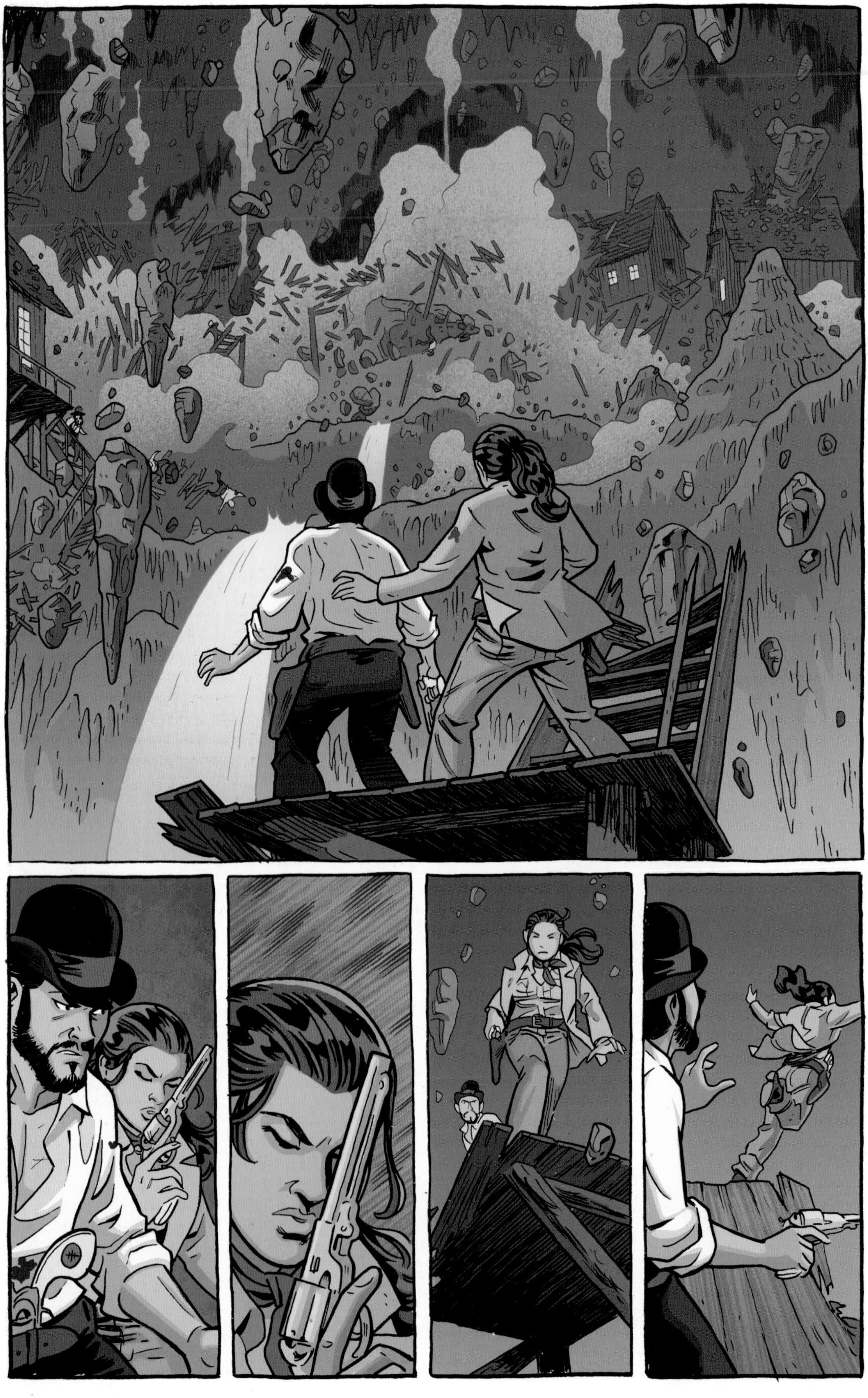

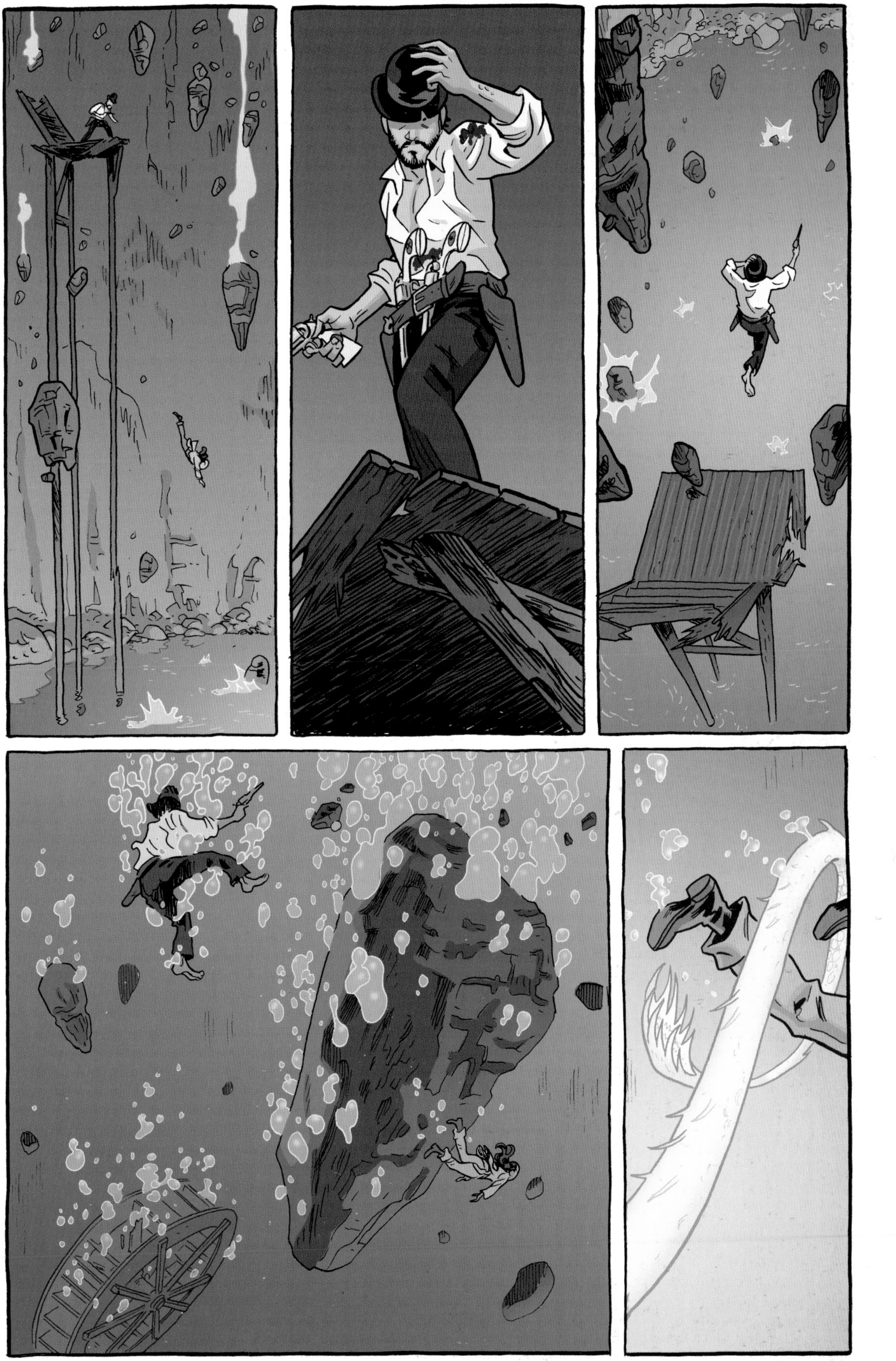

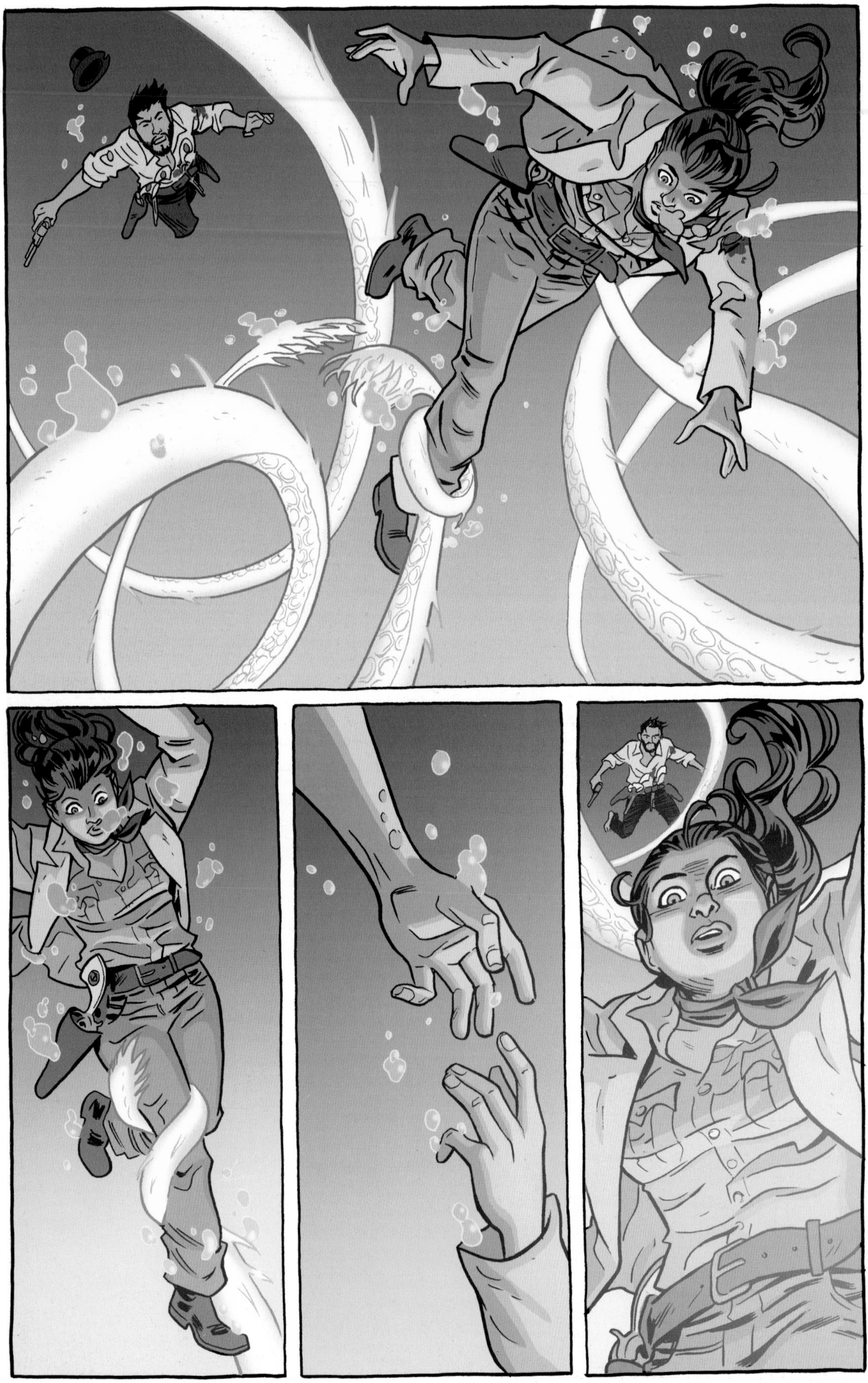

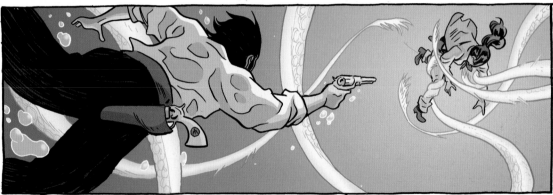

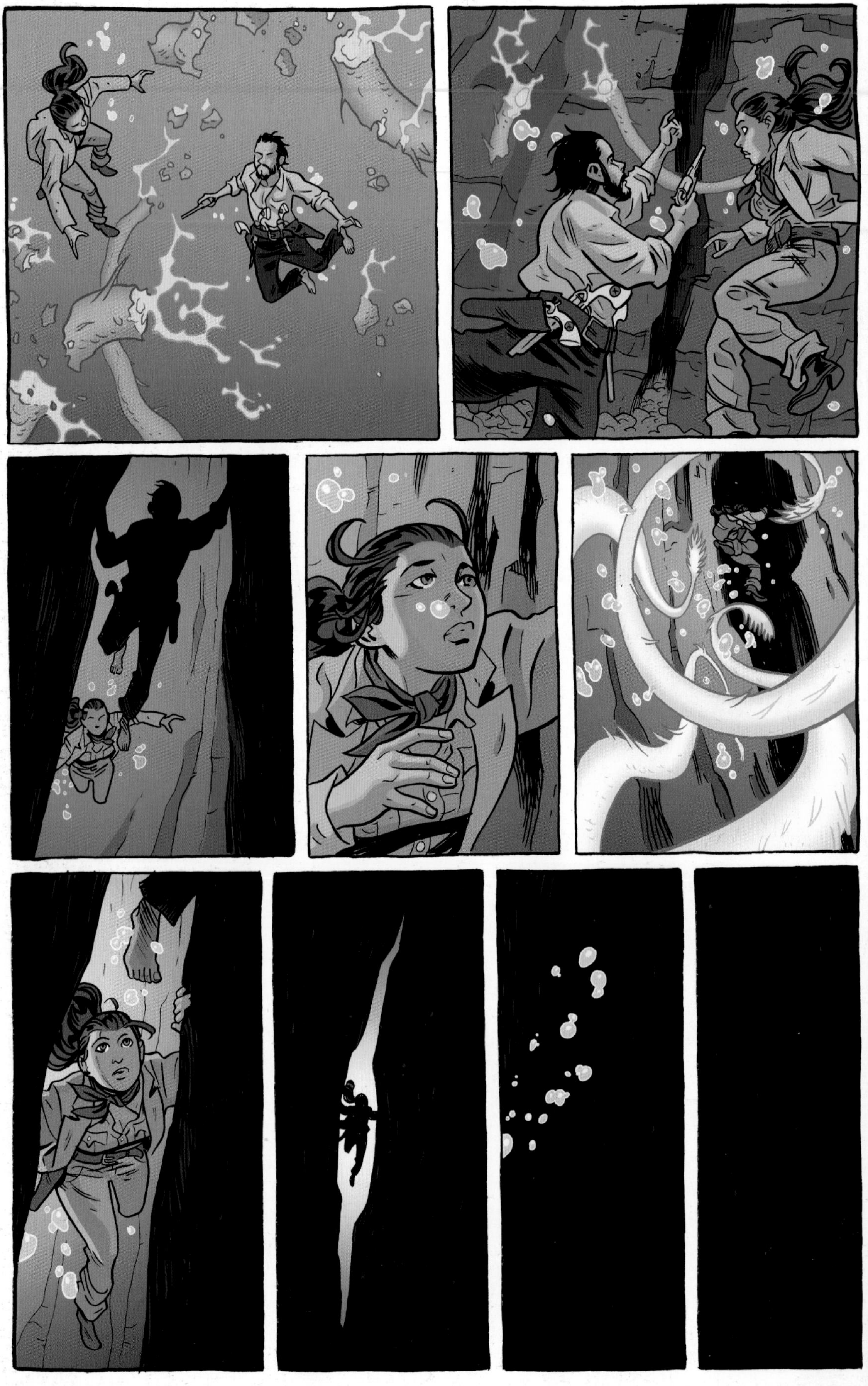

CHAPTER FIVE

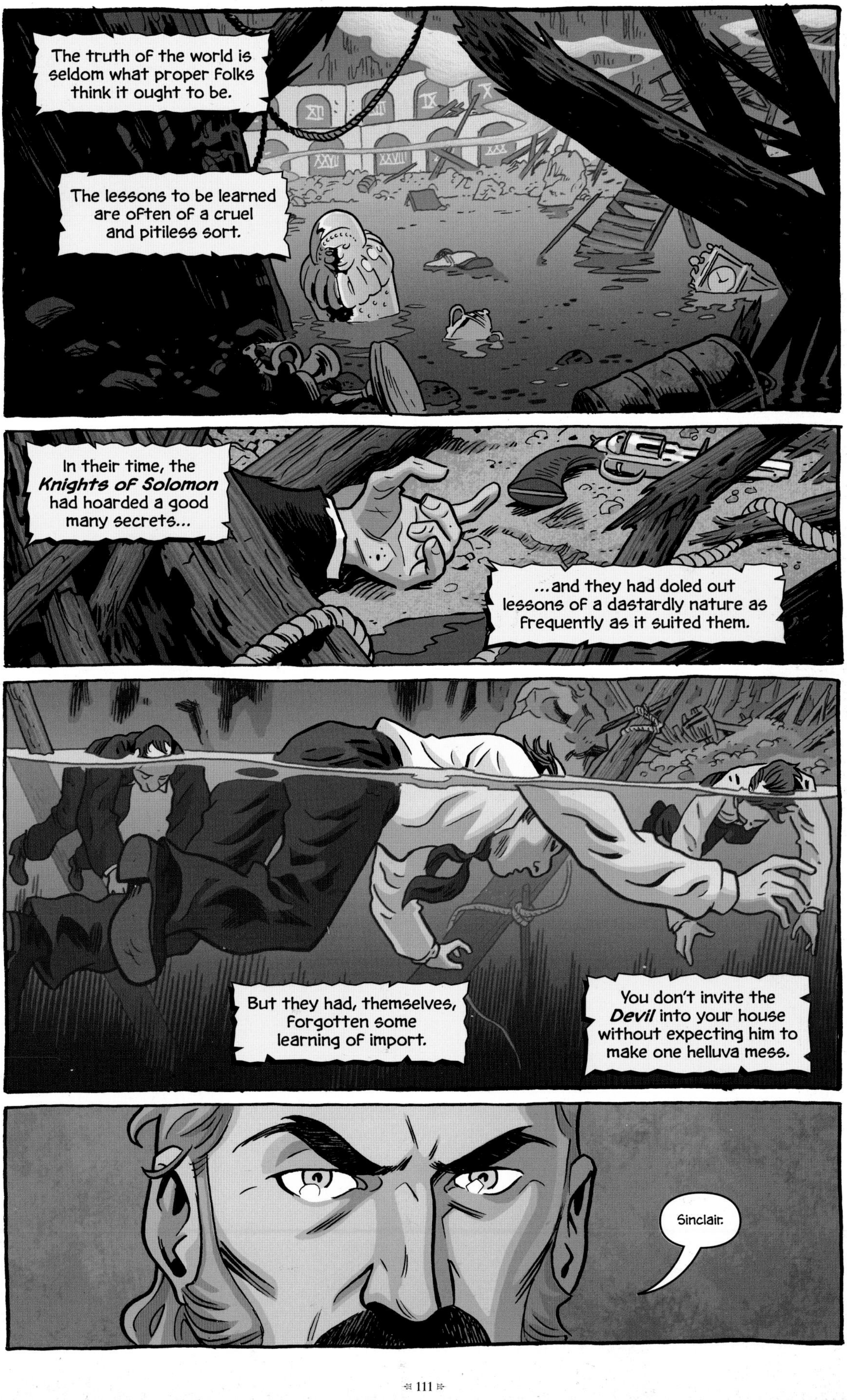
The truth of the world is seldom what proper folks think it ought to be.
The lessons to be learned are often of a cruel and pitiless sort.
In their time, the *Knights of Solomon* had hoarded a good many secrets...
...and they had doled out lessons of a dastardly nature as frequently as it suited them.
But they had, themselves, forgotten some learning of import.
You don't invite the *Devil* into your house without expecting him to make one helluva mess.
Sinclair.

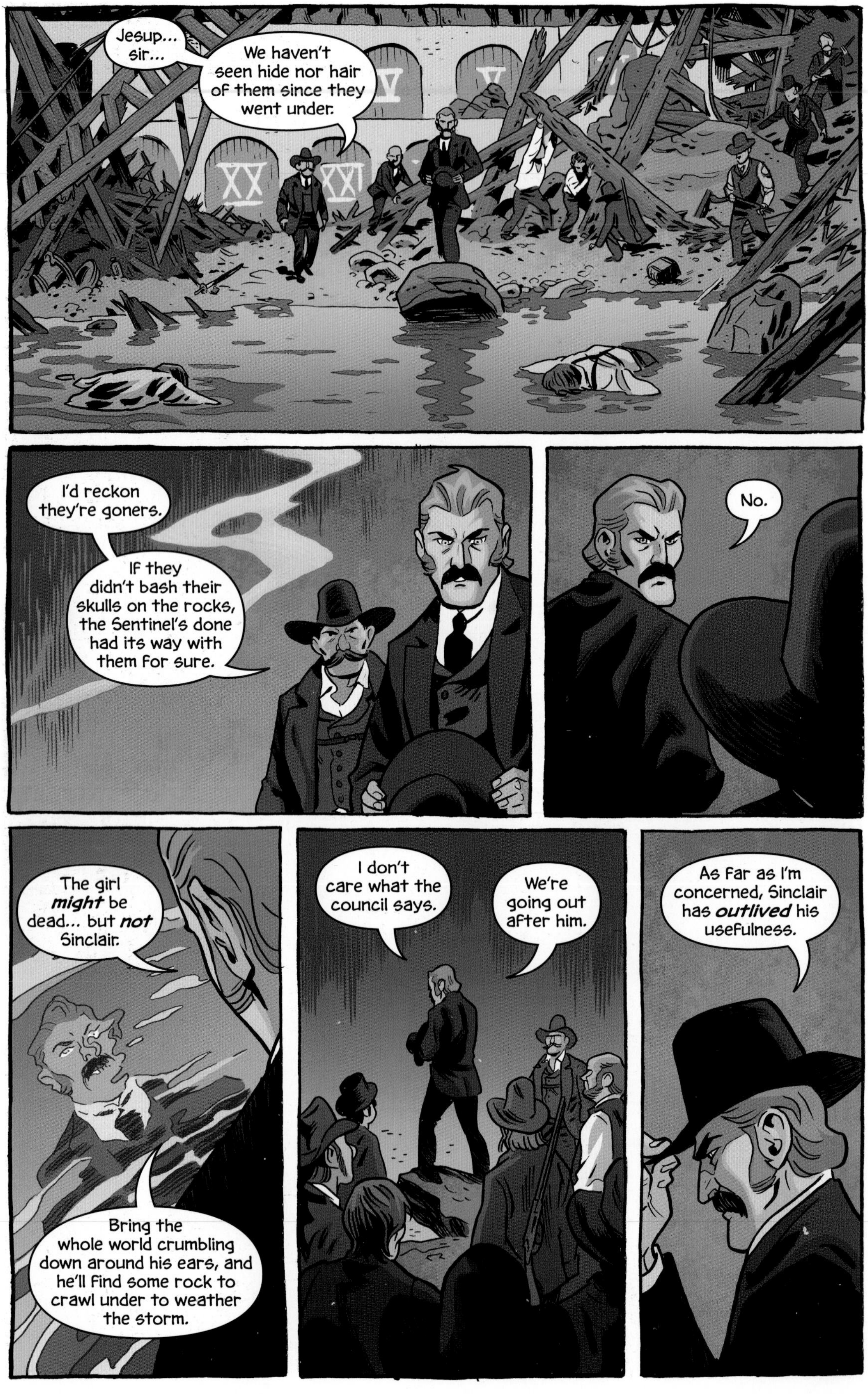
Jesup... sir...
We haven't seen hide nor hair of them since they went under.
I'd reckon they're goners.
If they didn't bash their skulls on the rocks, the Sentinel's done had its way with them for sure.
No.
The girl *might* be dead... but *not* Sinclair.
Bring the whole world crumbling down around his ears, and he'll find some rock to crawl under to weather the storm.
I don't care what the council says.
We're going out after him.
As far as I'm concerned, Sinclair has *outlived* his usefulness.

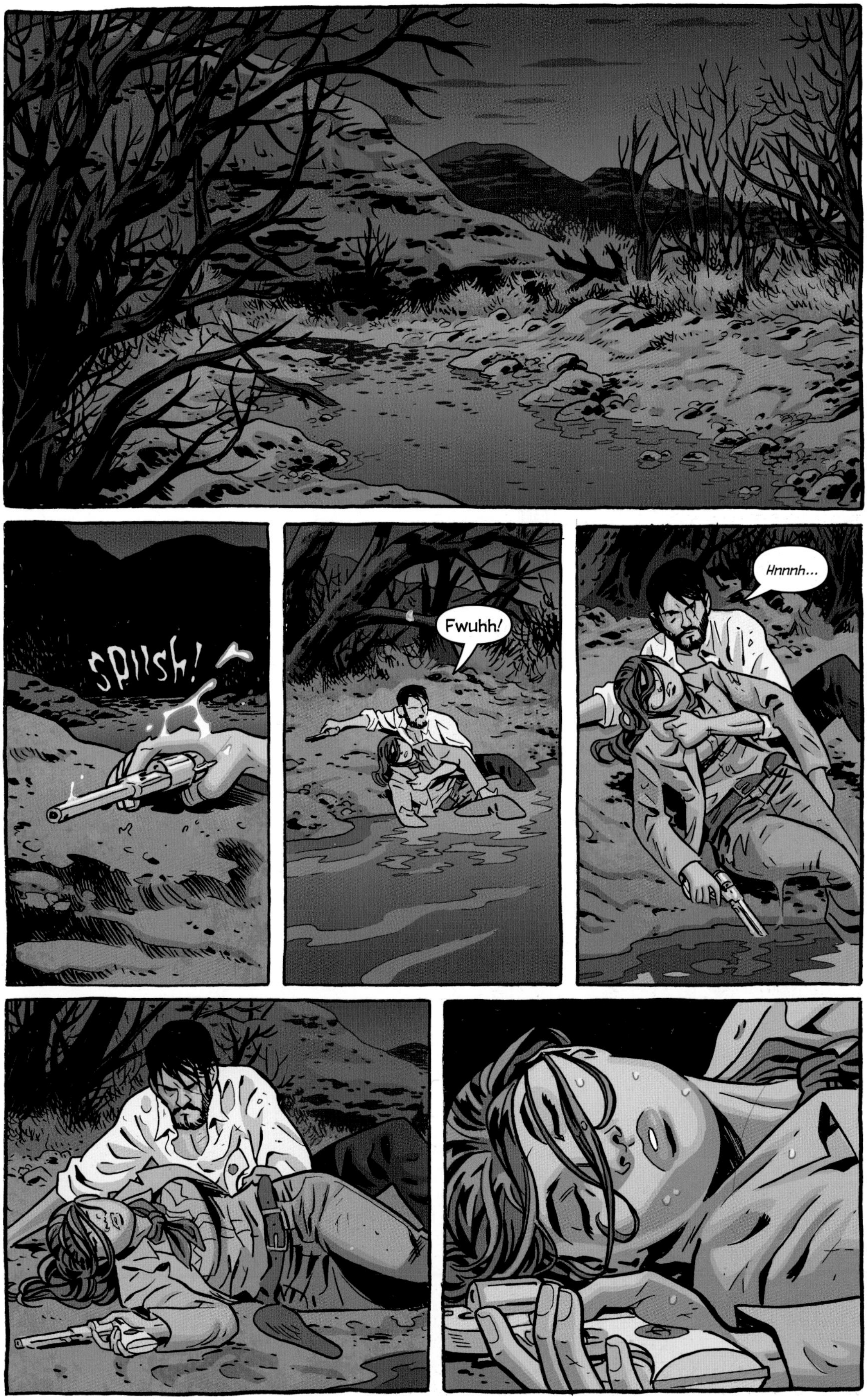
SPLISH!
Fwuhh!
Hnnnh...

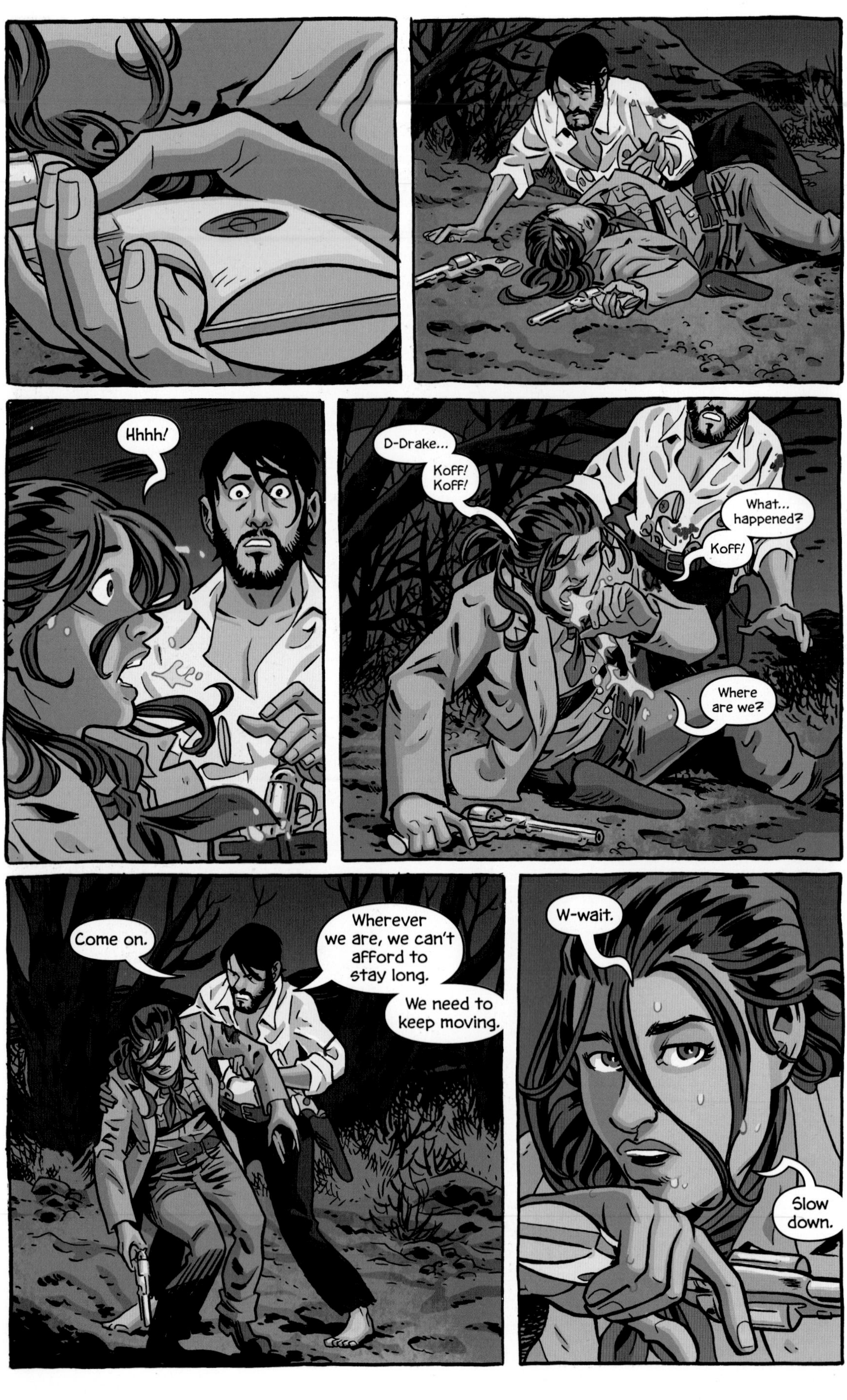

Hhhh!
D-Drake...
Koff! Koff!
What... happened?
Koff!
Where are we?
Come on.
Wherever we are, we can't afford to stay long.
We need to keep moving.
W-wait.
Slow down.

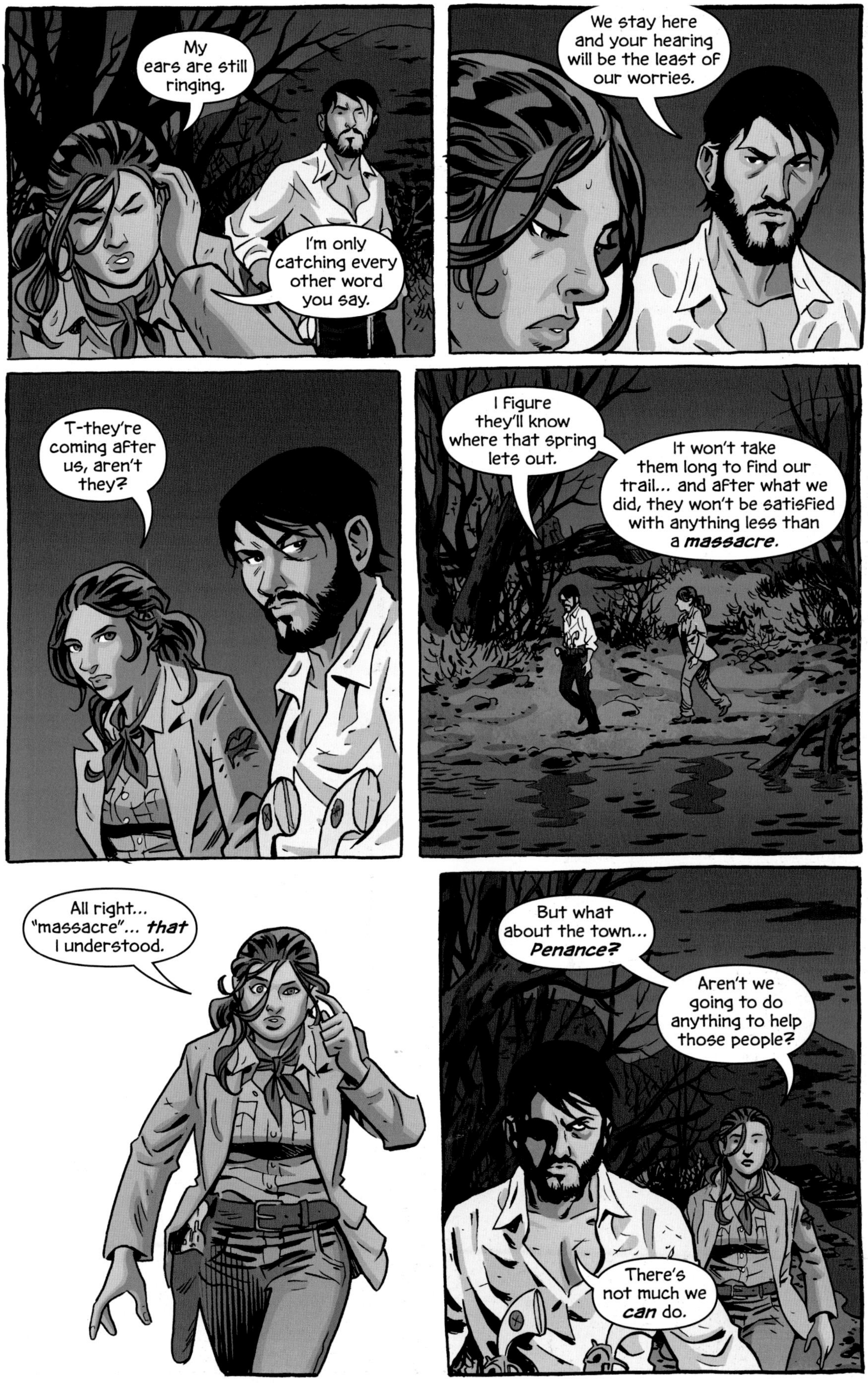
My ears are still ringing.
I'm only catching every other word you say.
We stay here and your hearing will be the least of our worries.
T-they're coming after us, aren't they?
I figure they'll know where that spring lets out.
It won't take them long to find our trail... and after what we did, they won't be satisfied with anything less than a *massacre.*
All right... "massacre"... *that* I understood.
But what about the town... *Penance?*
Aren't we going to do anything to help those people?
There's not much we *can* do.

"Near as I can tell, the water the townsfolk have been drinking... it's tainted by that seal...

"By drinking it... they've bound themselves to it... and that's just what the Knights wanted.

"The water changed those people... and it will keep changing them... but they'll die if they stop drinking it now.

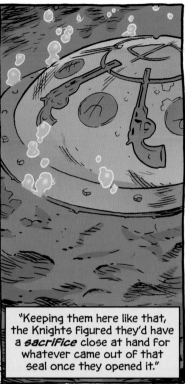

"Keeping them here like that, the Knights figured they'd have a *sacrifice* close at hand for whatever came out of that seal once they opened it."

What do we do when they catch us?

They want a *massacre?*

"I'll oblige them."

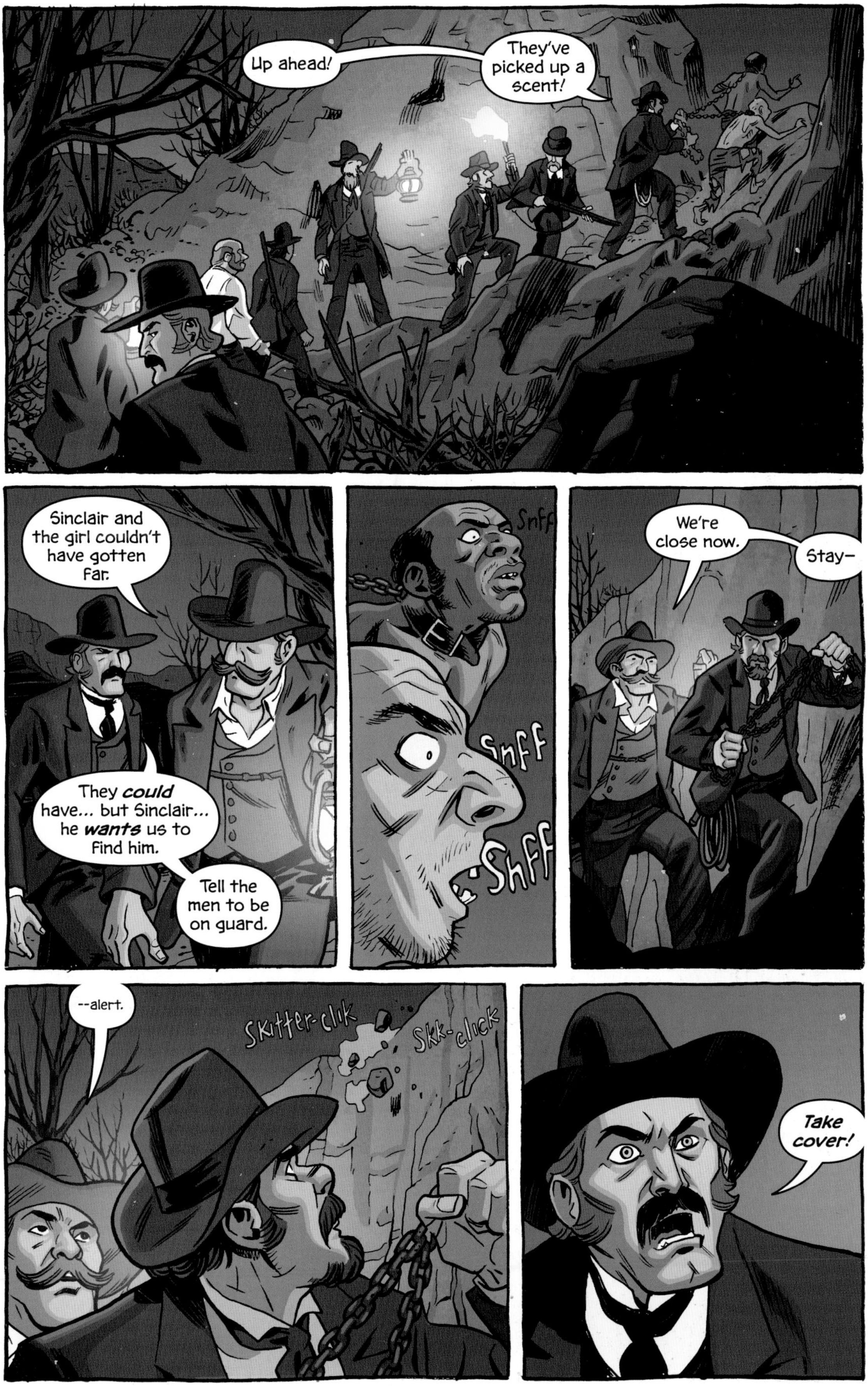

Up ahead!
They've picked up a scent!
Sinclair and the girl couldn't have gotten far.
They *could* have... but Sinclair... he *wants* us to find him.
Tell the men to be on guard.
Snff
Snff
Shff
We're close now.
Stay–
--alert.
Skitter-clik
Skk-click
Take cover!

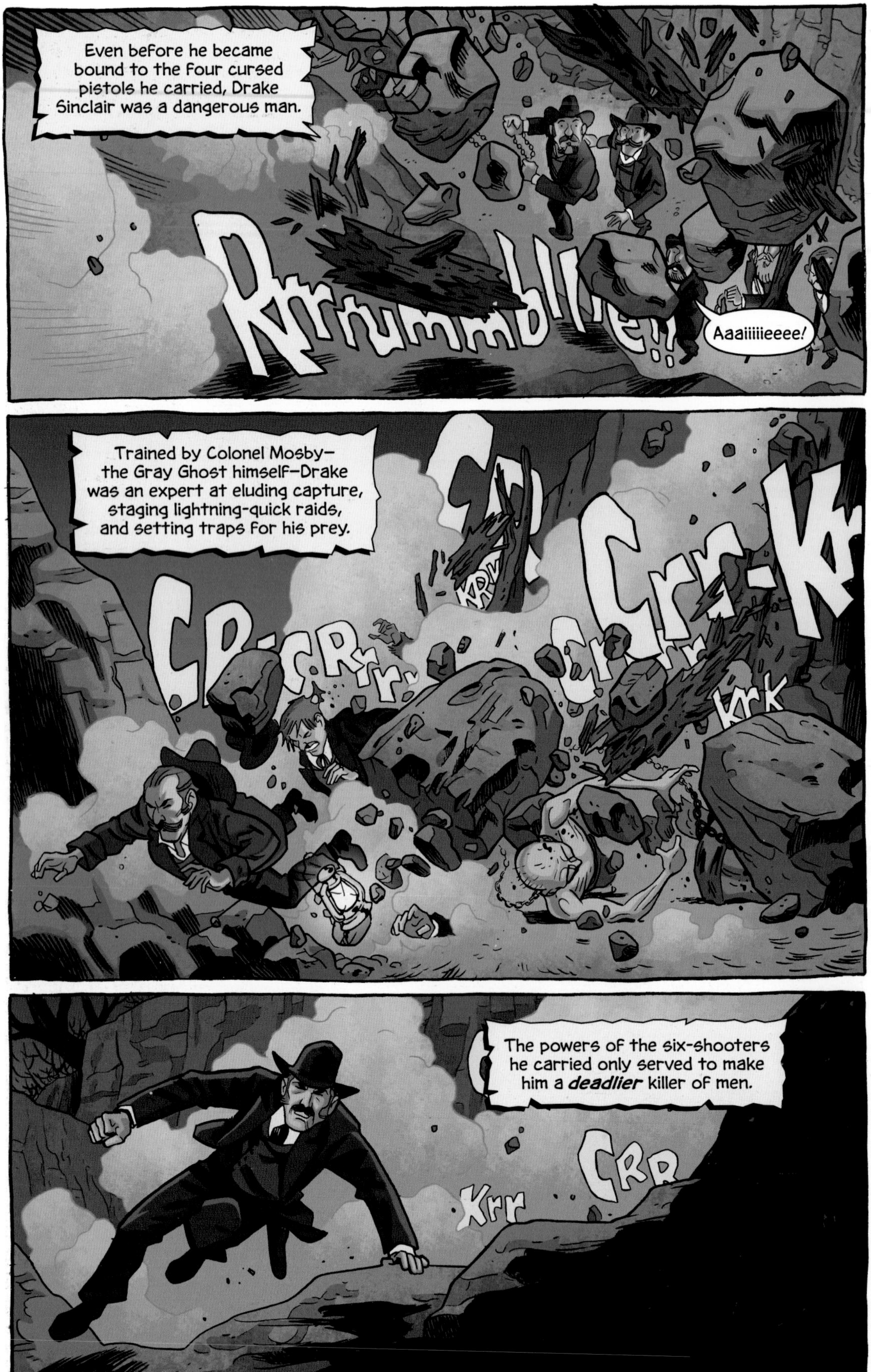
Even before he became bound to the four cursed pistols he carried, Drake Sinclair was a dangerous man.
Aaaiiiiieeee!
Trained by Colonel Mosby—the Gray Ghost himself—Drake was an expert at eluding capture, staging lightning-quick raids, and setting traps for his prey.
Krk
The powers of the six-shooters he carried only served to make him a *deadlier* killer of men.
Krr

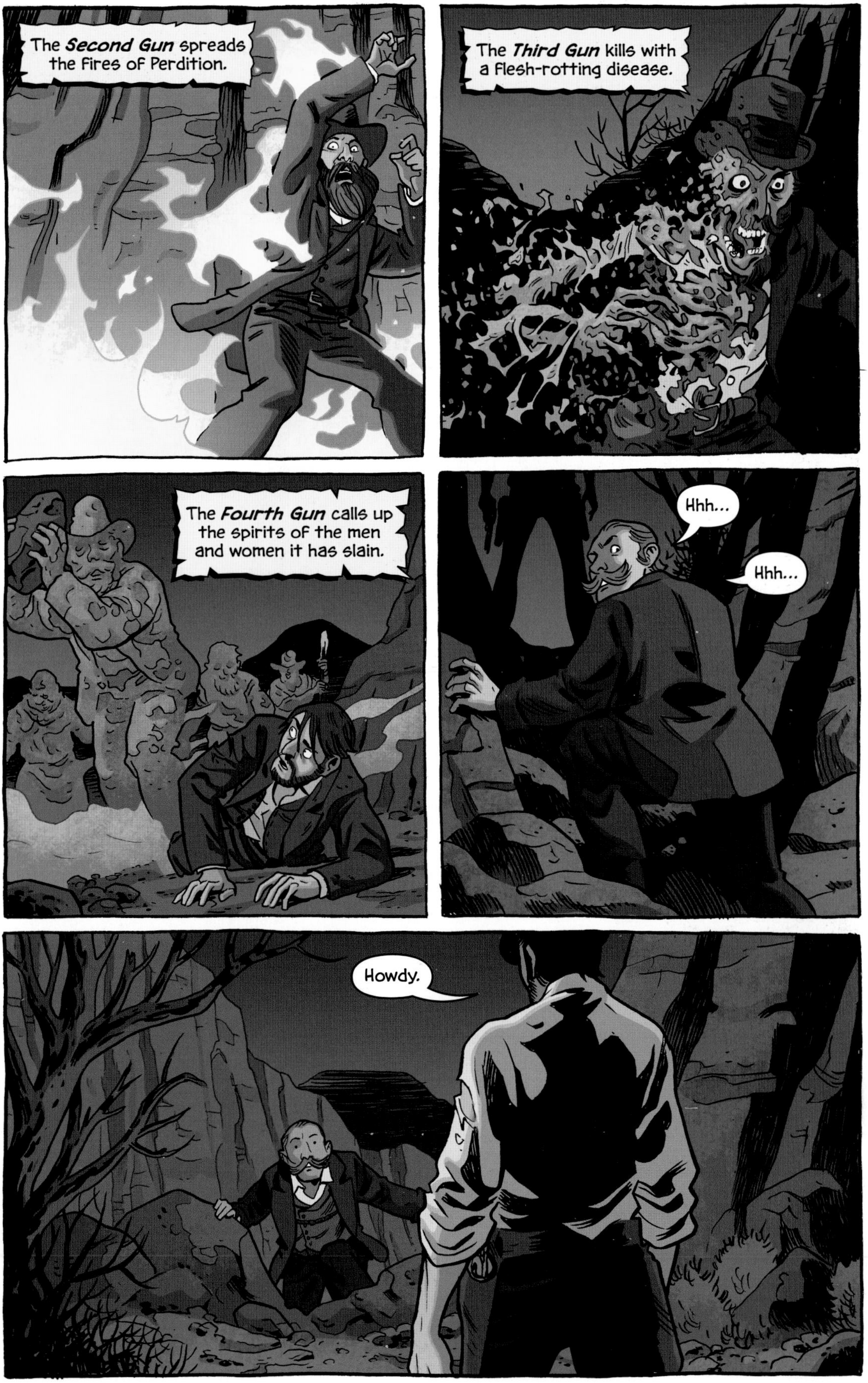
The Second Gun spreads the Fires of Perdition.
The Third Gun kills with a flesh-rotting disease.
The Fourth Gun calls up the spirits of the men and women it has slain.
Hhh...
Hhh...
Howdy.

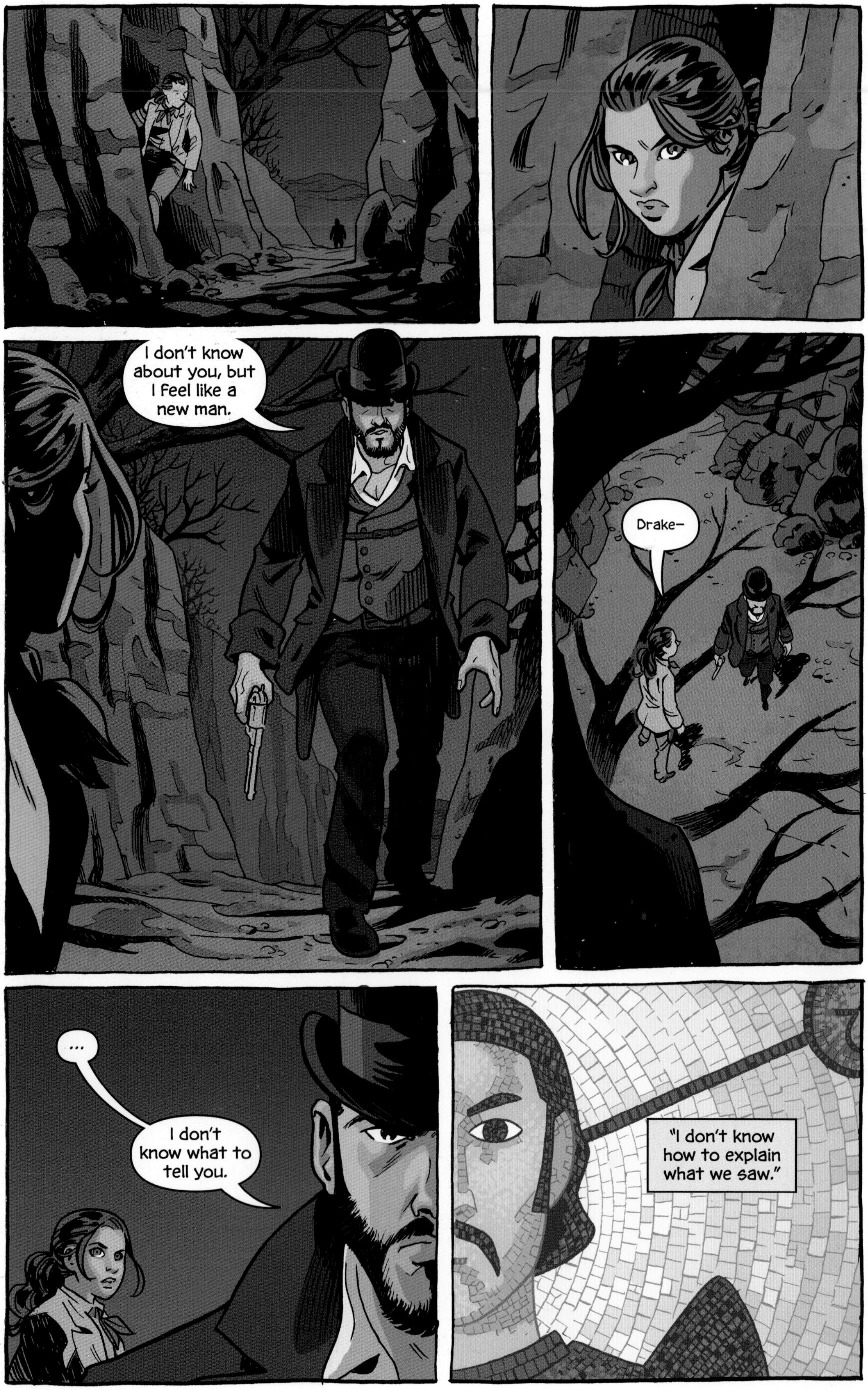
I don't know about you, but I feel like a new man.
Drake–
...
I don't know what to tell you.
"I don't know how to explain what we saw."

Not just what we saw...

...there's more.

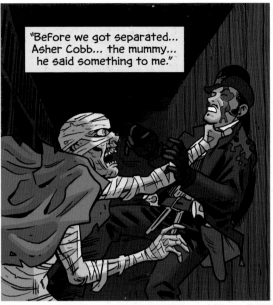

"Before we got separated... Asher Cobb... the mummy... he said something to me."

I know what you're going to do... what you're going to do with those guns...

But what he said—

What he said didn't make a lick of sense.

Becky!

KA-BLAM!

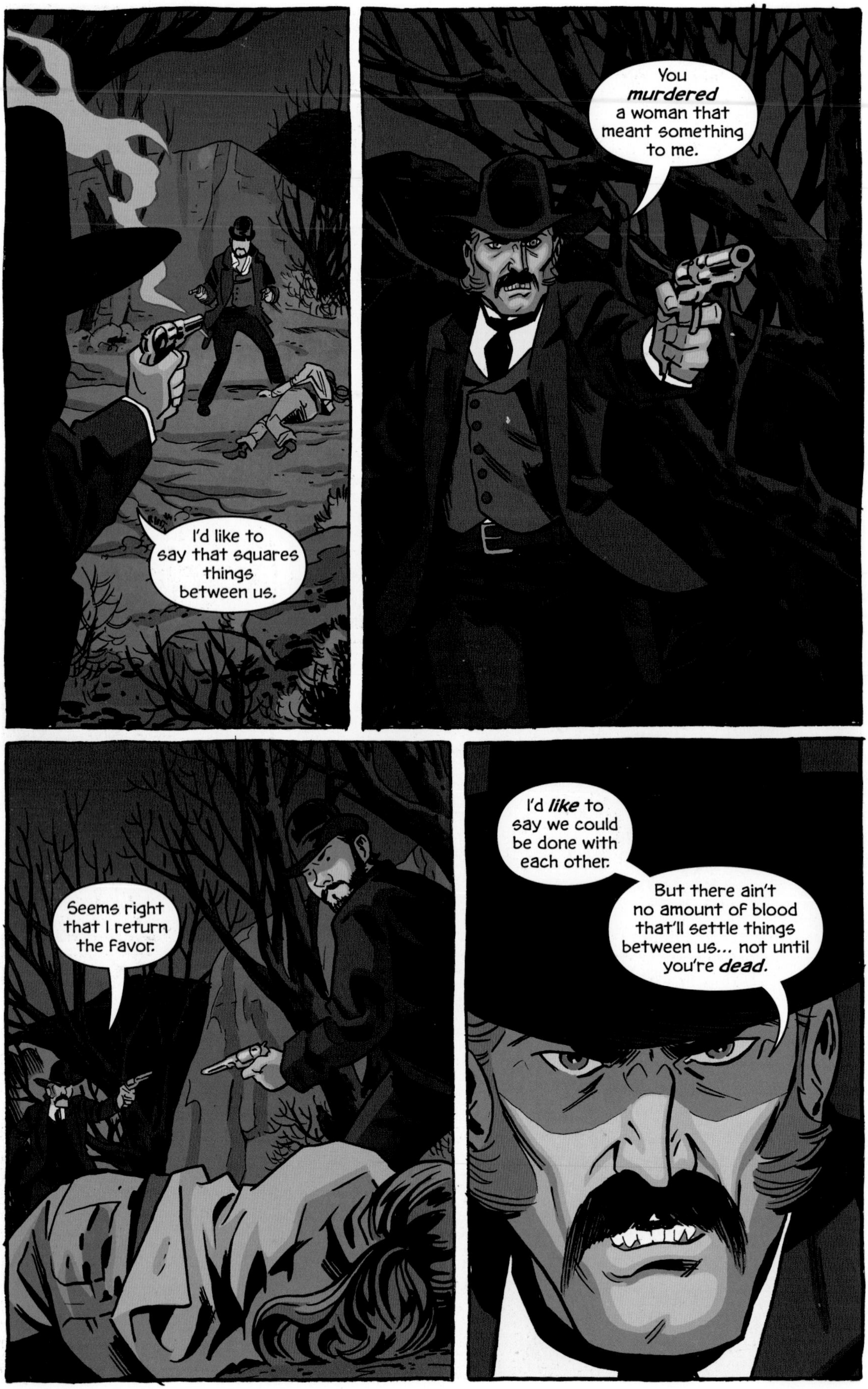
I'd like to say that squares things between us.
You *murdered* a woman that meant something to me.
Seems right that I return the favor.
I'd *like* to say we could be done with each other.
But there ain't no amount of blood that'll settle things between us... not until you're *dead.*

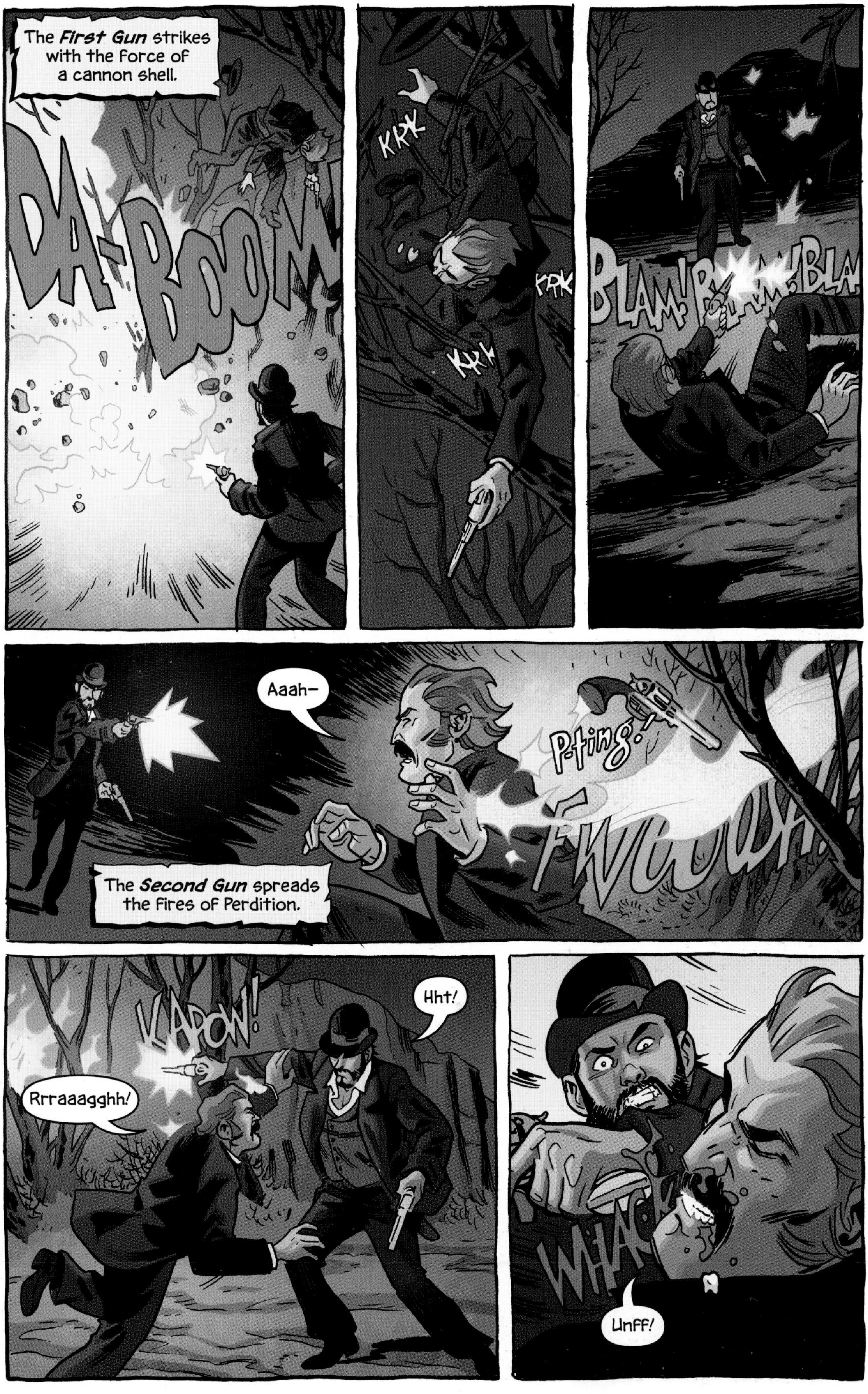
The *First Gun* strikes with the force of a cannon shell.
DA-BOOM
KRK
KRK
KRK
BLAM!
BLAM!
Aaah–
P-ting!
FWOOSH
The *Second Gun* spreads the fires of Perdition.
KAPOW!
Hht!
Rrraaagghh!
Unff!

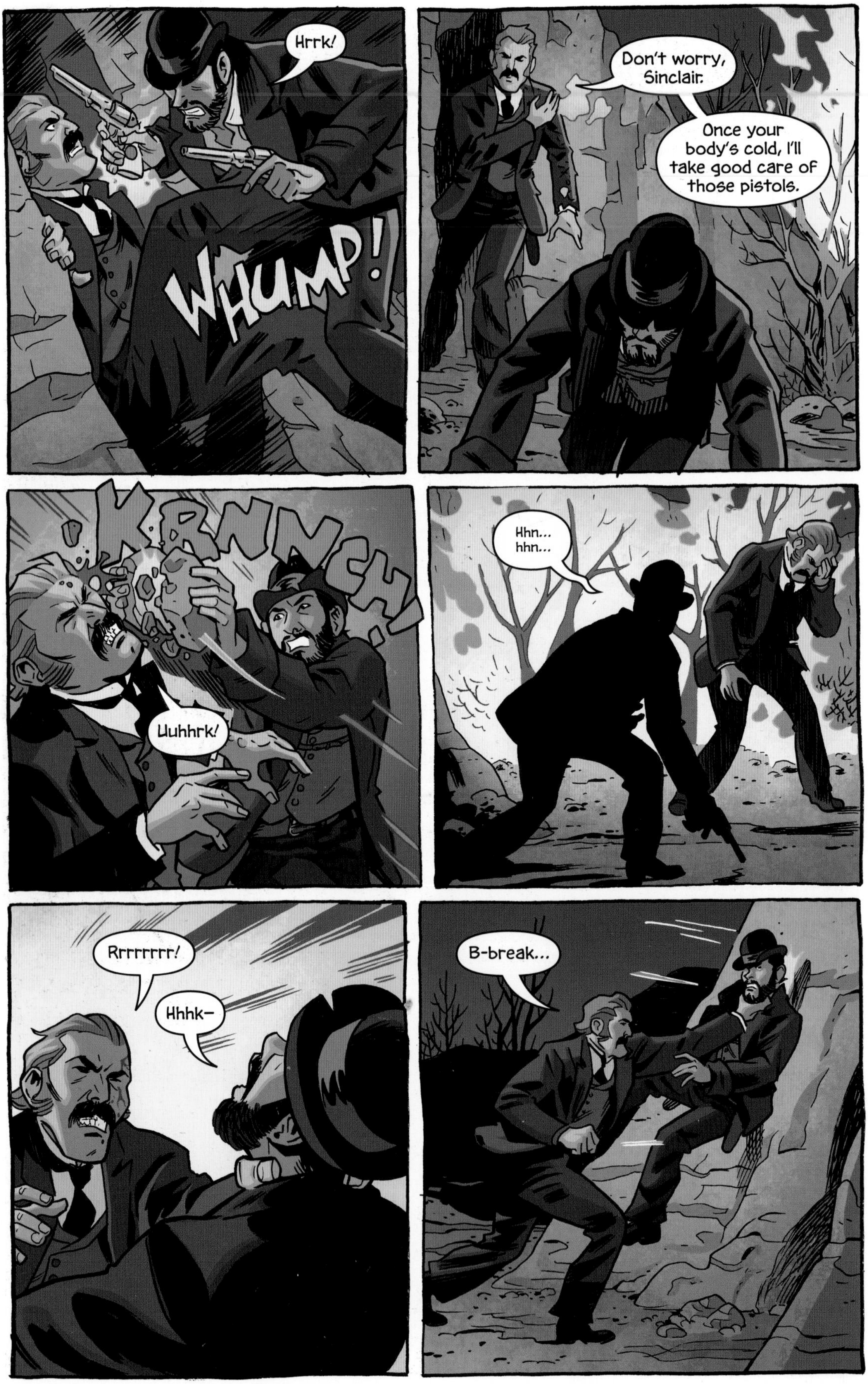
Hrrk!
WHUMP!
Don't worry, Sinclair.
Once your body's cold, I'll take good care of those pistols.
KRNNCH!
Uuhhrk!
Hhn... hhn...
Rrrrrrrr!
Hhhk-
B-break...

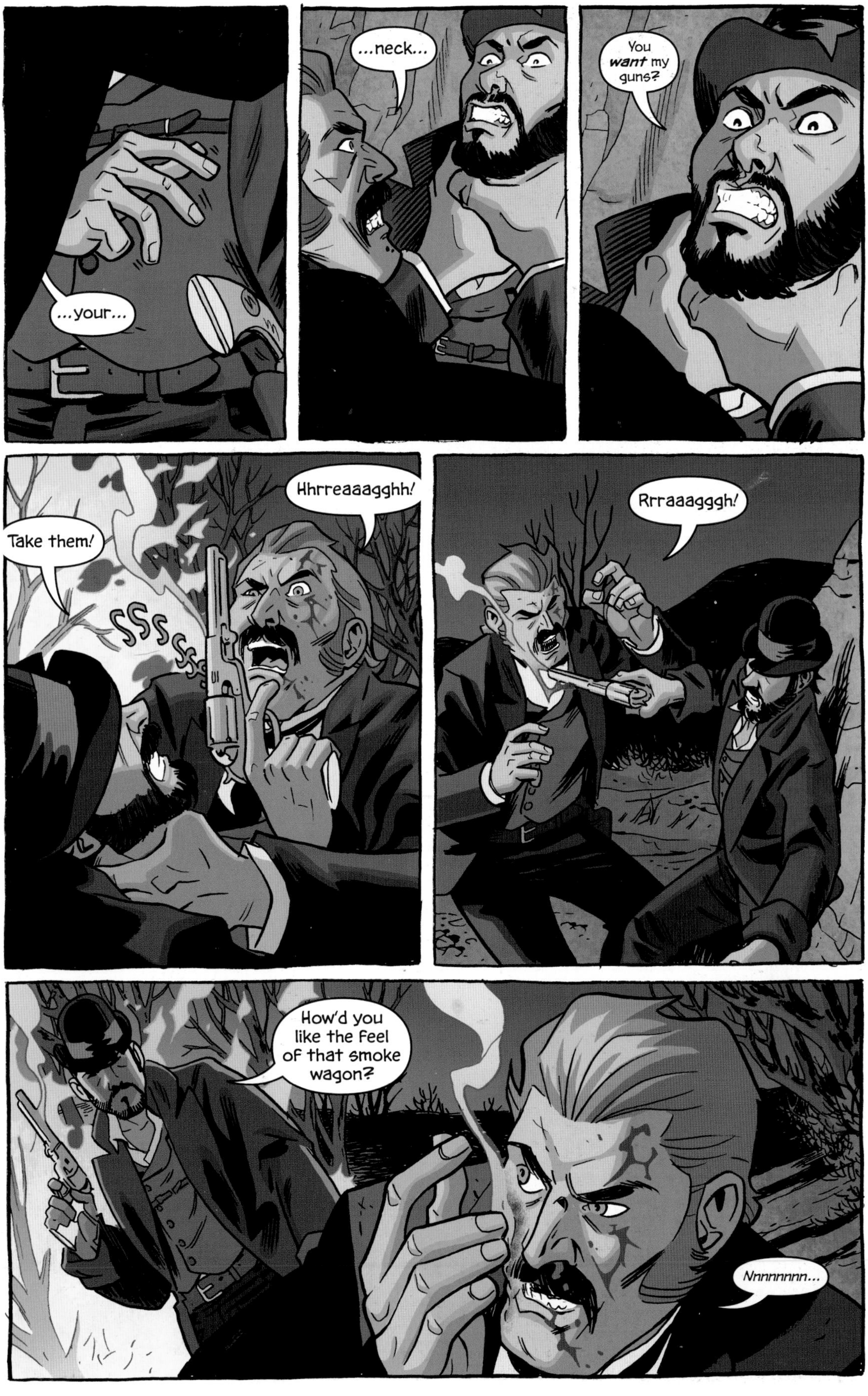
...your...
...neck...
You *want* my guns?
Take them!
Hhrreaaagghh!
SSSSSS
Rrraaagggh!
How'd you like the feel of that smoke wagon?
Nnnnnnnn...

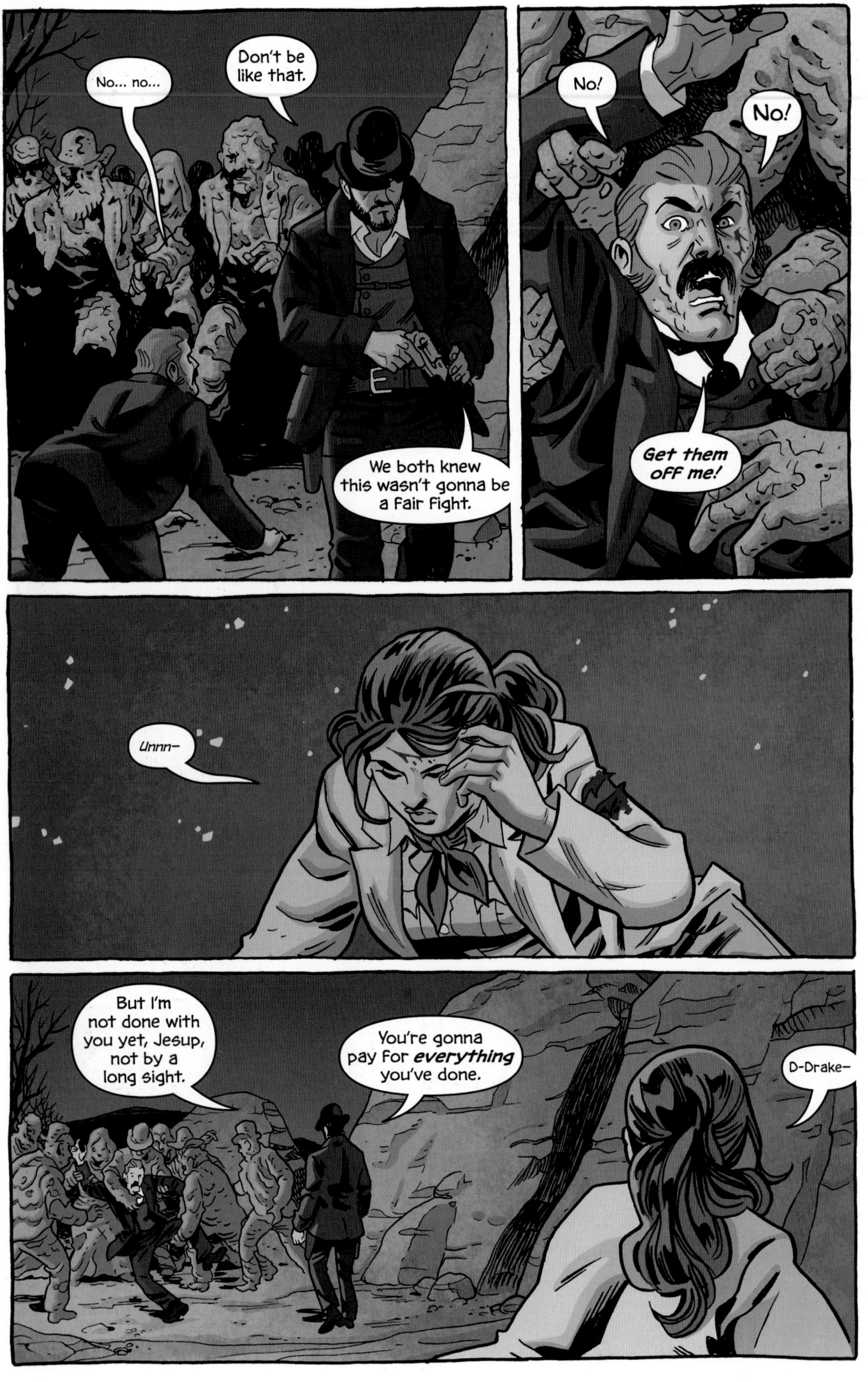
No... no...
Don't be like that.
We both knew this wasn't gonna be a fair fight.
No!
No!
Get them off me!
Unnn-
But I'm not done with you yet, Jesup, not by a long sight.
You're gonna pay for *everything* you've done.
D-Drake-

Drake... wait!

I'm all right.

The bullet just grazed me!

I know.

It's almost funny, Jesup.

I could tell you that you aren't worth wasting a bullet.

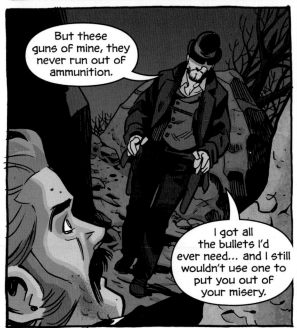

But these guns of mine, they never run out of ammunition.

I got all the bullets I'd ever need... and I still wouldn't use one to put you out of your misery.

Misery.

Heh.

Let me show you what I'm talking about.

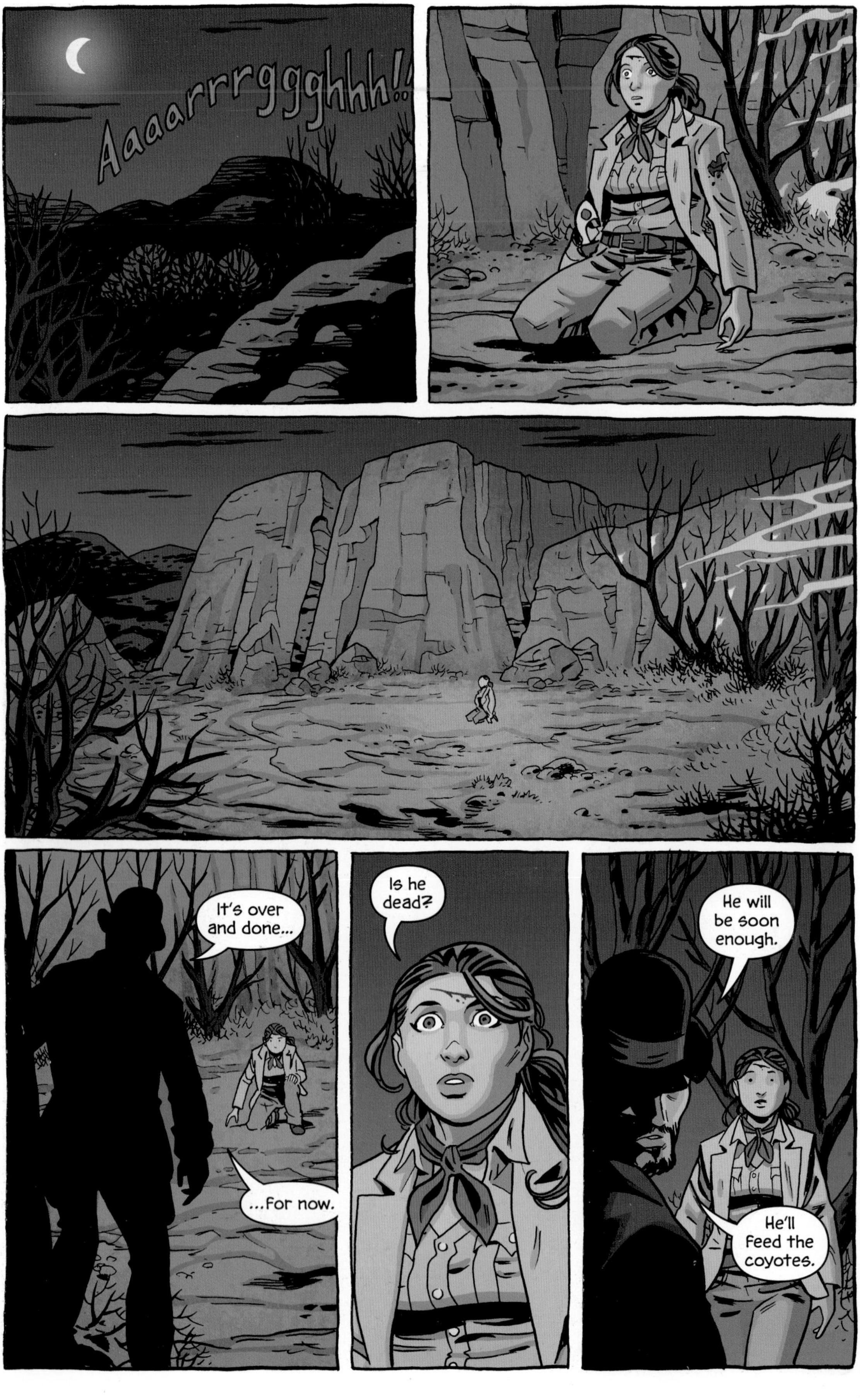
Aaaarrrggghhh!!
It's over and done...
...For now.
Is he dead?
He will be soon enough.
He'll feed the coyotes.

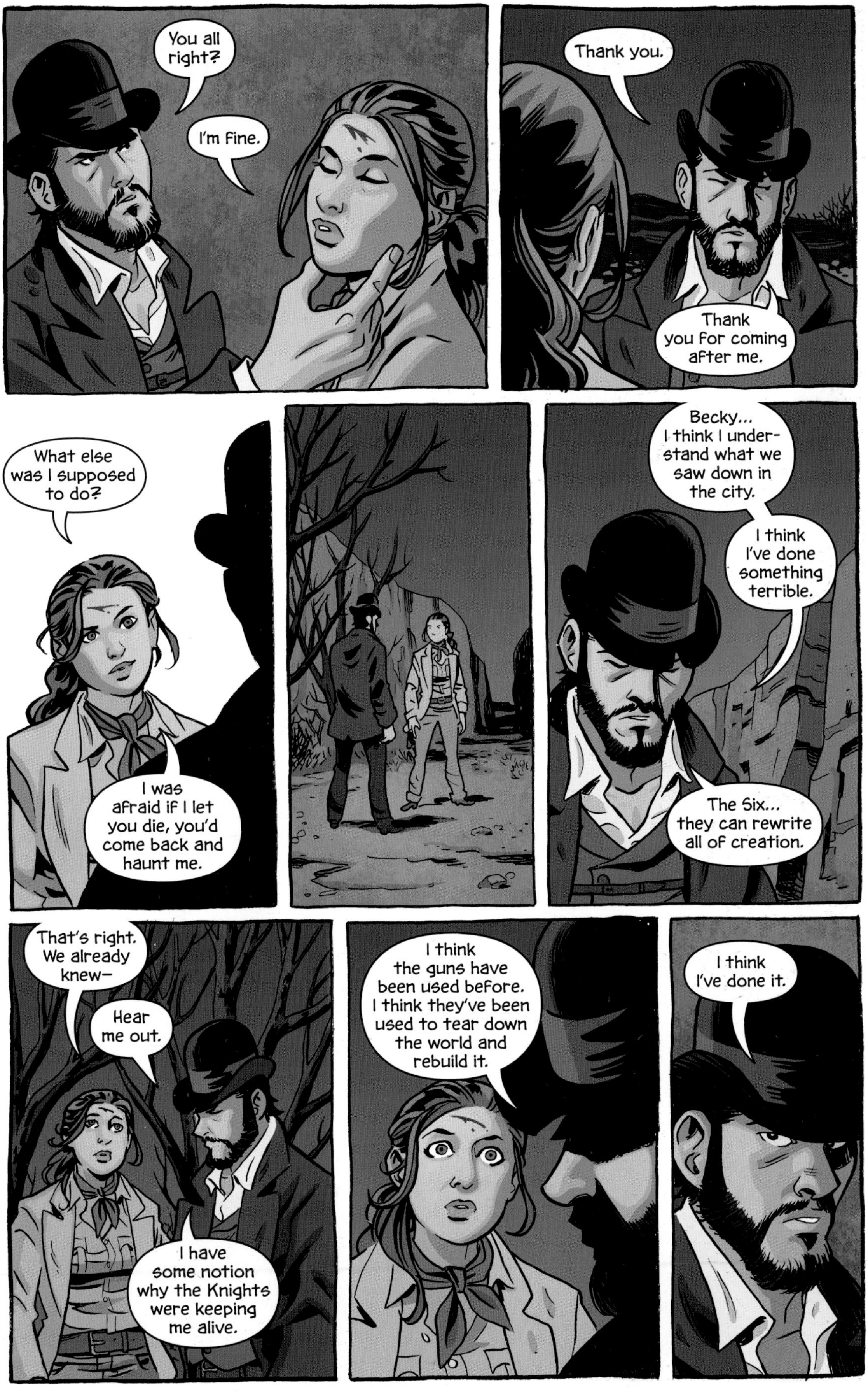
You all right?
I'm fine.
Thank you.
Thank you for coming after me.
What else was I supposed to do?
I was afraid if I let you die, you'd come back and haunt me.
Becky... I think I understand what we saw down in the city.
I think I've done something terrible.
The Six... they can rewrite all of creation.
That's right. We already knew—
Hear me out.
I have some notion why the Knights were keeping me alive.
I think the guns have been used before. I think they've been used to tear down the world and rebuild it.
I think I've done it.

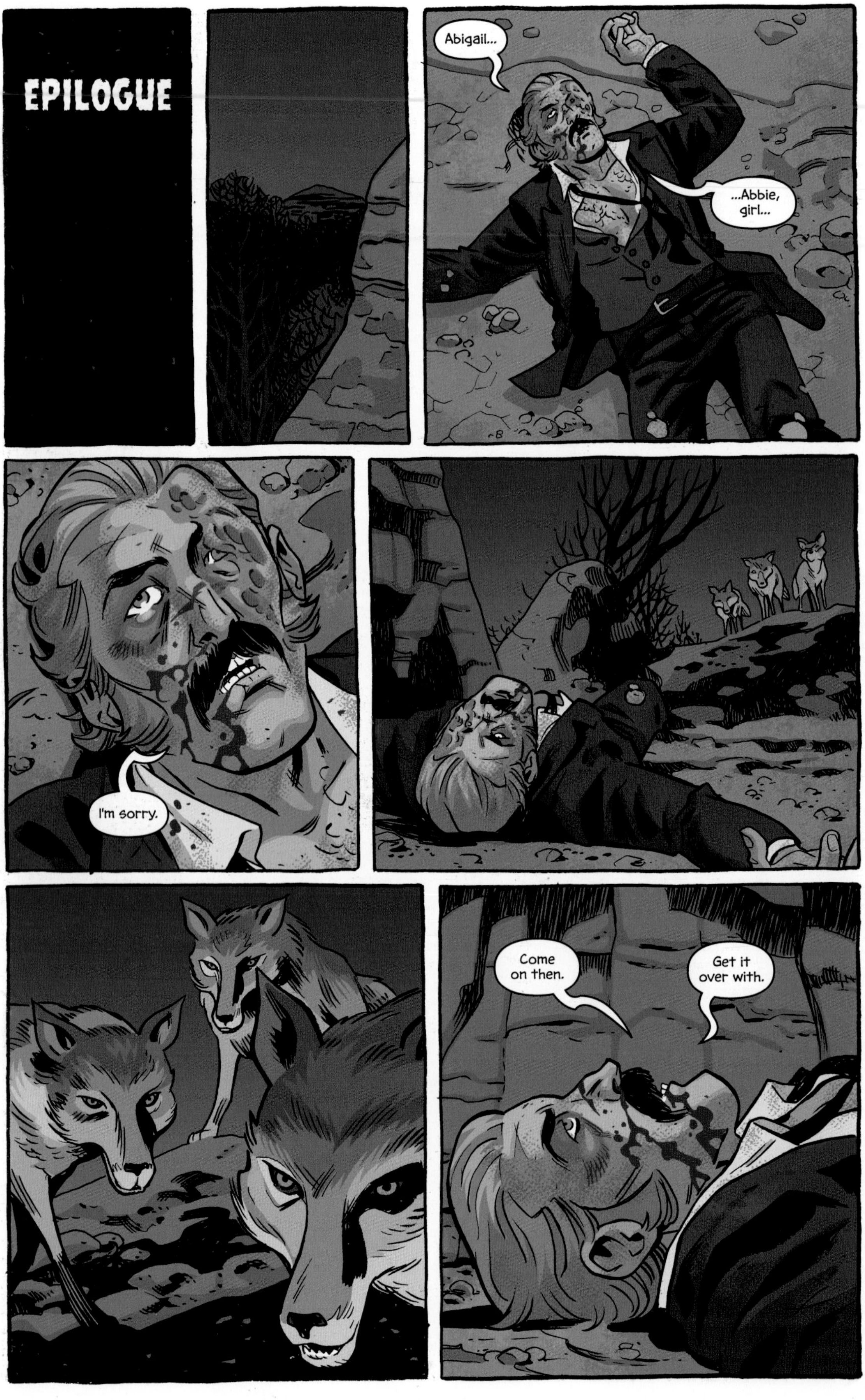
EPILOGUE
Abigail...
...Abbie, girl...
I'm sorry.
Come on then.
Get it over with.

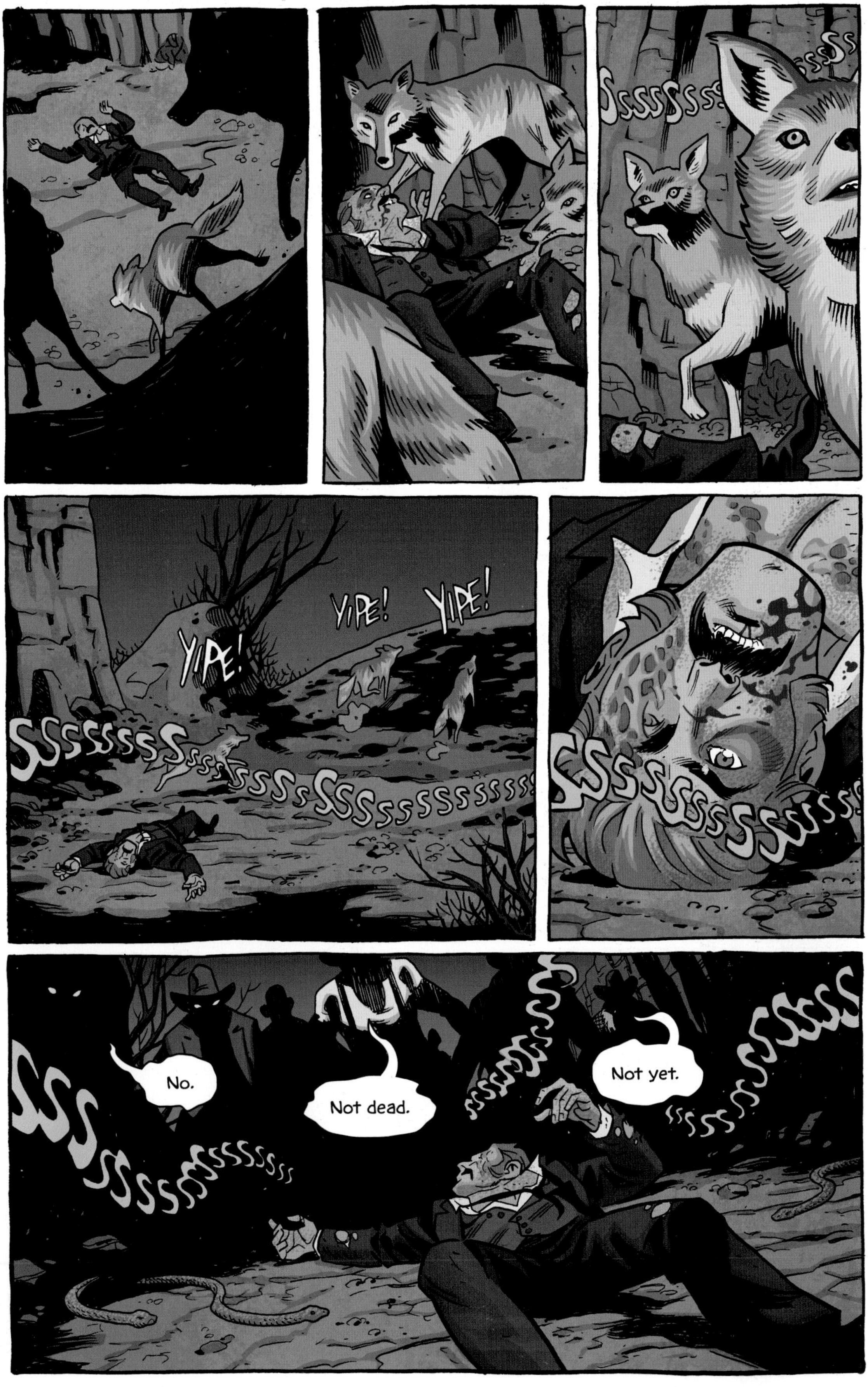
SSSSSSS
YIPE!
YIPE!
YIPE!
No.
Not dead.
Not yet.

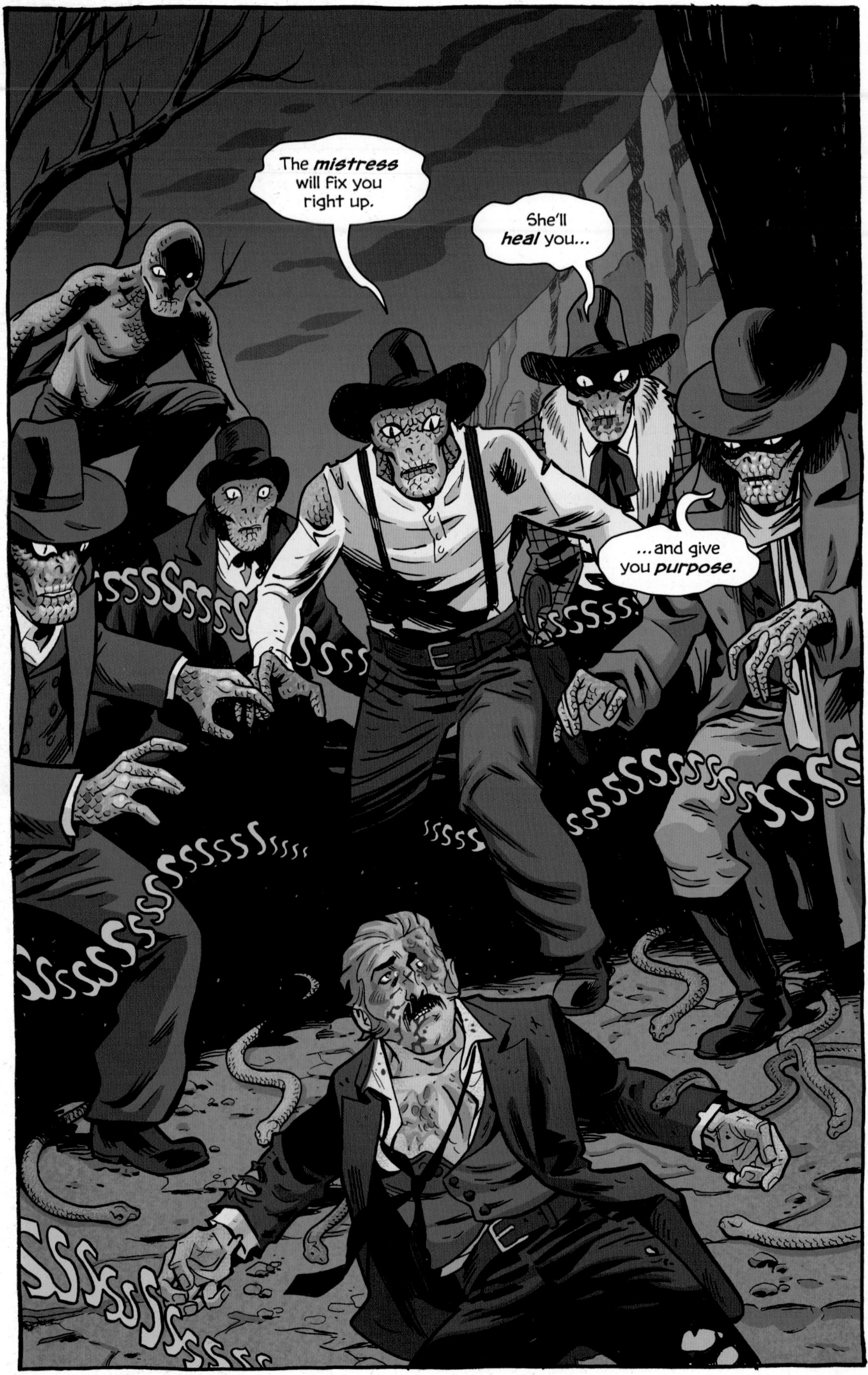
The *mistress* will fix you right up.
She'll *heal* you...
...and give you *purpose.*

CHAPTER SIX

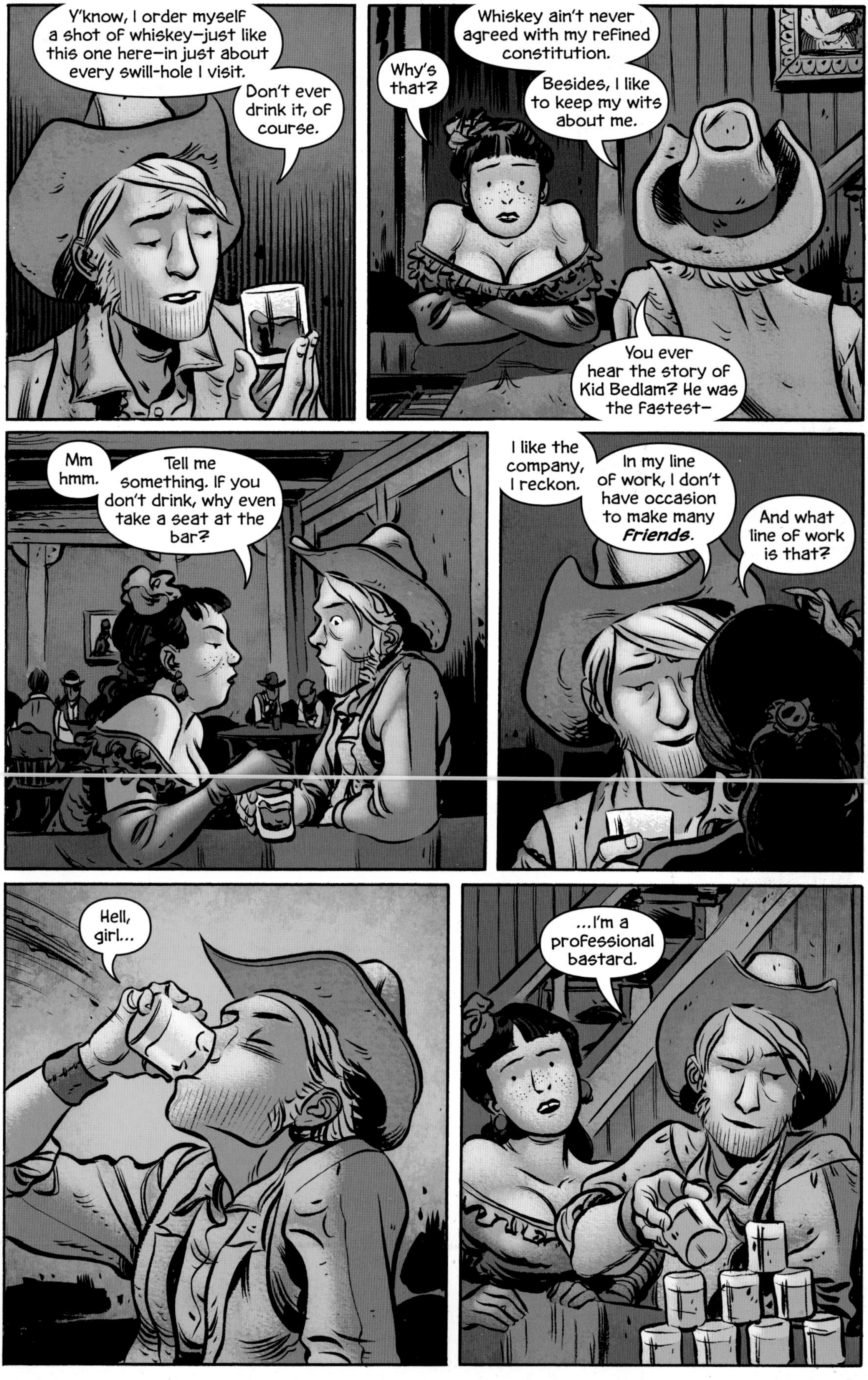

Y'know, I order myself a shot of whiskey—just like this one here—in just about every swill-hole I visit.
Don't ever drink it, of course.
Why's that?
Whiskey ain't never agreed with my refined constitution.
Besides, I like to keep my wits about me.
You ever hear the story of Kid Bedlam? He was the fastest—
Mm hmm.
Tell me something. If you don't drink, why even take a seat at the bar?
I like the company, I reckon.
In my line of work, I don't have occasion to make many *Friends*.
And what line of work is that?
Hell, girl...
...I'm a professional bastard.

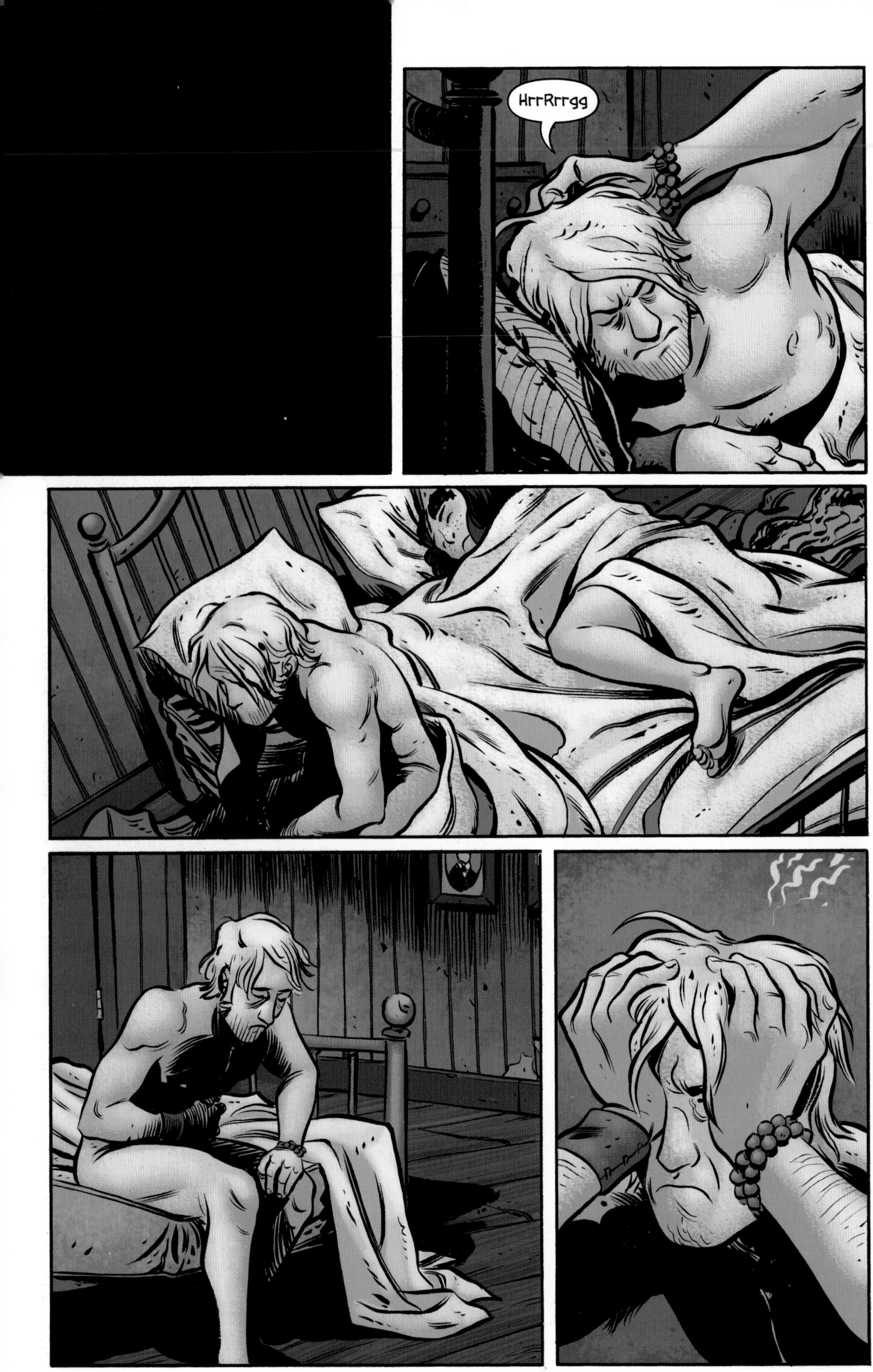
HrrRrrgg

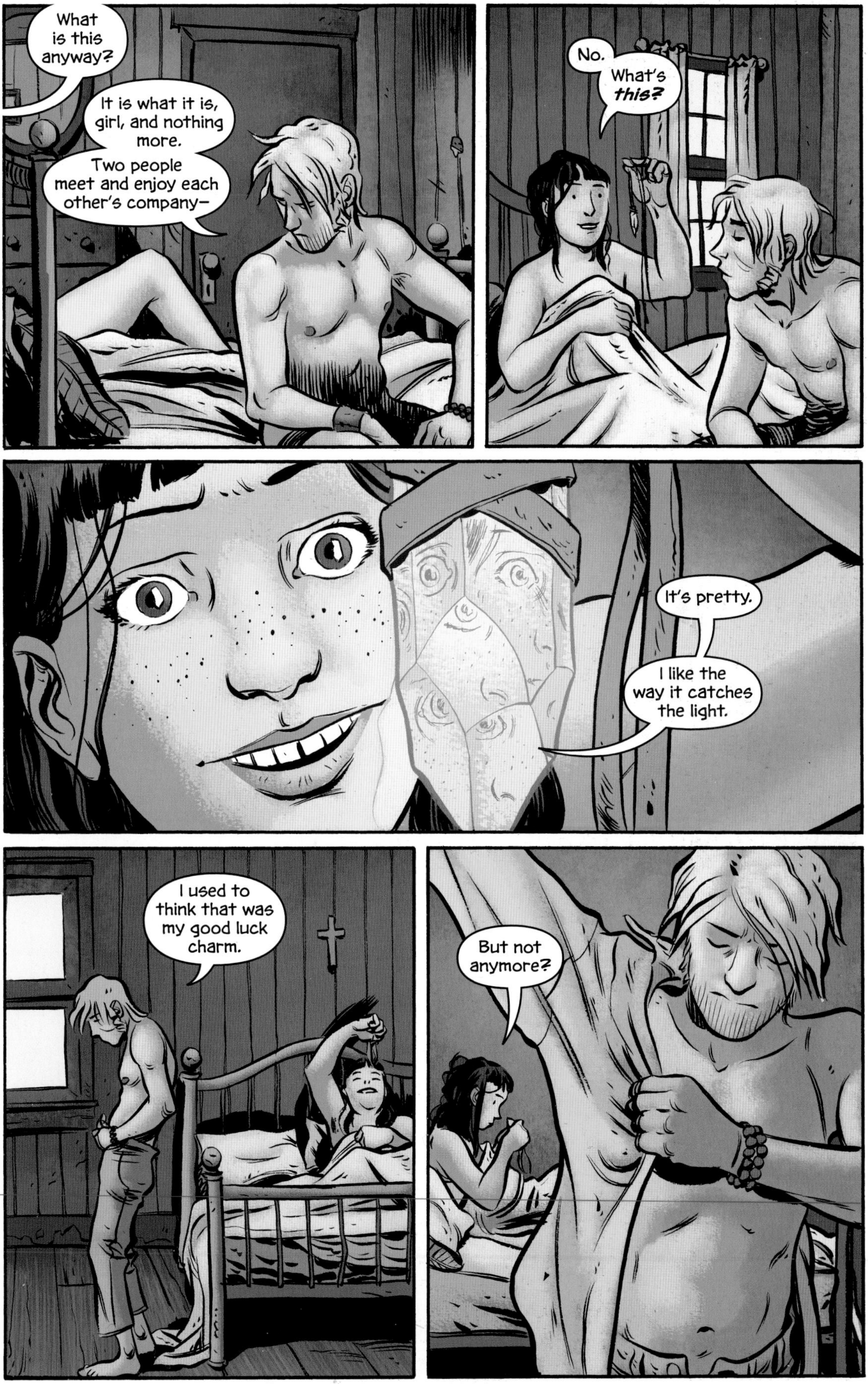
What is this anyway?
It is what it is, girl, and nothing more.
Two people meet and enjoy each other's company—
No.
What's *this?*
It's pretty.
I like the way it catches the light.
I used to think that was my good luck charm.
But not anymore?

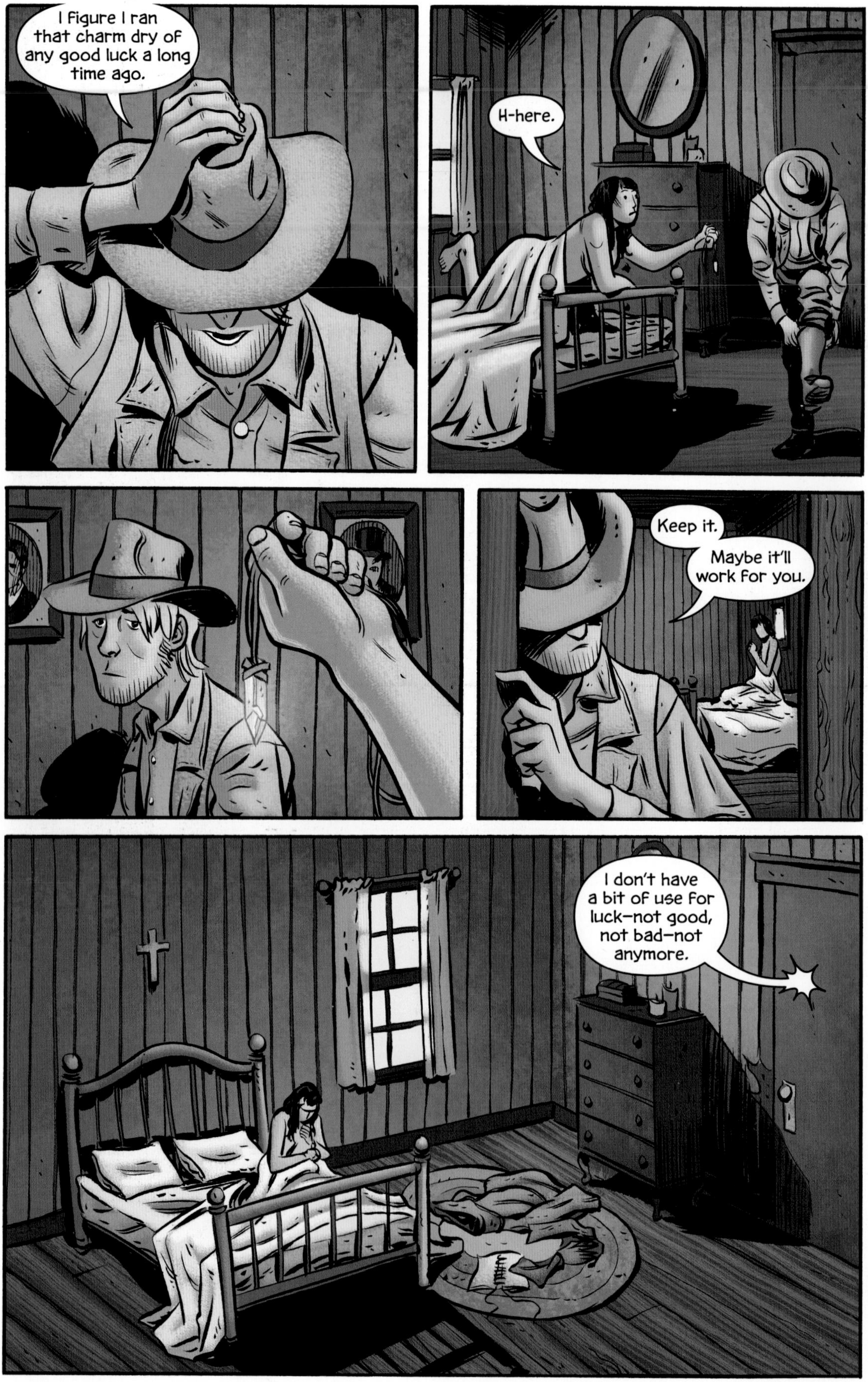
I figure I ran that charm dry of any good luck a long time ago.
H-here.
Keep it.
Maybe it'll work for you.
I don't have a bit of use for luck—not good, not bad—not anymore.

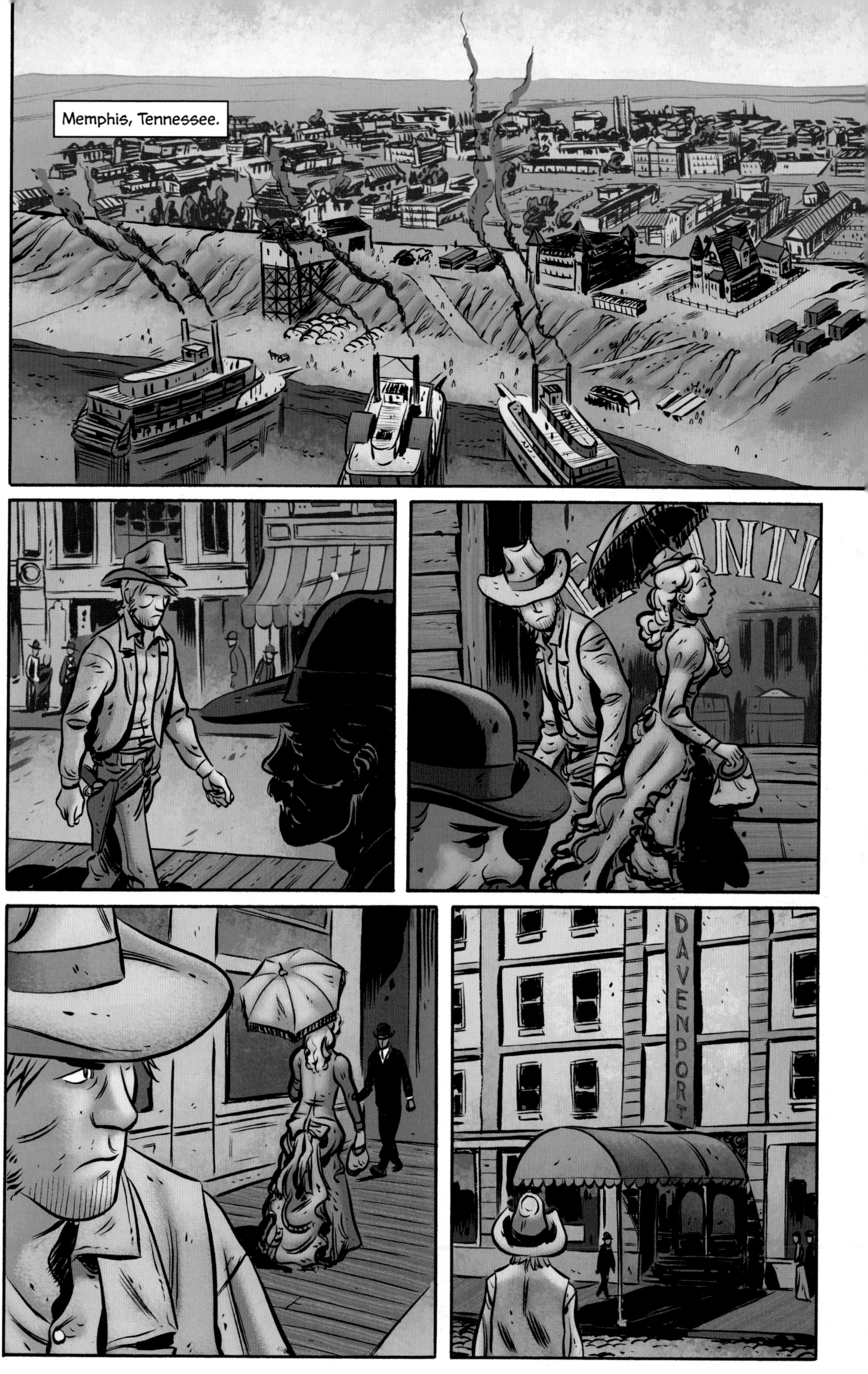
Memphis, Tennessee.
DAVENPORT

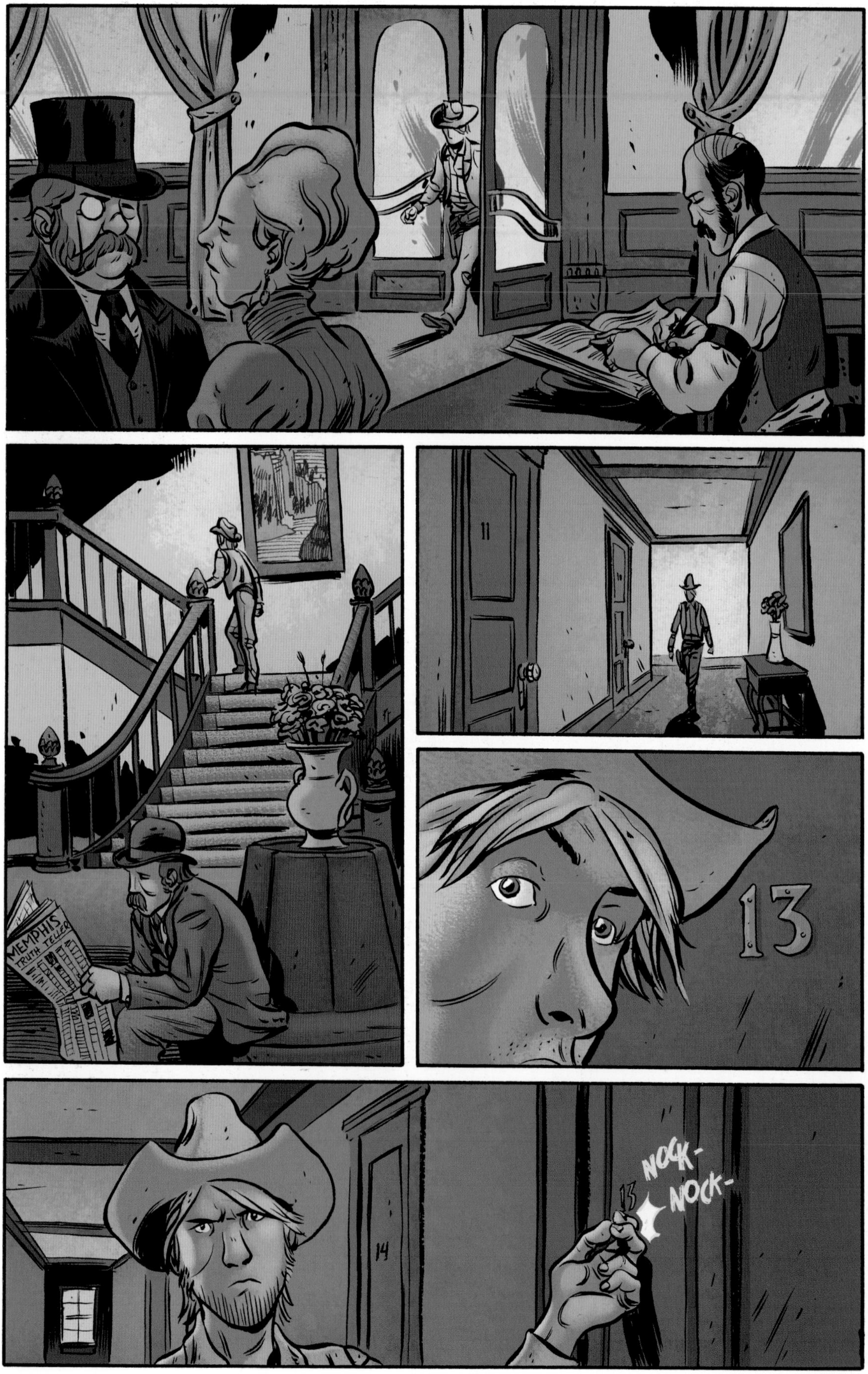
MEMPHIS
TRUTH TELLER
11
13
14
13
NOCK-
NOCK-

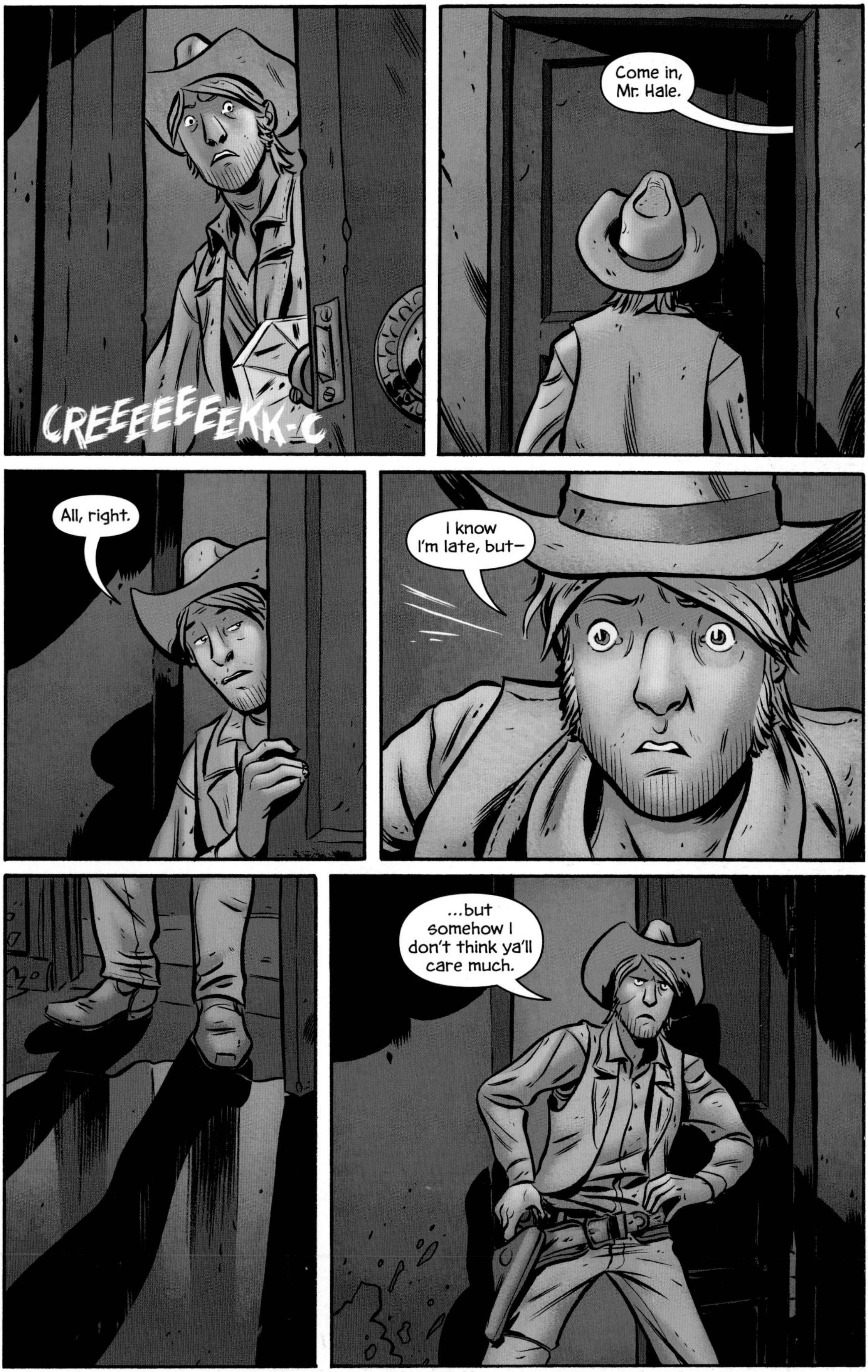
CREEEEEEEEKK-C
Come in, Mr. Hale.
All, right.
I know I'm late, but–
...but somehow I don't think ya'll care much.

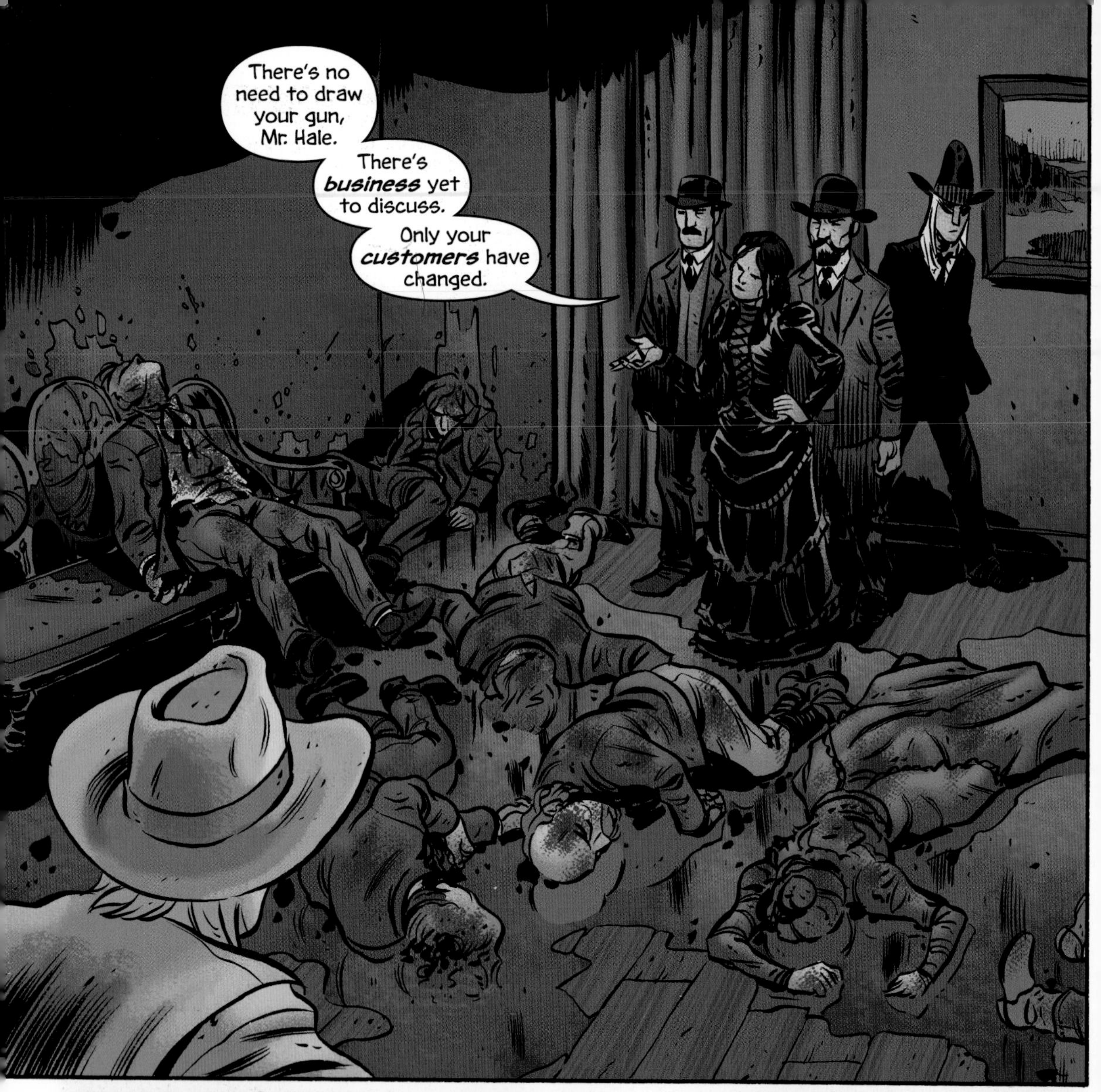
There's no need to draw your gun, Mr. Hale.
There's *business* yet to discuss.
Only your *customers* have changed.

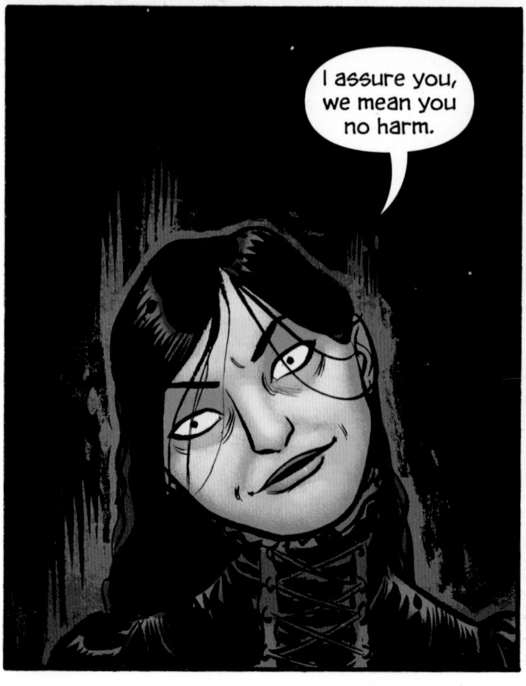
I assure you, we mean you no harm.

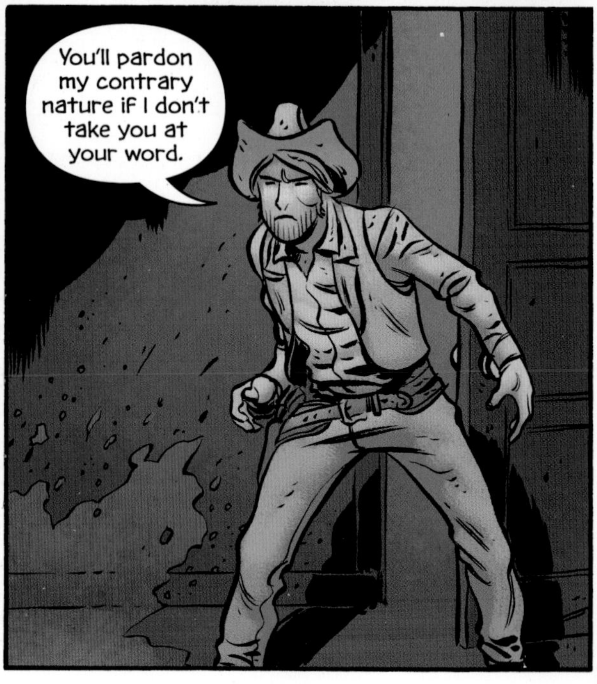
You'll pardon my contrary nature if I don't take you at your word.

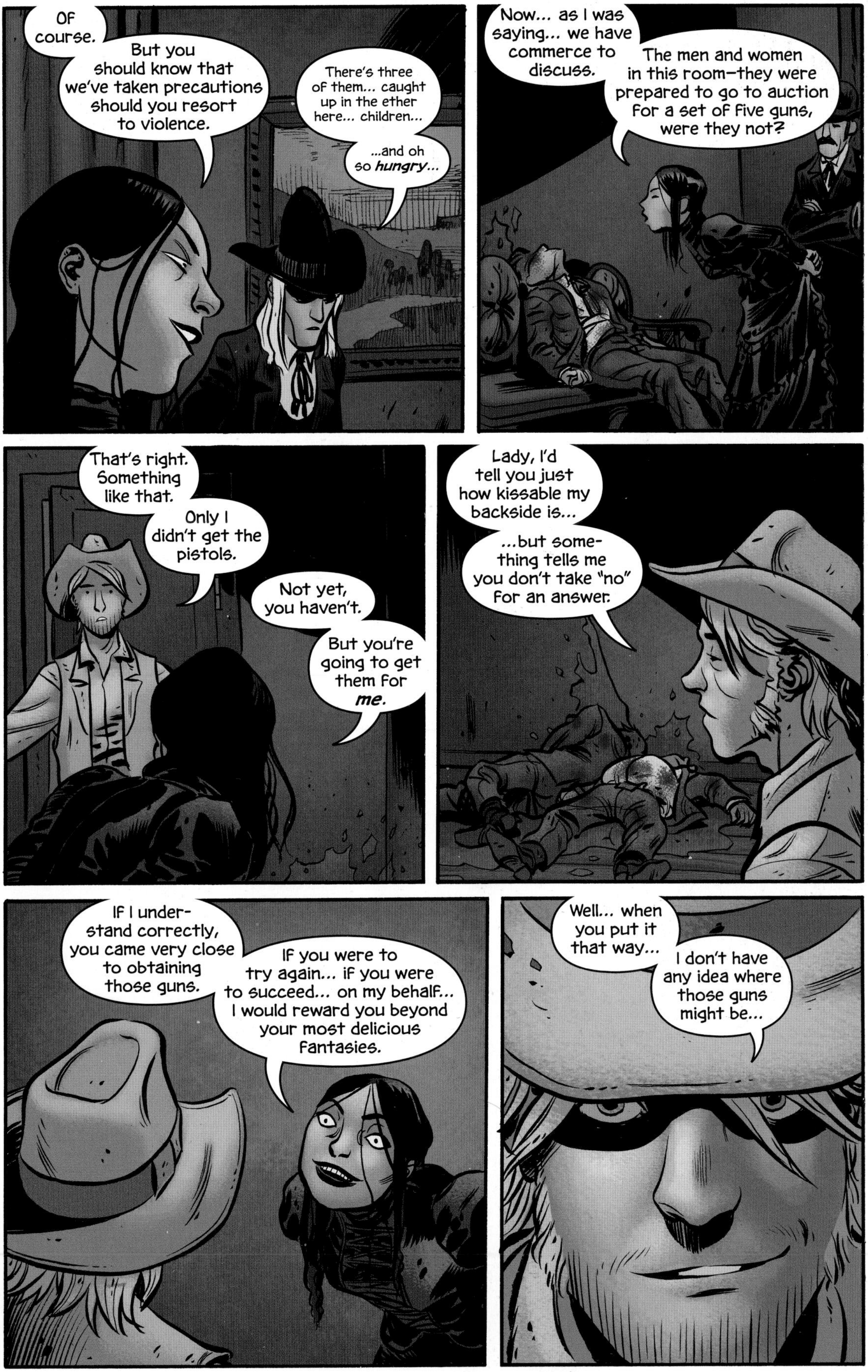
Of course.
But you should know that we've taken precautions should you resort to violence.
There's three of them... caught up in the ether here... children...
...and oh so *hungry*...
Now... as I was saying... we have commerce to discuss.
The men and women in this room—they were prepared to go to auction for a set of five guns, were they not?
That's right. Something like that.
Only I didn't get the pistols.
Not yet, you haven't.
But you're going to get them for *me*.
Lady, I'd tell you just how kissable my backside is...
...but some-thing tells me you don't take "no" for an answer.
If I under-stand correctly, you came very close to obtaining those guns.
If you were to try again... if you were to succeed... on my behalf... I would reward you beyond your most delicious fantasies.
Well... when you put it that way...
I don't have any idea where those guns might be...

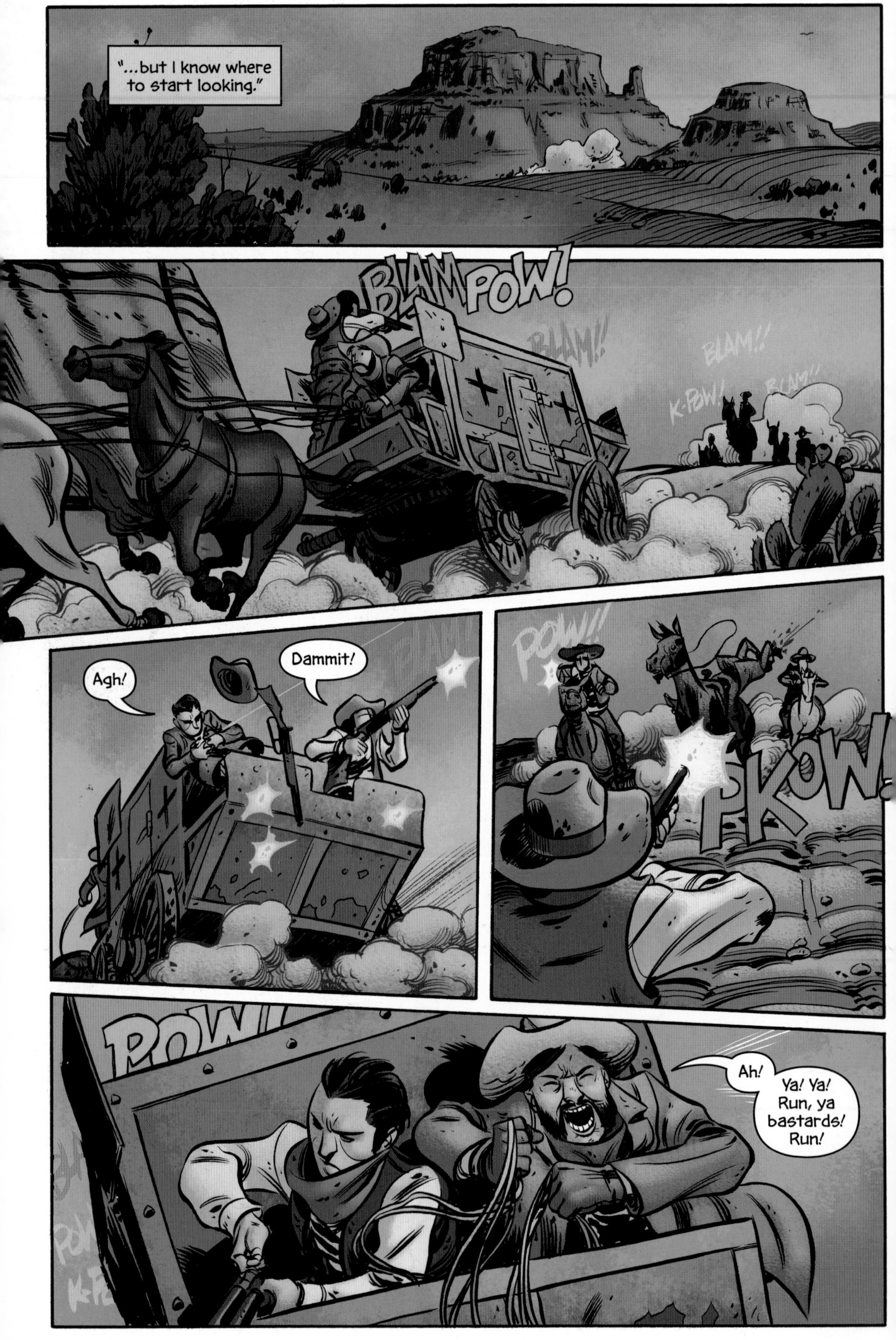
"...but I know where to start looking."
BLAMPOW!
BLAM!!
BLAM!!
K-POW!
BLAM!!
Agh!
Dammit!
POW!!
PKOW!
Ah!
Ya! Ya! Run, ya bastards! Run!

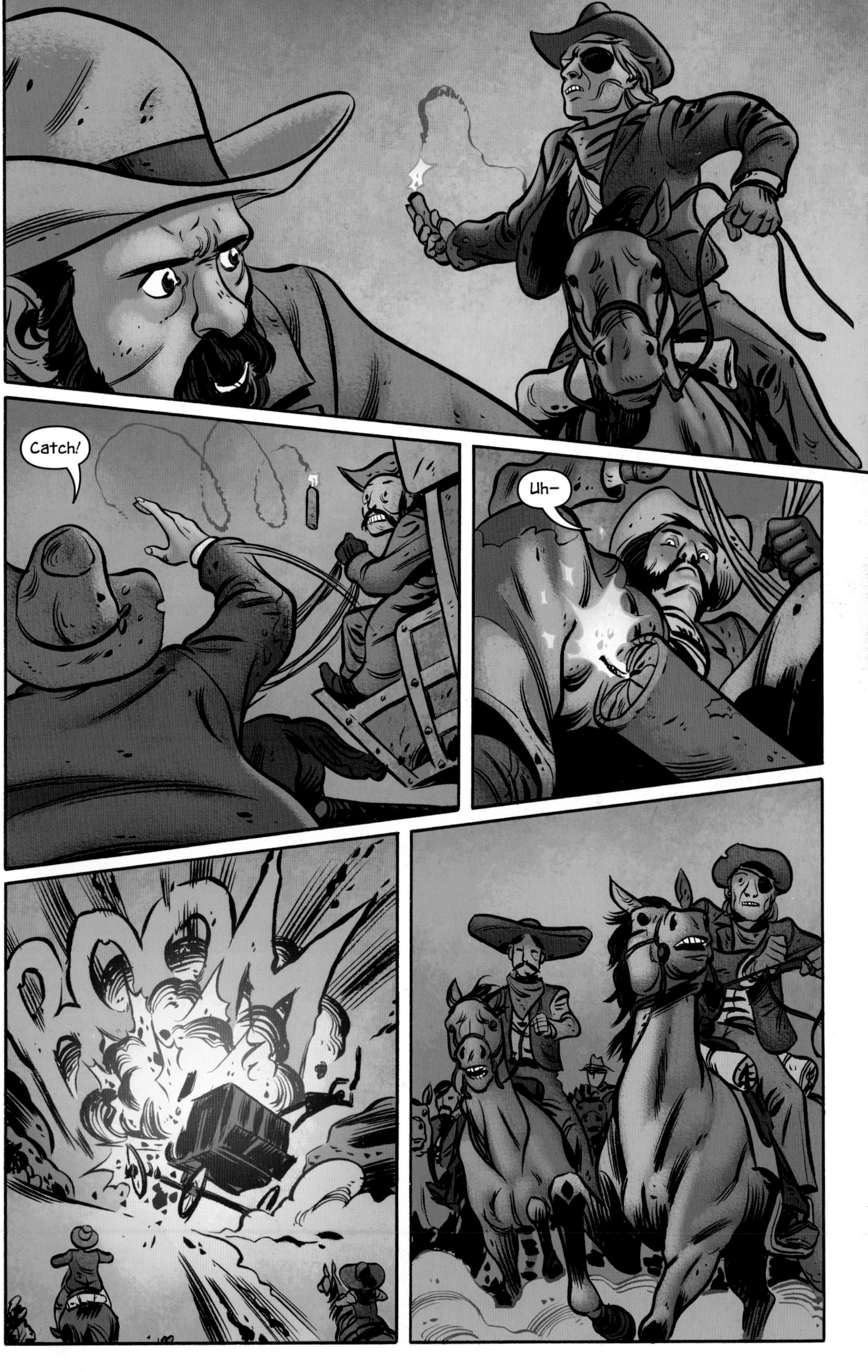
Catch!
Uh–

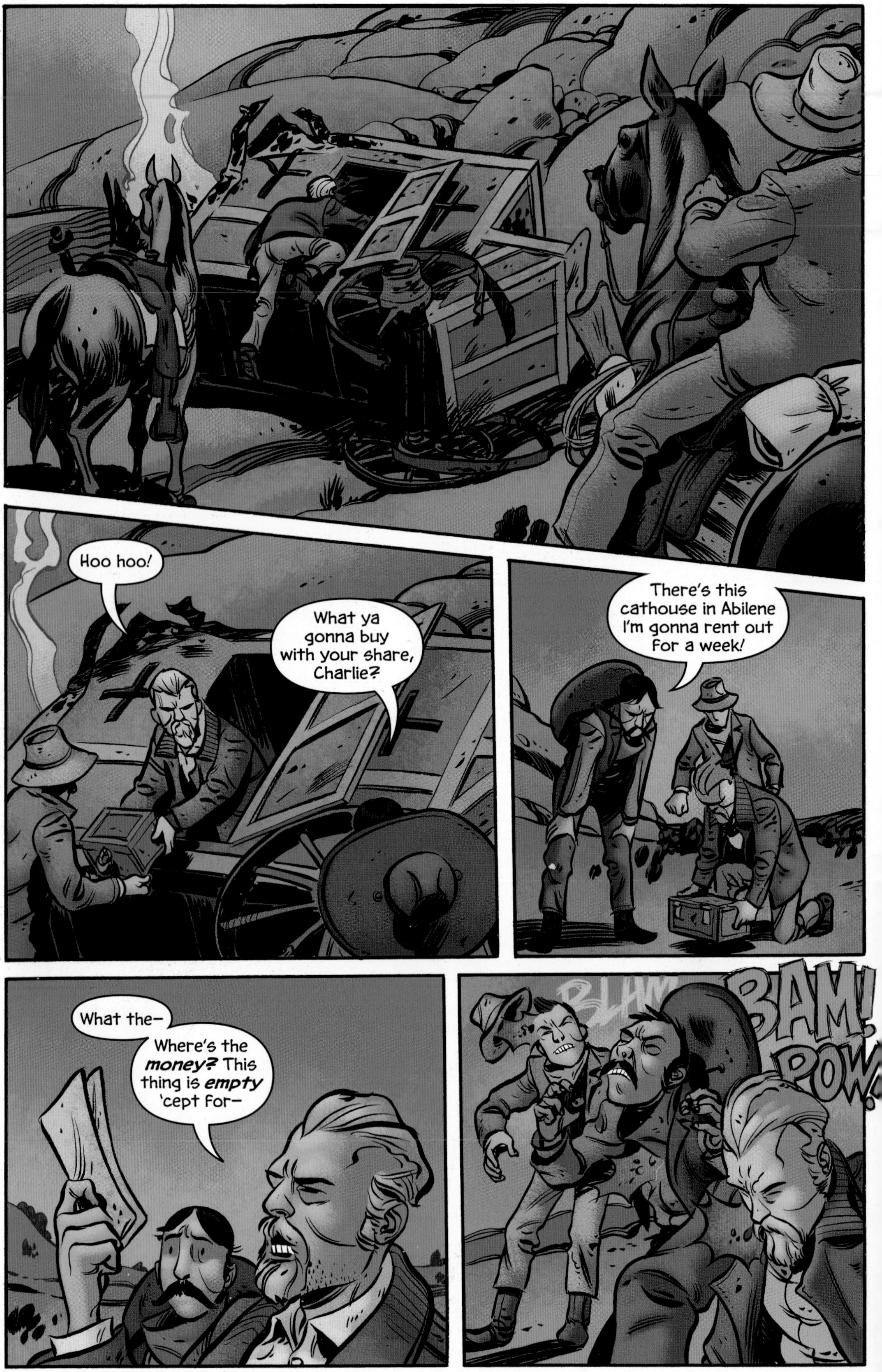
Hoo hoo!
What ya gonna buy with your share, Charlie?
There's this cathouse in Abilene I'm gonna rent out for a week!
What the–
Where's the *money?* This thing is *empty* 'cept for–
BLAM
BAM!
POW!

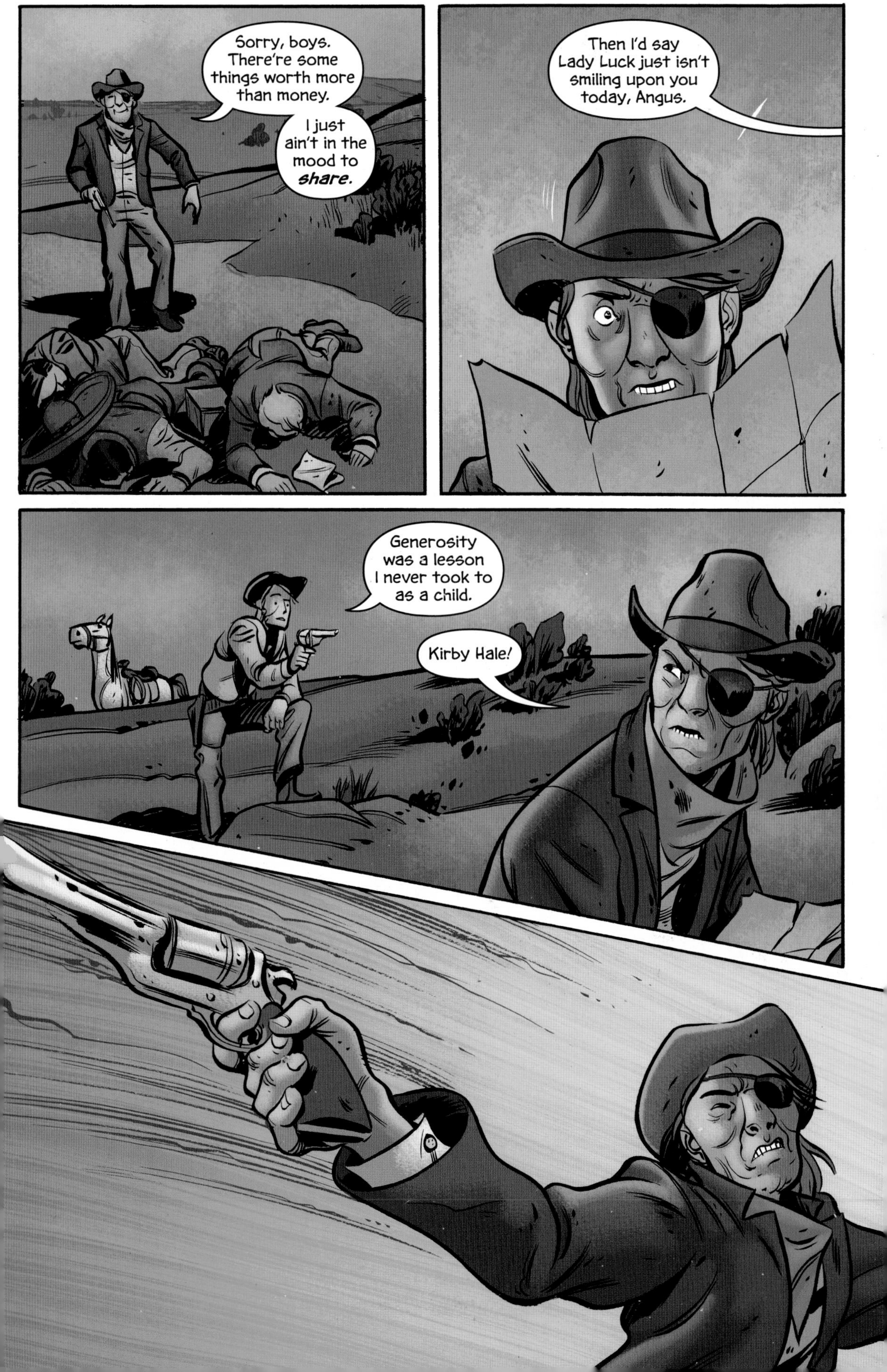
Sorry, boys. There're some things worth more than money.
I just ain't in the mood to *share.*
Then I'd say Lady Luck just isn't smiling upon you today, Angus.
Generosity was a lesson I never took to as a child.
Kirby Hale!

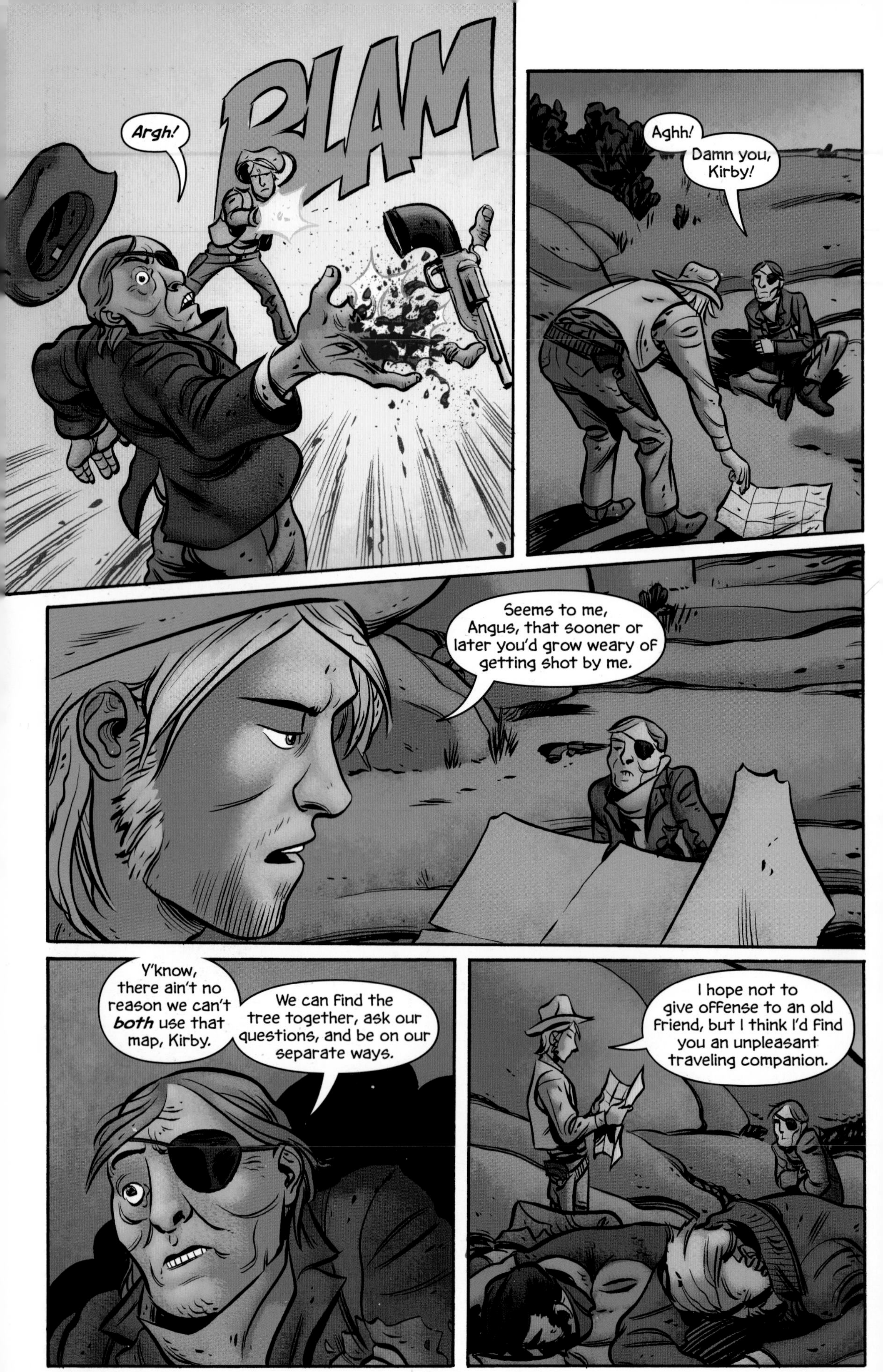

BLAM
Argh!
Aghh!
Damn you, Kirby!
Seems to me, Angus, that sooner or later you'd grow weary of getting shot by me.
Y'know, there ain't no reason we can't *both* use that map, Kirby.
We can find the tree together, ask our questions, and be on our separate ways.
I hope not to give offense to an old friend, but I think I'd find you an unpleasant traveling companion.

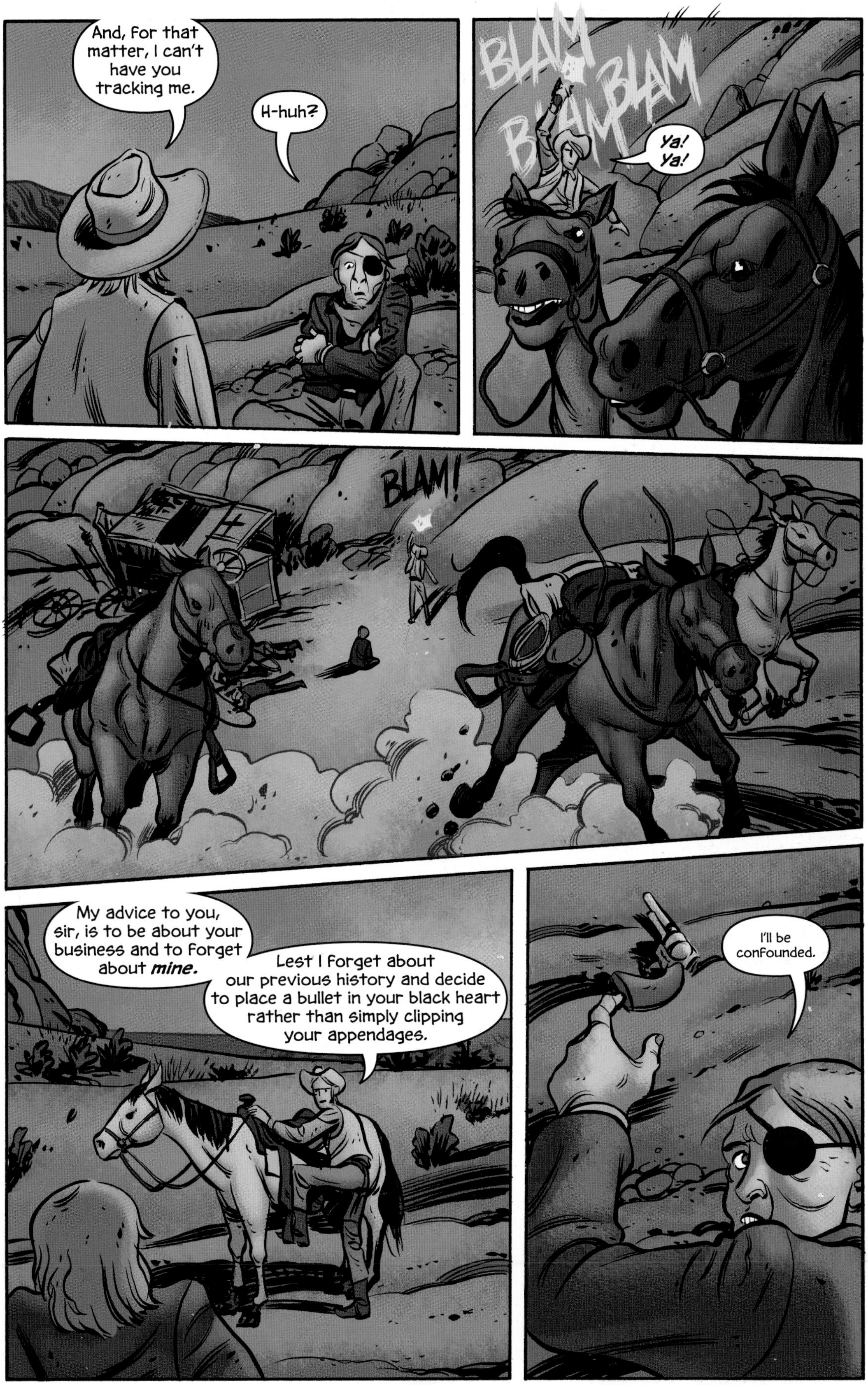
And, for that matter, I can't have you tracking me.
H-huh?
BLAM BLAM BLAM BLAM
Ya! Ya!
BLAM!
My advice to you, sir, is to be about your business and to forget about *mine.*
Lest I forget about our previous history and decide to place a bullet in your black heart rather than simply clipping your appendages.
I'll be confounded.

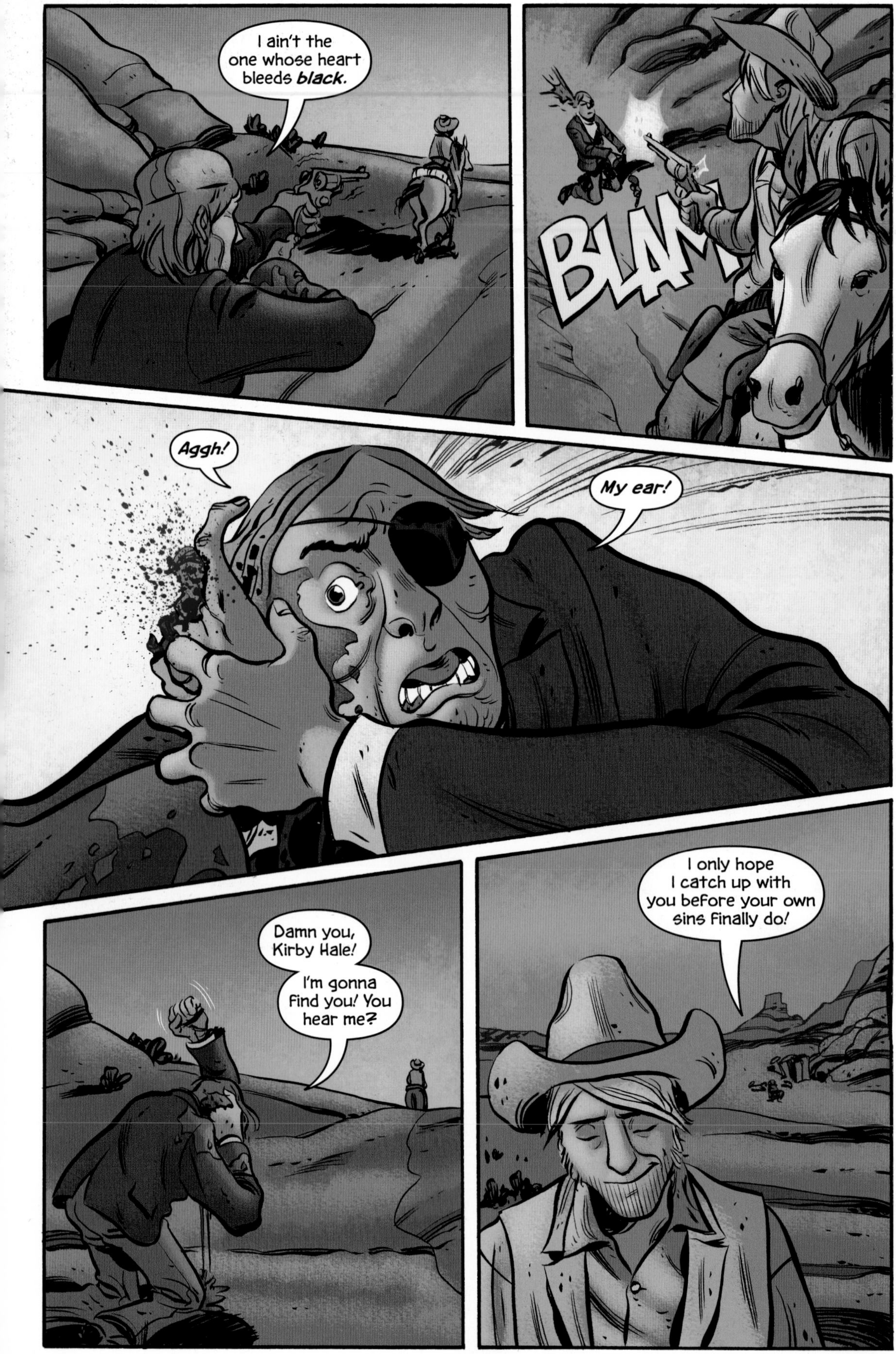
I ain't the one whose heart bleeds *black*.
BLAM
Aggh!
My ear!
Damn you, Kirby Hale!
I'm gonna find you! You hear me?
I only hope I catch up with you before your own sins finally do!

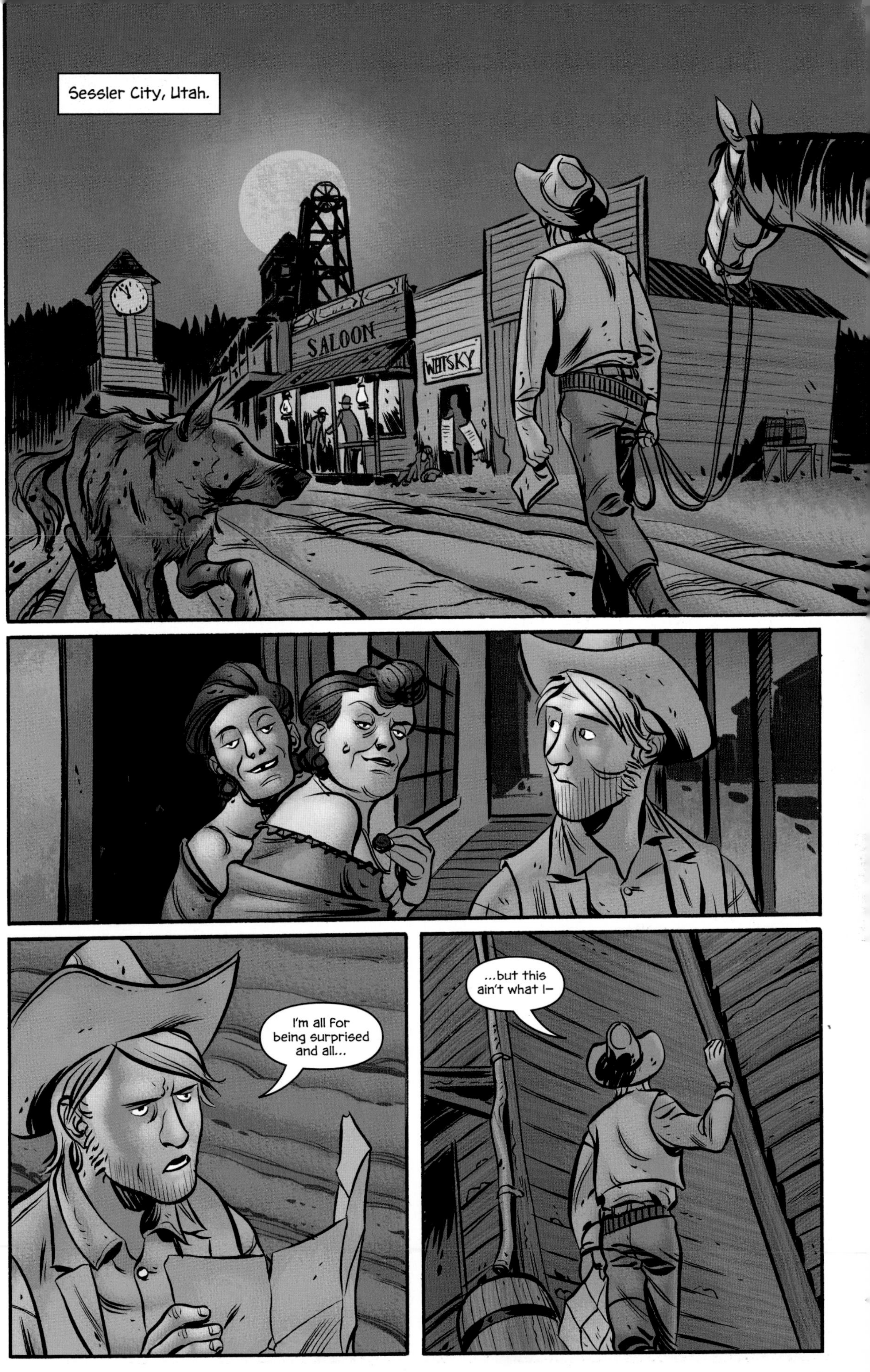
Sessler City, Utah.
SALOON
WHISKY
I'm all for being surprised and all...
...but this ain't what I—

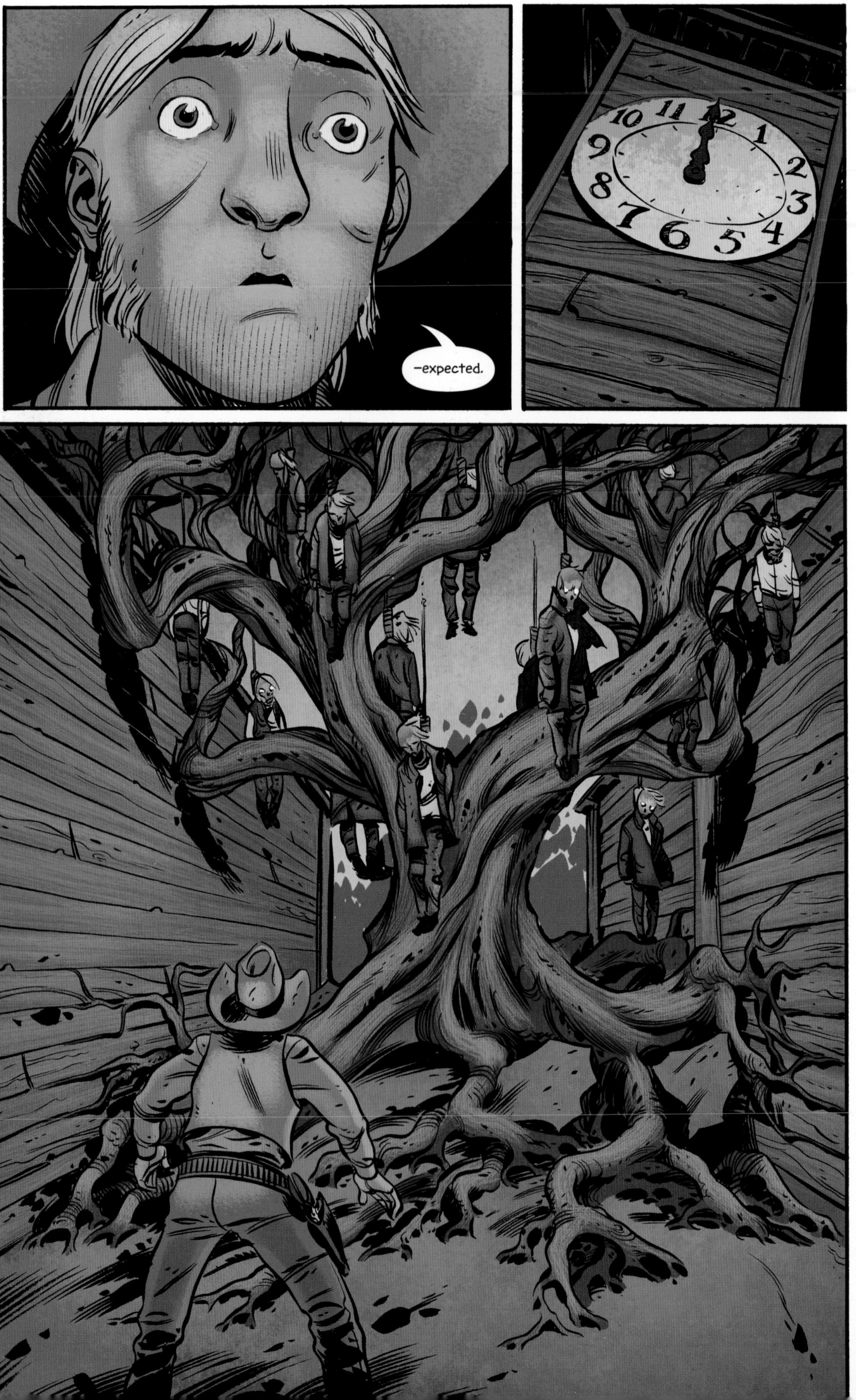
—expected.

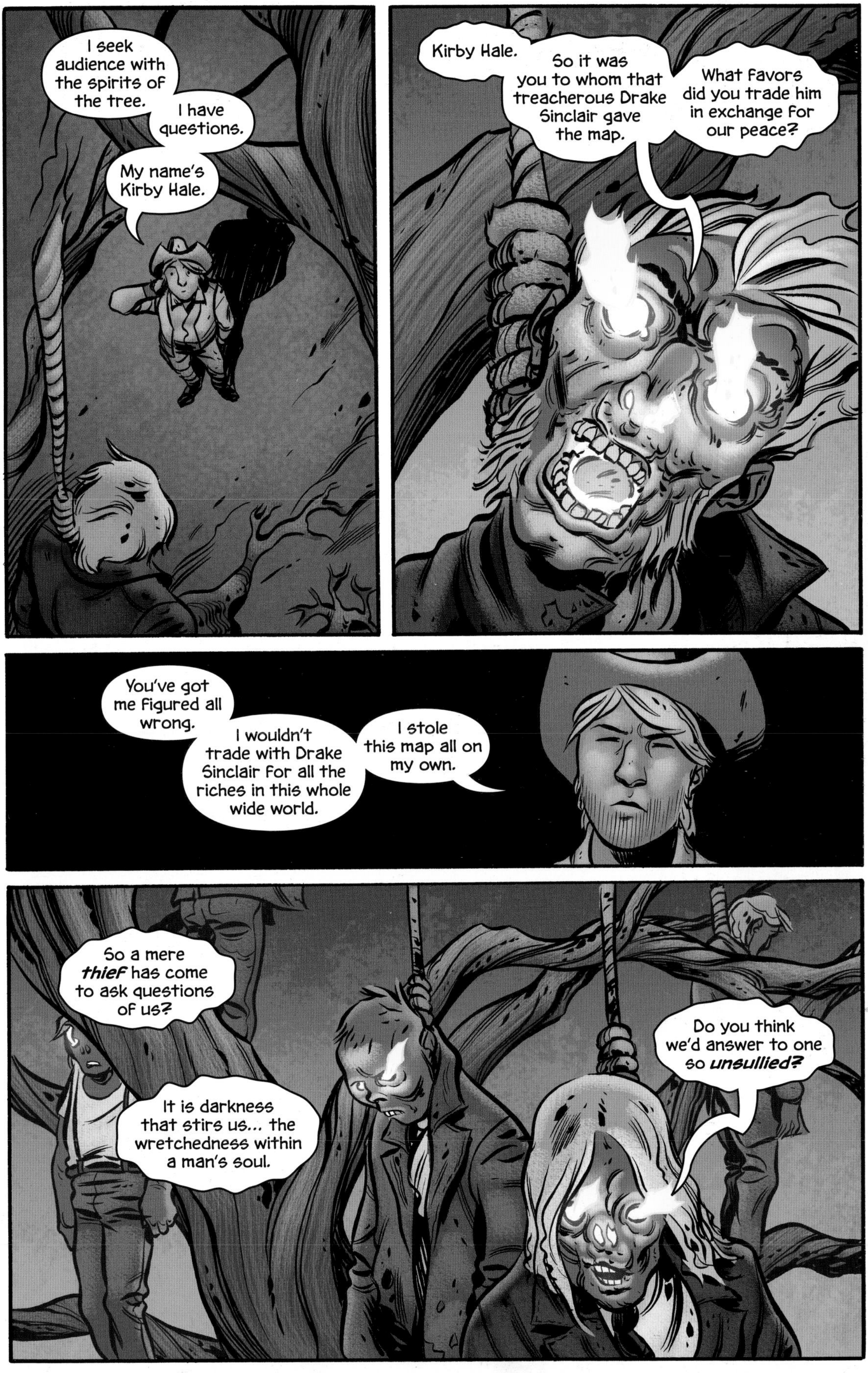
I seek audience with the spirits of the tree.
I have questions.
My name's Kirby Hale.
Kirby Hale.
So it was you to whom that treacherous Drake Sinclair gave the map.
What favors did you trade him in exchange for our peace?
You've got me figured all wrong.
I wouldn't trade with Drake Sinclair for all the riches in this whole wide world.
I stole this map all on my own.
So a mere *thief* has come to ask questions of us?
It is darkness that stirs us... the wretchedness within a man's soul.
Do you think we'd answer to one so ***unsullied?***

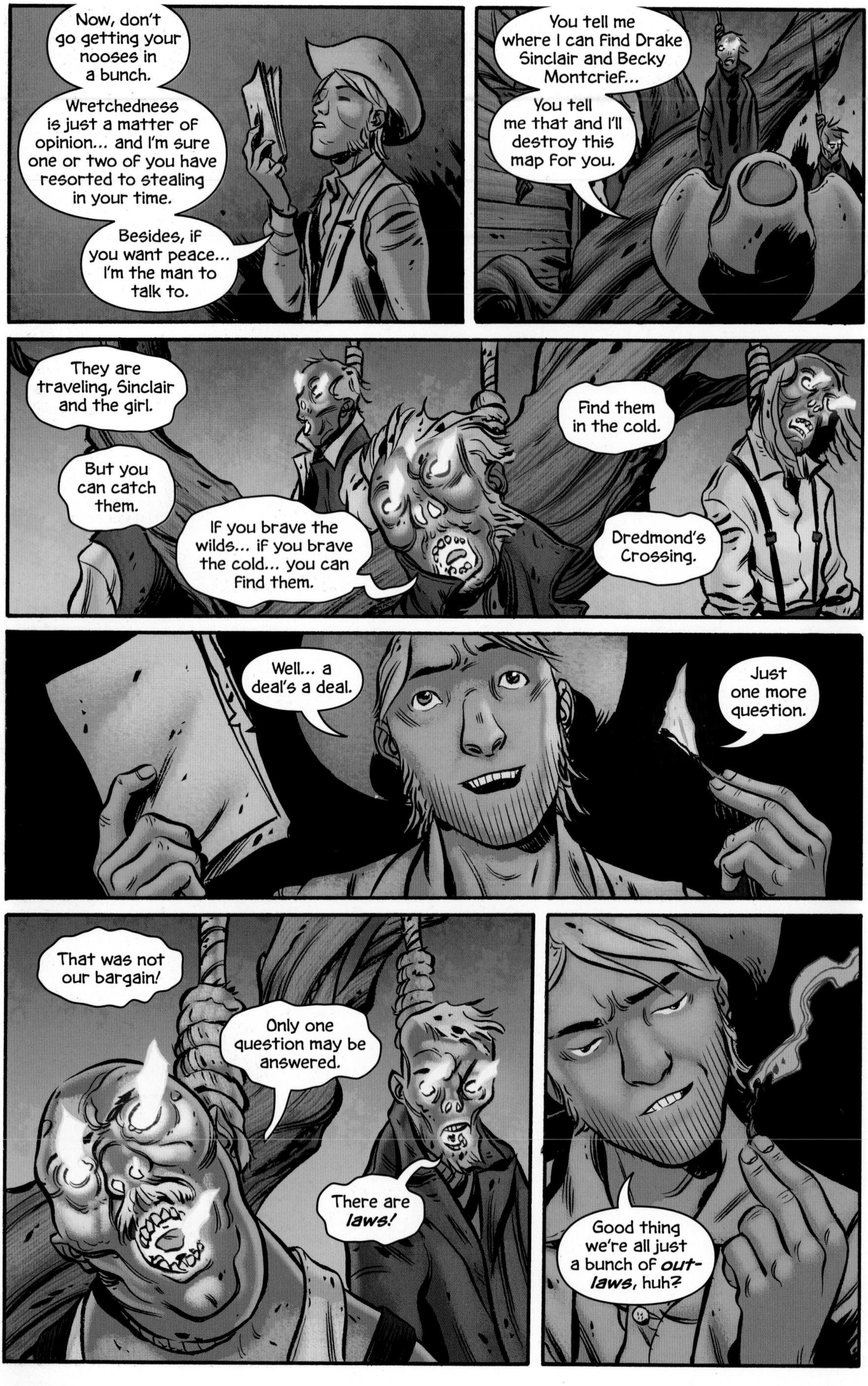
Now, don't go getting your nooses in a bunch.
Wretchedness is just a matter of opinion... and I'm sure one or two of you have resorted to stealing in your time.
Besides, if you want peace... I'm the man to talk to.
You tell me where I can find Drake Sinclair and Becky Montcrief...
You tell me that and I'll destroy this map for you.
They are traveling, Sinclair and the girl.
But you can catch them.
If you brave the wilds... if you brave the cold... you can find them.
Find them in the cold.
Dredmond's Crossing.
Well... a deal's a deal.
Just one more question.
That was not our bargain!
Only one question may be answered.
There are *laws!*
Good thing we're all just a bunch of *out-laws*, huh?

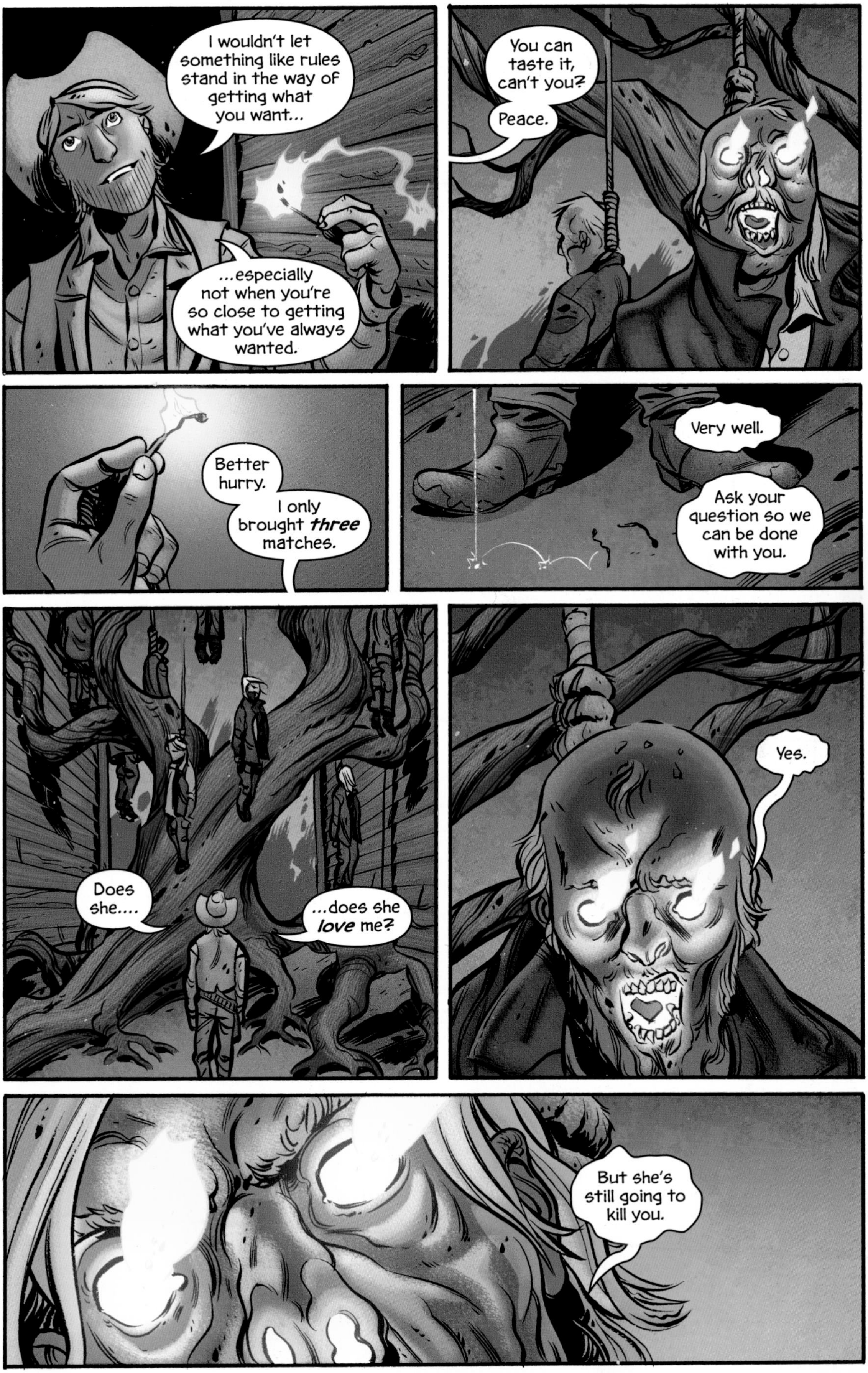
I wouldn't let something like rules stand in the way of getting what you want...
...especially not when you're so close to getting what you've always wanted.
You can taste it, can't you?
Peace.
Better hurry.
I only brought *three* matches.
Very well.
Ask your question so we can be done with you.
Does she....
...does she *love* me?
Yes.
But she's still going to kill you.

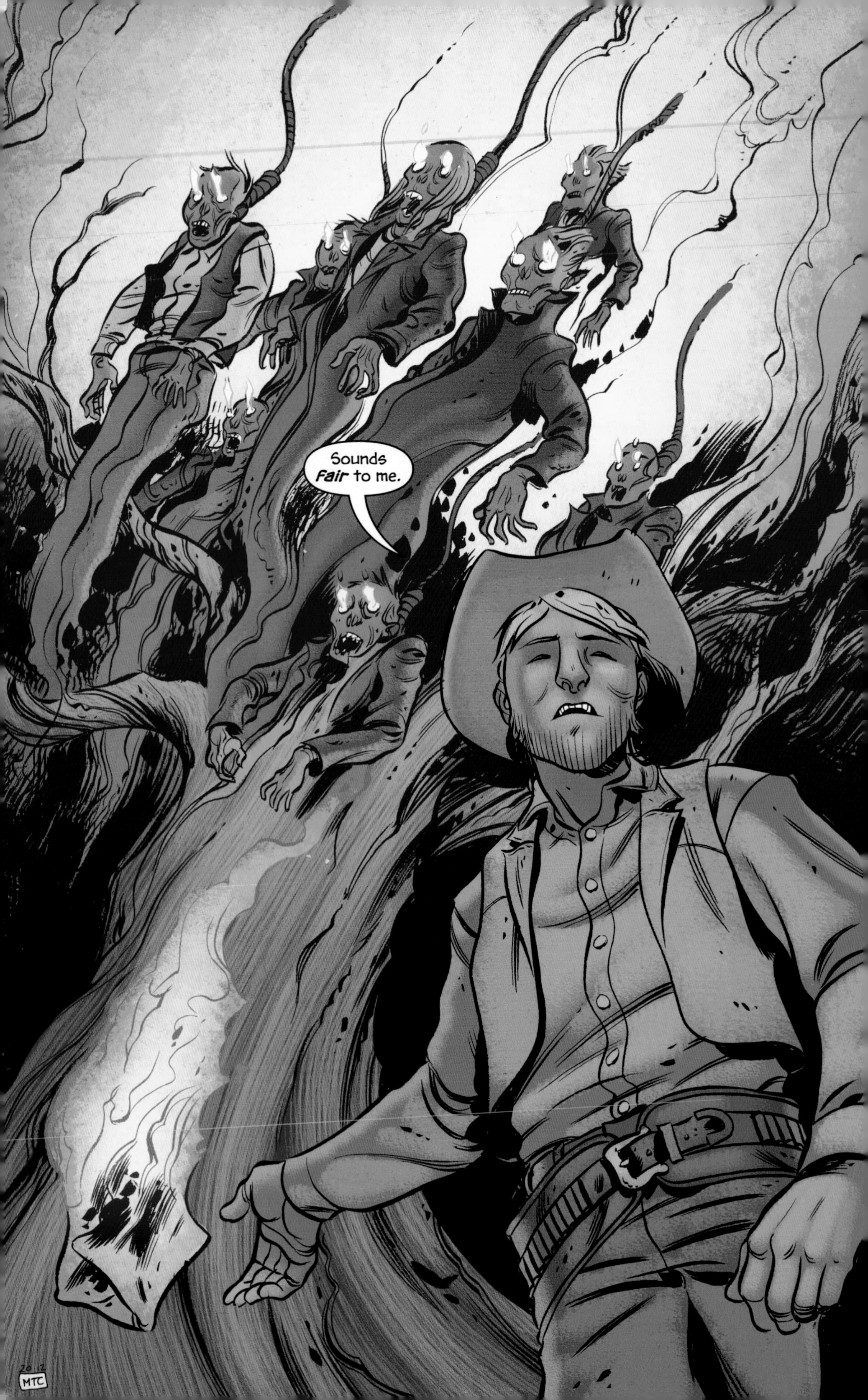
Sounds fair to me.
20.12
MTC

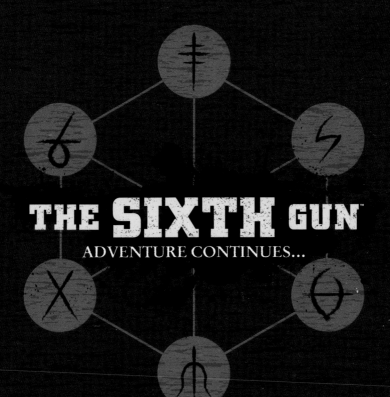

THE SIXTH GUN™

ADVENTURE CONTINUES...

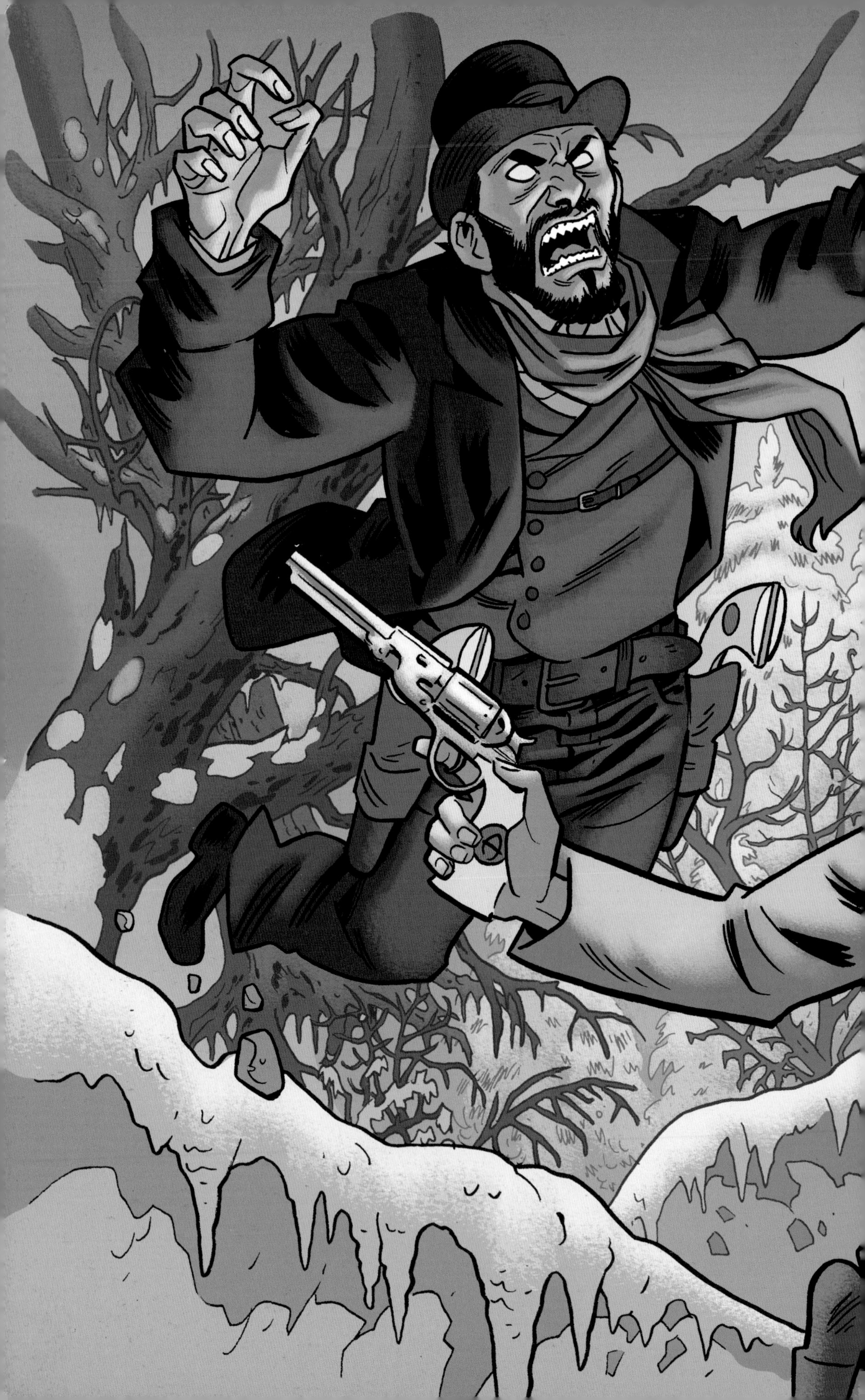

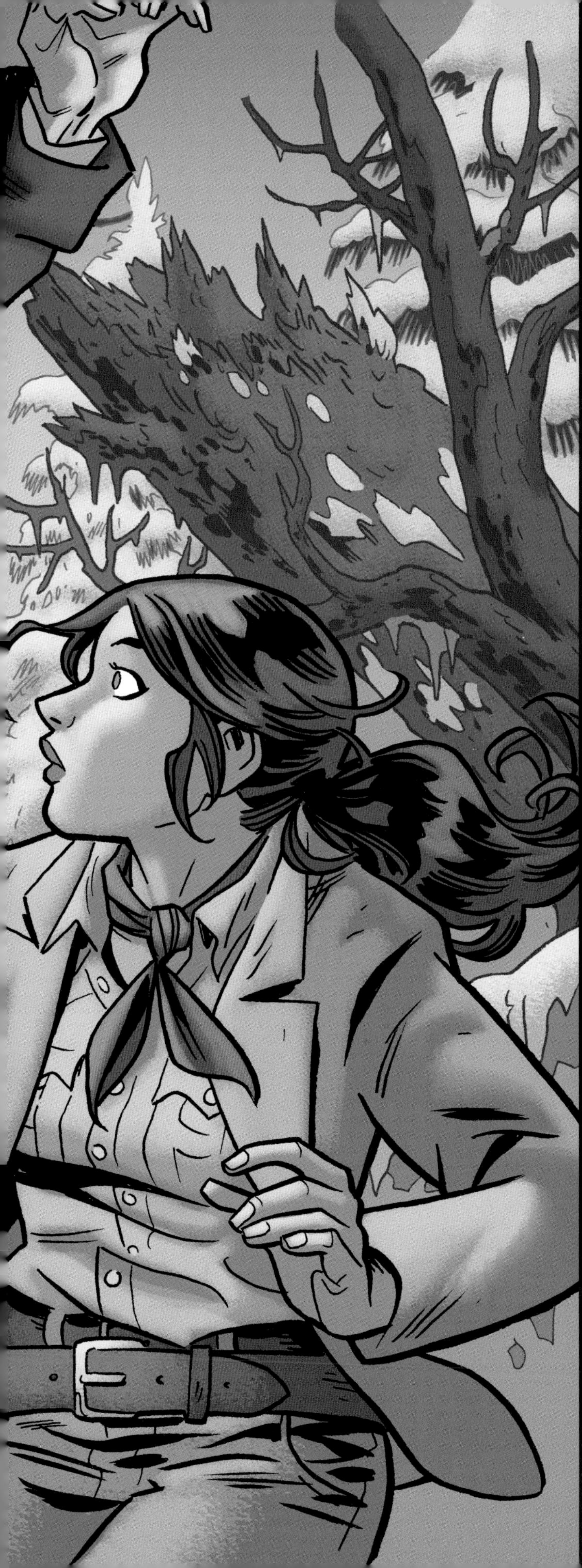

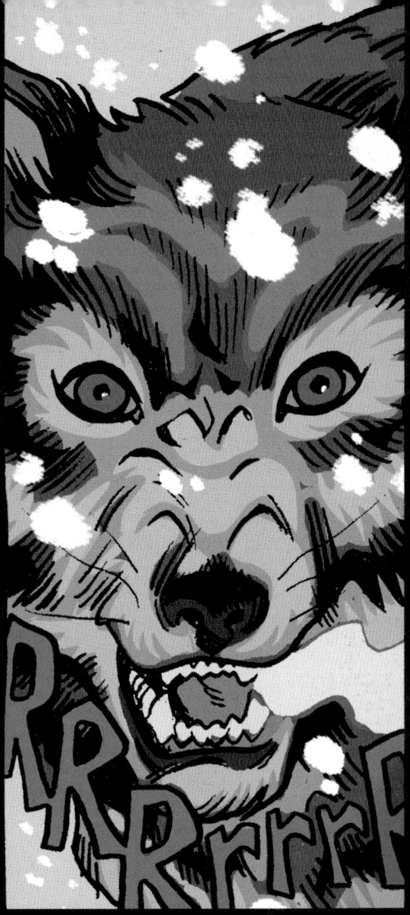

THE ADVENTURE CONTINUES EVERY MONTH!

Becky Montcrief and Drake Sinclair have finally escaped the Knights of Solomon, but they are far from safe. Without warning, they find themselves trapped in a frozen wasteland and attacked by a primeval, unkillable creature. If they hope to survive, they will be forced to make a terrible sacrifice.

Meanwhile, Gord Cantrell races to find his friends. He has attained the knowledge needed to destroy the Six once and for all, but he is being pursued by the Sword of Abraham, religious zealots who misjudge his intentions. And he travels with a most unexpected pair of allies—allies who have other plans for the six guns destined to change the world.

Don't miss a single exciting issue and follow the continuing adventures of Drake Sinclair, Becky Montcrief, and Gord Cantrell. Ancient spirits stir, the powers of the Sixth Gun expand, and both the living and the dead grow restless. Available at finer comic book shops everywhere!

Cullen Bunn grew up in rural North Carolina, but now lives
in the St. Louis area with his wife Cindy and Jackson, his
son. His noir/horror comic (and first collaboration with
Brian Hurtt), *The Damned*, was published in 2007 by Oni Press.
The follow-up, *The Damned: Prodigal Sons*, was released in 2008. In
addition to *The Sixth Gun*, his current projects include *The Tooth*,
an original graphic novel from Oni Press; *Crooked Hills*, a middle
reader horror prose series from Evileye Books; and various work
for Marvel and DC. Somewhere along the way, Cullen founded
Undaunted Press and edited the critically acclaimed small press
horror magazine, *Whispers from the Shattered Forum*.

All writers must pay their dues, and Cullen has worked various
odd jobs, including Alien Autopsy Specialist, Rodeo Clown, Professional Wrestler Manager, and Sasquatch Wrangler.

And, yes, he has fought for his life against mountain lions and he
did perform on stage as the World's Youngest Hypnotist. Buy him
a drink sometime, and he'll tell you all about it.

Visit his website at www.cullenbunn.com.

Author portrait illustrations by Jason Latour, jasonlatour.com

Brian Hurtt got his start in comics pencilling the second arc of Greg Rucka's *Queen & Country*. This was followed by art duties on several projects including *Queen & Country: Declassified*, *Three Strikes*, and Steve Gerber's critically acclaimed series *Hard Time*.

In 2006, Brian teamed with Cullen Bunn to create the Prohibition-era monster-noir sensation *The Damned*. The two found that their unique tastes and storytelling sensibilities were well-suited to one another and were eager to continue that relationship.

The Sixth Gun is their sophomore endeavor together and the next in what looks to be many years of creative collaboration.

Brian lives in St. Louis where the summers are too hot, the winters too cold, but the rent is just right.

He can be found online at thehurttlocker.blogspot.com

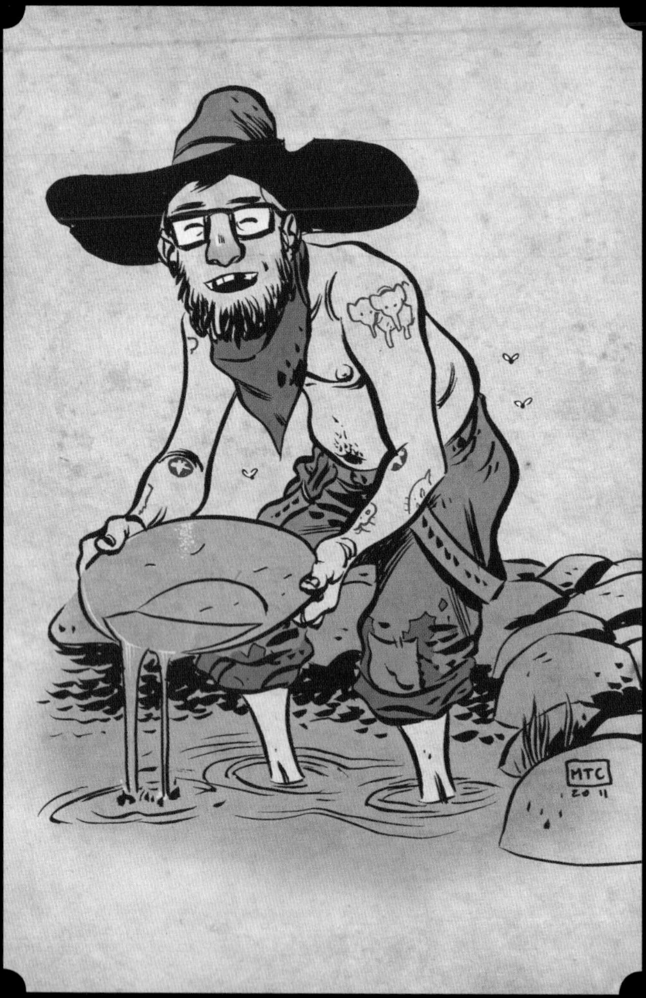

MTC
2011

Illustration by Tyler Crook.

Mr. Tyler Crook is an American artist living in the 21st century. For twelve years he lived in an unlit cubicle making art for sports video games. This left him bearded and almost completely translucent. Then in 2011, he struck gold, *comic book gold*, with the release of *Petrograd*, an original graphic novel he illustrated and which was written by Philip Gelatt and published by Oni Press. He is survived by his wife and many pets, but he's not dead... yet. In fact, he is currently very busy working on *B.P.R.D. Hell on Earth* for Dark Horse Comics.

Visit him on the Universal Hive Brain at www.mrcrook.com

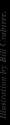
Illustration by Bill Crabtree.

Bill Crabtree's career as a colorist began in 2003 with the launch of Image Comic's *Invincible* and *Firebreather*. He would go on to color the first 50 issues of *Invincible*, which would become a flagship Image Comics title, along with garnering Bill a Harvey Awards nomination.

He continues to color *Firebreather*, which was recently made into a feature film on Cartoon Network, as well as *Godland* and *Jack Staff*.

Perhaps the highlight of his comics career, his role as colorist on *The Sixth Gun* began with issue 6, and has since been described as "like Christmas morning, but with guns."

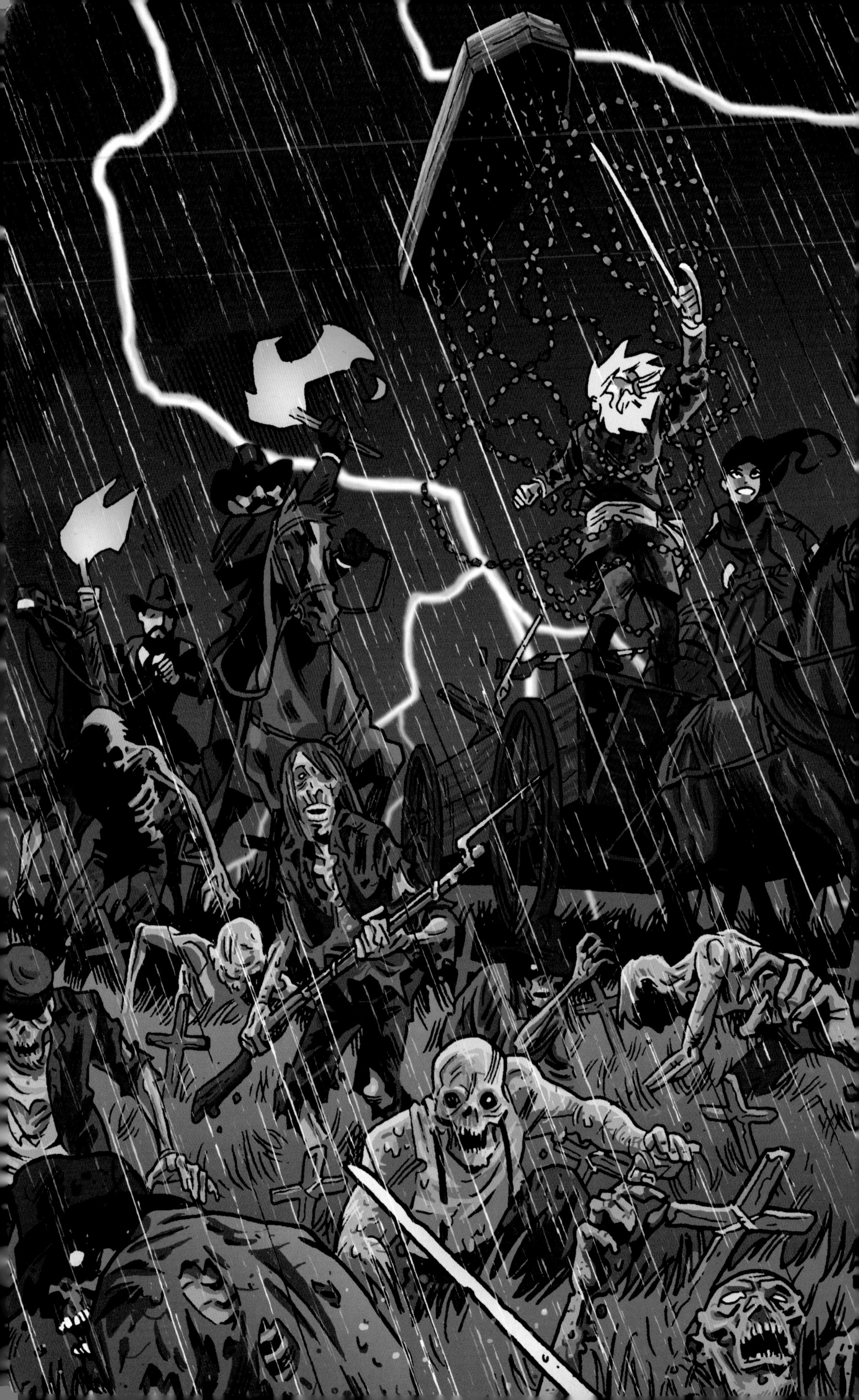

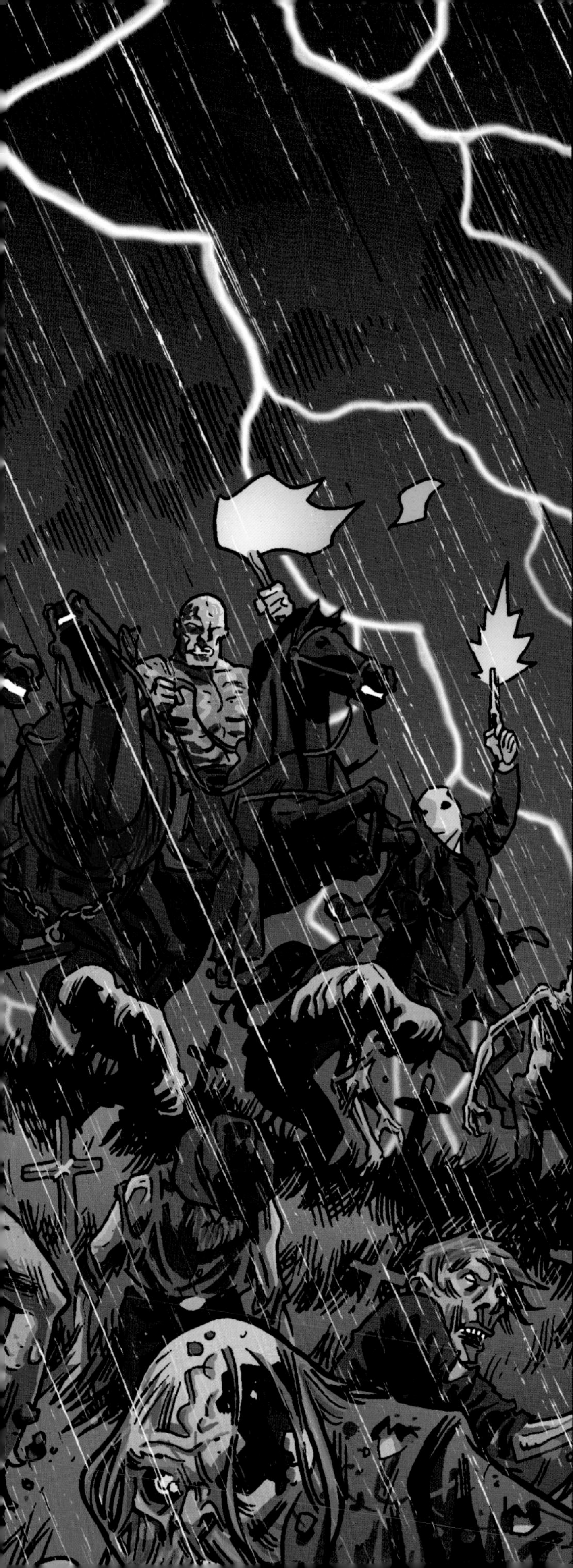

Also Available...

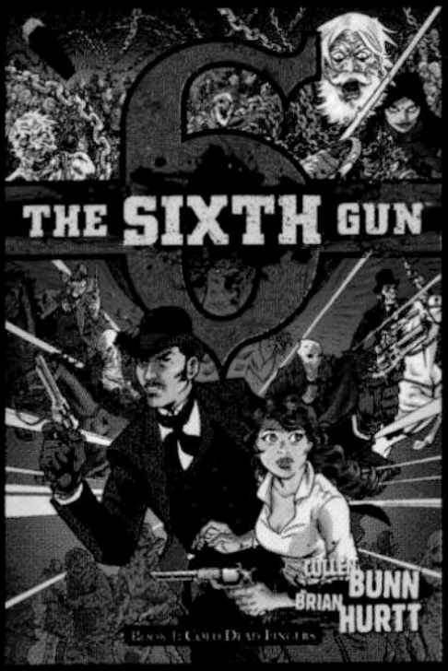
THE SIXTH GUN
CULLEN BUNN
BRIAN HURTT

THE SIXTH GUN, VOLUME 1:
COLD DEAD FINGERS
By Cullen Bunn & Brian Hurtt
176 pages • Trade Paperback
Color • $19.99
ISBN 978-1-934964-60-6

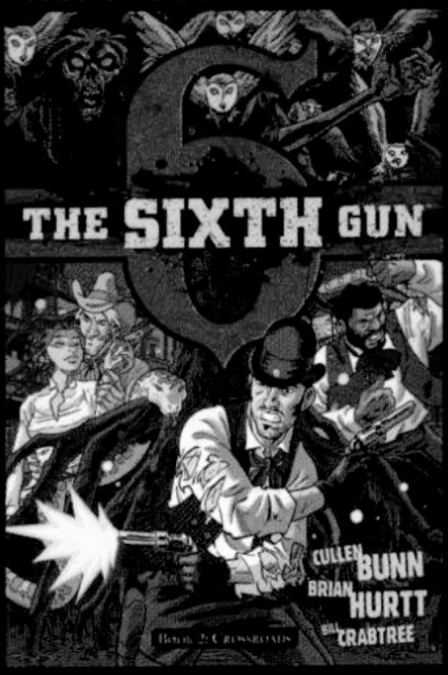
THE SIXTH GUN
CULLEN BUNN
BRIAN HURTT
BILL CRABTREE

THE SIXTH GUN, VOLUME 2:
CROSSROADS
By Cullen Bunn & Brian Hurtt
136 pages • Trade Paperback
Color • $19.99
ISBN 978-1-934964-67-5

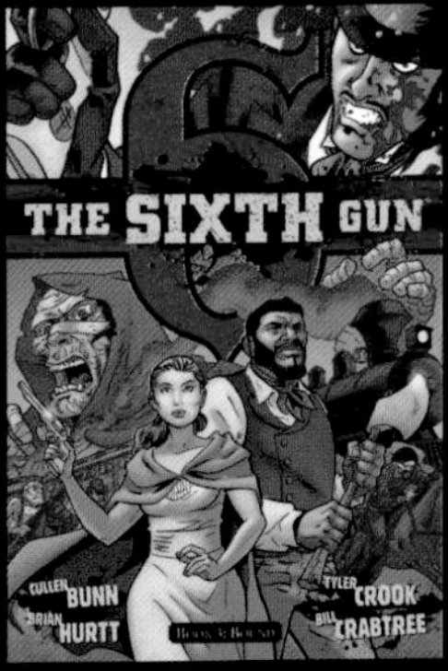
THE SIXTH GUN
CULLEN BUNN
BRIAN HURTT
TYLER CROOK
BILL CRABTREE

THE SIXTH GUN, VOLUME 3:
BOUND
By Cullen Bunn & Brian Hurtt with
Tyler Crook
136 pages • Trade Paperback
Color • $19.99
ISBN 978-1-934964-78-1

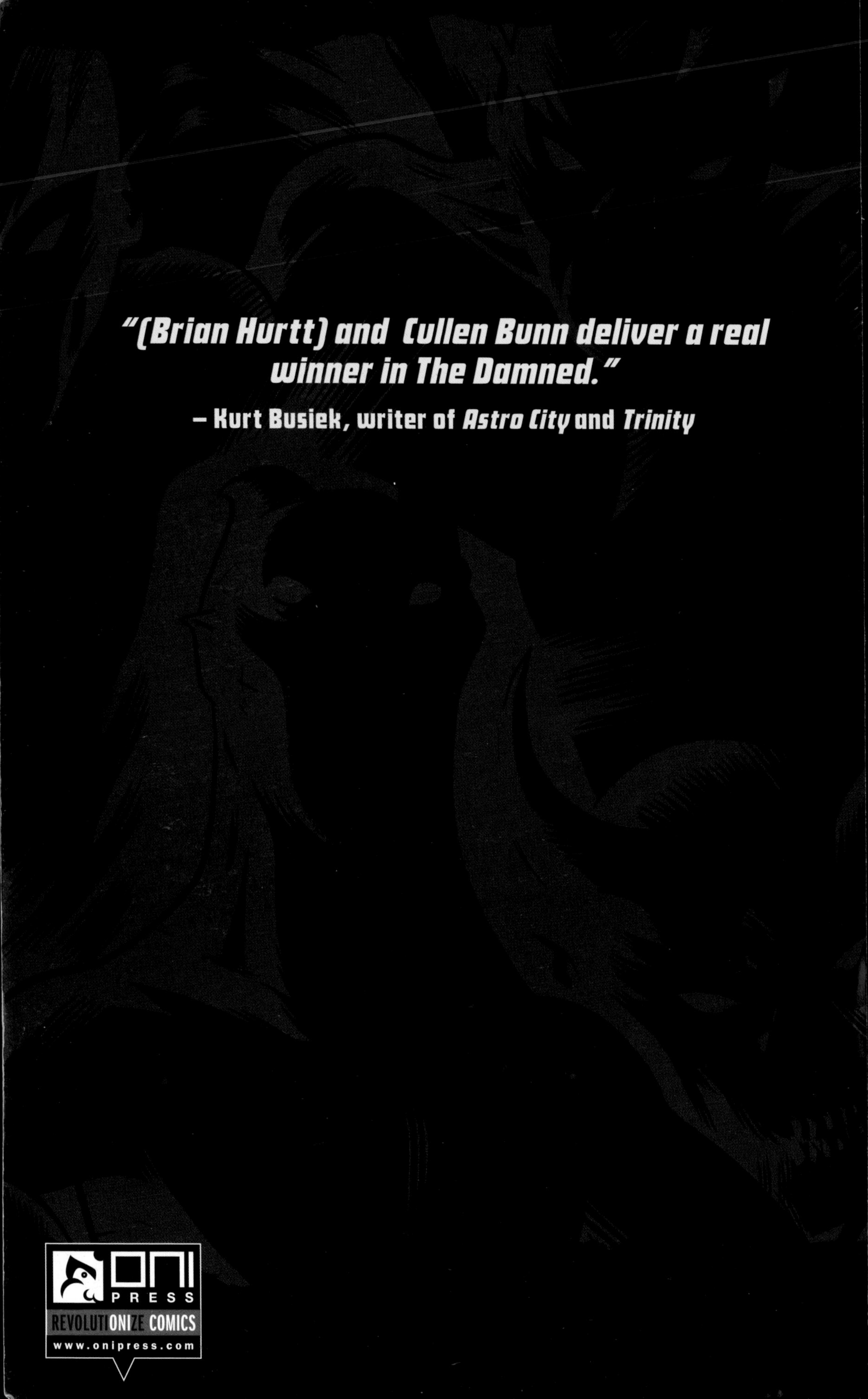

"(Brian Hurtt) and Cullen Bunn deliver a real winner in The Damned."

– Kurt Busiek, writer of *Astro City* and *Trinity*

ONI PRESS
REVOLUTIONIZE COMICS
www.onipress.com

CULLEN BUNN BRIAN HURTT
THE DAMNED
VOLUME ONE
"THREE DAYS DEAD"
brian hurtt 2007
"This is an absolutely terrific book. Tough guys, mobsters, and demons from hell. A bluesy, bitter mood and a fascinating, mysterious world. It's great to see Brian Hurtt back after the much-missed Hard Time, and it's even better to have him doing something beautifully realized. He and Cullen Bunn deliver a real winner in The Damned."
– Kurt Busiek (Superman, Conan, Astro City)

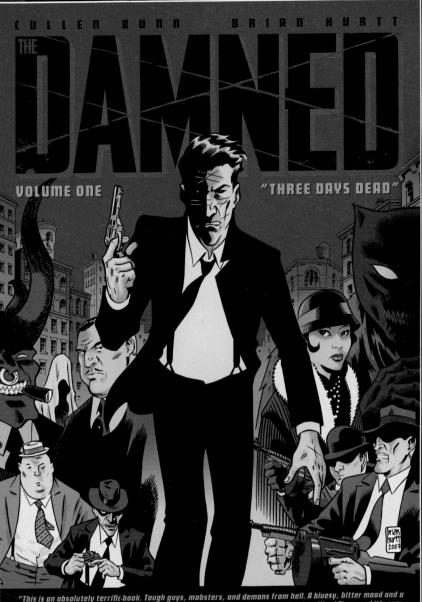

ALSO AVAILABLE FROM ONI PRESS...

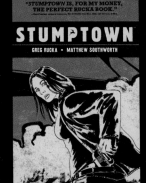

www.onipress.com

For more information on these and other fine Oni Press comic books and graphic novels visit www.onipress.com. To find a comic shop specialty store in your area visit www.comicshops.us.